Passage to India

Passage to India

*Abhishiktānanda and the Retrieval of
the Supernatural in Roman Catholicism*

Enrico Beltramini

FOREWORD BY
Leonard Fernando

☙PICKWICK *Publications* · Eugene, Oregon

PASSAGE TO INDIA
Abhishiktānanda and the Retrieval of the Supernatural in Roman Catholicism

Copyright © 2021 Enrico Beltramini. All rights reserved. Except for brief quotations in critical publications or reviews, no part of this book may be reproduced in any manner without prior written permission from the publisher. Write: Permissions, Wipf and Stock Publishers, 199 W. 8th Ave., Suite 3, Eugene, OR 97401.

Pickwick Publications
An Imprint of Wipf and Stock Publishers
199 W. 8th Ave., Suite 3
Eugene, OR 97401

www.wipfandstock.com

PAPERBACK ISBN: 978-1-6667-0159-3
HARDCOVER ISBN: 978-1-6667-0160-9
EBOOK ISBN: 978-1-6667-0161-6

Cataloguing-in-Publication data:

Names: Beltramini, Enrico, author. | Fernando, Leonard, foreword writer.

Title: Passage to India : Abhishiktānanda and the retrieval of the supernatural in Roman Catholicism / by Enrico Beltramini ; foreword by Leonard Fernando.

Description: Eugene, OR: Pickwick Publications, 2021 | Includes bibliographical references and index.

Identifiers: ISBN 978-1-6667-0159-3 (paperback) | ISBN 978-1-6667-0160-9 (hardcover) | ISBN 978-1-6667-0161-6 (ebook)

Subjects: LCSH: Abhishiktananda, Swami, 1910–1973 | Catholic Church—Doctrines | Catholic Church—Relations—Hinduism | Hinduism—Relations—Christianity | Christianity and other religions—Hinduism

Classification: BX4705.A214 B45 2021 (print) | BX4705.A214 (ebook)

11/10/21

To
Reverend Franco Mosconi OSB Cam
Amicitiae Sacramentum

CONTENTS

Foreword by Leonard Fernando | ix
Acknowledgements | xiii
Abbreviations | xvii
Preface | xix

Introduction | 1
1 The Recovery of the Supernatural | 13
2 Escaping Extrinsicism | 31
3 Meeting Monchanin | 50
4 A Theologian? | 65
5 Reintroducing Abhishiktānanda | 90
6 Abhishiktānanda's Priesthood | 110
7 Sacramental Ontology | 125
8 Sacramental Imagination | 140
   Conclusion | 152

Bibliography | 167
Index | 179

FOREWORD

I CONSIDER DR. ENRICO Beltramini's book *Passage to India: Abhishiktānanda and the Retrieval of the Supernatural in Roman Catholicism* as a bold venture that succeeds in portraying the life and writings of the Benedictine monk, Catholic priest, and Indian *Sannyāsi* Swami Abhishiktānanda (Henri Le Saux) in a new perspective. The person of Abhishiktānanda and his multifaceted life (1910–73) has remained for long an unfathomable mystery. In this book the author provides keys to solve the mystery. With great love and admiration for Abhishiktānanda and equally great regard for the scholars who have written on Abhishiktānanda, he has made bold claims about the person and the overriding intuition of his thought.

This book is a result of extensive, careful, and at the same time critical study of the writings of and on Abhishiktānanda against the backdrop of French Catholicism of the twentieth century, which Dr. Beltramini as a well-established church historian highlights as having a decisive influence in the personal search and writings of Henri Le Saux.

This new way of understanding and interpreting Abhishiktānanda may cause ripples in the theological circles of global Christianity accustomed to seeing him more as a spiritual seeker who emerged as a bridge between Western Christian monasticism and Indian Hindu Sannyasa and as someone who paved the way for monastic inter-religious dialogue. Moreover, some have judged him as unorthodox, especially in his acceptance of and approach to Hinduism. But as the author points out, Abhishiktānanda's mystical experience and appreciation of Advaita led him not only to dialogue between Advaita and Christianity but also caused him to go through inner conflict and struggle, though he claimed towards the end of his life to have overcome the conflict and achieved harmony and peace.

FOREWORD

Context, with its challenging questions demanding creative and adequate responses, influences one's theology. Many writers on Abhishiktānanda have focused on the Indian *Sannyāsi* Abhishiktānanda, delving deep into the rich ocean of Hinduism with its mysticism and Advaitic philosophy to explain his theological musings. On the contrary, to unveil the theology of Abhishiktānanda, the path that Dr. Beltramini has chosen is to vividly portray the French Catholicism in which he grew up. This was a period of great turmoil both in the political and ecclesiastical worlds. It also marked the emergence of intellectual stalwarts who were able to guide the church in the right path even when they were criticized and condemned. The author has used extensively the writings of Maurice Blondel, Henri de Lubac, and Hans Urs von Balthasar to explain extrincism, historicism, and the supernatural so as to portray the issues Abhishiktānanda was grappling with. He also brings Abhishiktānanda in conversation with Jules Monchanin and points out the difference in approach of these two monks at Shantivanam.

In his defense of Abhishiktānanda, Dr. Beltramini encourages admirers as well as critics of Abhishiktānanda not to look at him as a theologian but as an artist, a poet with a theological concern, and as a result to refrain from subjecting his life and writings to systematic theological scrutiny. He points out that Abhishiktānanda did not deny the dogmas of Christianity but laid great stress on spiritual experience, knowing full well that fundamental experience will lead later to articulation in concepts.

Against the oft-projected view of Abhishiktānanda as an acosmic monk, as an individualistic spiritual seeker Dr. Beltramini rightly corrects this view to portray him as a contemplative with social concerns; he points out that Abhishiktānanda was a monk and a priest and his spiritual search was a combination of both these two vocations, not only as a monk, as Raimon Panikkar sometimes reduces him to.

Dr. Beltramini presents the "supernatural, that is unity in distinction of supernatural and nature," as the important concept that influenced the thought of Abhishiktānanda. And Abhishiktānanda, convinced of the sacramental ontology of Being, sought the renewal of sacramental imagination in Catholicism. He gave prime importance to the experience of the divine. That remained the goal and guiding force of his life. Paradoxically, he achieved what he already longed for as a monk in France in the cave of Arunachala in India. Spending weeks in a cave as a Christian hermit among Hindu ascetics in Arunachala, Abhishiktānanda experienced "the realization of the all-pervading Presence of God," something that he failed

FOREWORD

to achieve as member of the Solesmes Congregation at the Abbey of Sainte Anne de Kergonan as well as in Shantivanam ashram. The most important masters who facilitated his reaching this extraordinary level of spiritual experience and who led him into the richness of Advaita Vedanta were Sri Rama'a Maharishi and Gnananda.

This book is a well-researched and scholarly. All the available writings of Abhishiktānanda have been critically studied—the originals in French have also been studied. The difficulty of using these writings as a source because of the editing of the text done by others is also discussed to highlight the difficulty in knowing what exactly Abhishiktānanda's position is.

To present Abhishiktānanda life story and writings, more than 100 writings on Abhishiktānanda by different writers have been discussed in the book. Besides these writings, more than seventy-five writings on connected themes have been also studied. The discussion of these writings has helped portray the cultural and religious milieu of Henri Le Saux in a precise way.

The author has assessed the current state of scholarship on Abhishiktānanda. Though aware that Abhishiktānanda remains a mystery and puzzle to many, the author has succeeded in reinterpreting Abhishiktānanda by focusing on the supernatural as the intuition that can help us understand him better and look at him from the French Catholic situation, including his monastic life.

The author has presented Abhishiktānanda in the context of his contribution to global Christianity through his intuitive recovery of the supernatural and fervent appeal for a renaissance of sacramental imagination in Roman Catholicism. I congratulate the author, whose doctoral thesis I had the privilege to guide, for this scholarly book throwing new light on the person and writings of Swami Abhishiktānanda.

Leonard Fernando, SJ
Rector, St. Joseph's College, Trichy
President, Church History Association of India

ACKNOWLEDGEMENTS

THE FIRST TIME I read one of Abhishiktānanda's works was nearly twenty years ago, when I was at the Camaldolese community in Bardolino, on top of the chain of morainic hills to the east of Lake Garda. There, in a hermitage that combines solitude and natural beauty, located at an altitude of approximately 2,300 feet (700 meters), monks and visitors can enjoy a spectacular view of the shores of the lake, while the vineyards of Bardolino (there is a well-known wine of the same name) cover the surrounding hillsides behind the lake coastline. The hermitage was founded by the Camaldolese congregation—the only monastic stream in the Benedictine order to pursue the eremitical tradition of monastic life, although integrated with that of the *cenobium*—during the first Counter-Reformation era; it was abandoned and reestablished, and now lives a spiritual renaissance. In the 30,000-book library of the hermitage, the books of and on Abhishiktānanda are placed near those of the founder , the Italian monk Saint Romuald (ca. 950–1025/27), and the other giants of the congregation—from Saint Peter Damian (c. 1007–72/73) to Cyprian Vagaggini, who was at the Vatican Council II as *peritus* (1909–99). The congregation has provided one pope, six cardinals, three archbishops, and eleven bishops to the Roman Catholic Church across nearly 1,000 years of history. Notably, a contemporary Camaldolese monk is Bede Griffiths, who in 1980 affiliated the Saccidananda Ashram (Shantivanam), founded by Abhishiktānanda and Jules Monchanin, with the Camaldolese congregation. The ashram has ever since been under the Camaldolese congregation's jurisdiction. Here a connection lies between Abhishiktānanda and the Camaldolese hermits. Another connection between Abhishiktānanda and the Camaldolese genius is subtler. The solitude and silent life of the

ACKNOWLEDGEMENTS

hermits who live on the border of the church places them at the very heart of the church and the world, because solidarity comes with contemplation, in the paradoxical way that turns solitude with God into total solidarity with humanity. The same is true with Abhishiktānanda. He ministered to the world through his solitude and silence, while his eschatological horizon embraced the whole of humankind. In India, at the borders of the church, he showed concern for the future of the whole church, always maintaining an organic presence within the church.

This book originated as a doctoral dissertation (DTh) at Vidyajyoti College of Theology in Delhi. I wish to express my deepest gratitude to Leonard Fernando, SJ, former principal and professor of church history and systematic theology at Vidyajyoti College of Theology, now rector at St. James's College, Tiruchirappalli, India. I benefited enormously from his invaluable support, guidance, encouragement, and patience throughout my DTh. I want to thank him especially for ensuring that I immediately felt at home at Vidyajyoti. I am grateful to all the other members of the faculty at Vidyajyoti, especially P. R. John, SJ, the recently appointed principal, and the late George Gispert-Sauch, SJ, who reflected with me on the circumstances that occasioned his personal encounters with Abhishiktānanda. I want to offer particular thanks to Rev. Dr. Monodeep Daniel, Secretary of the Delhi Brotherhood Society in New Delhi, who introduced me to Abhishiktānanda archive at the Abhishiktānanda Centre for Interreligious Dialogue and offered me precious assistance and gracious help.

One of the few advantages of taking as long to write a book as I have taken to write this one is that I have had benefited from the generosity of many people. I was fortunate to have the help of Gavin Flood, professor of Hindu Studies and comparative religion at the University of Oxford and academic director of the Oxford Centre for Hindu Studies. Under his supervision, I prepared my first work on Abhishiktānanda, which eventually became the MPhil thesis in Religious Studies at the University of Stirling. Although he did not participate in any formal or informal role in the development of this DTh thesis, I have benefited from regular personal conversation with Professor Flood when we both were in Stirling, usually late in the afternoon, when the Scottish sky becomes like a kaleidoscope. I maintain to him a debt of gratitude that I recognize here. I definitely need to recognize the gentle gesture of Jacob Riyeff, who sent me a copy of his English translation of Abhishiktānanda's French poems, before publication, at a crucial phase of my research. I am indebted to Marianne

ACKNOWLEDGEMENTS

Delaporte, who hired me at Notre Dame de Namur University and for many years chaired the Department of Philosophy and Religious Studies there. Her passionate and constant support helped me beyond words in the period in which this book was conceived and written. I must recognize the precious, clever, ultimately indispensable assistance of Sarah Tyrrell, who reviewed this manuscript several times and made it better. Finally, I thank my wife Laura, the leading partner in our daily work of weaving the sacramental tapestry of our marriage.

I can't forget that the very first time I discussed the life and work of Abhishiktānanda was not with an academic but with a monk, Franco Mosconi, OSB Cam. Franco has been a practicing Benedictine monk for over half a century and is a highly respected author and spiritual leader who has received the personal congratulations of Pope Emeritus Benedict XVI for his practice of *lectio divina*. Although he has many fine biblical credentials, he can be described as a contemplative person who revels in playfulness and the lightness of Being. His guide and example helped deepen and enrich my understanding of monastic life and spiritual search. This book is dedicated to him.

During my work on Abhishiktānanda, I have presented papers at conferences and published essays in academic journals. In particular, the main argument of this book was anticipated in an academic paper: "Abhiṣiktānanda and Roman Catholicism's Retrieval of the Sacramental Order of Reality," *Vidyajyoti Journal of Theological Reflection* 83, no. 1 (2019) 106–23. An article complementing the argument of this book was published as "Abhishiktānanda: A Reception History," *Journal of Hindu-Christian Studies* 31, no. 10 (2018). Elements of *The Unknown Christ of Christianity*, a previous book of mine, have been used to compose chapter 6 of this book.

This is ideally the first of a two-book series on the mid-twentieth century project of contemplative mission pursued by Jules Monchanin and Abhishiktānanda that culminated in the establishment of the Saccidananda Ashram at Shantivanam, in Namir Tamil. In this series, Monchanin and Abhishiktānanda's project is understood in the context of the evolution and spread of so-called Roman Catholic French *ressourcement* theology. In this book I investigate a specific ramification of this topic—that is, the relationship between Abhishiktānanda's project of contemplative mission and the French *ressourcement* theology's concern for a sacramental order of reality. In the second book, still to be written, I will address the relationship between Monchanin's project of spiritual assimilation and the French *ressourcement* theology's notion of living tradition.

I borrowed the title of the work from Walt Whitman's 1870 poem "Passage to India" in *Leaves of Grass*. In Whitman's poem, the world of physical reality, the physical journey to India, is only a prelude to the spiritual pathway to India, the East, and, ultimately, to God. The poet, therefore, sings of "a worship new," a spiritual passage to India. A passage to India is indeed a journey of the soul "to primal thought"; it is a passage back to the creation, to innocence, "to realms of budding bibles." It is a journey "back to wisdom's birth, to innocent intuitions." The words "passage" and "India" both have a symbolic meaning and significance for *recovery* that I thought very much encompasses Abhishiktānanda's message that this work aims to unlock.

ABBREVIATIONS

BOOK TITLES
(BY Abhishiktānanda)

(For complete citations, see Bibliography at the end of the volume. Books quoted only occasionally receive abbreviated citation in the footnotes.)

Arunachala	*The Secret of Arunachala*
Diary	*Ascent to the Depth of the Heart* (original: *La montée au fond du coeur*)
Eyes	*The Eyes of Light*
Further	*The Further Shore*
Guru	*Guru and Disciple*
Hindu	*Hindu-Christian Meeting Point*
Letters	*Swami Abhishiktānanda: His Life Told through His Letters*
Memorial	*Swami Parama Arubi Anandam (Fr. J. Monchanin). A Memorial*
Mountain	*The Mountain of the Lord*
Prayer	*Prayer*
Saccidananda	*Saccidananda: A Christian Approach to Advaitic Experience*

ABBREVIATIONS

BOOK AND ARTICLE TITLES
(ON ABHISHIKTĀNANDA)

(For complete citations, see Bibliography at the end of the volume. Books quoted only occasionally receive abbreviated citation in the footnotes.)

Life *The Cave of the Heart: The Life of Swami Abhishiktānanda*

Letter Letter to Abhishiktānanda on Eastern–Western Monasticism

Letter 2 Foreword to *The Cave of the Heart*

PREFACE

IN 1790, WILLIAM BLAKE composed the manuscript *The Marriage of Heaven and Hell*, probably not completed until 1793. One of the main themes of this prose poem is the confrontation of the popular images of a dual world, exemplified in the opposition of heaven and hell. Against this imagery of contraries, Blake advocates a "marriage" in which heaven cannot exist without hell. Along this path to the reconstitution of a unified vision of reality, Plato is not the solution to the problem, but part of the problem itself.

> If the door of perception were cleansed, every thing would appear to man as it is, infinite. For man has closed himself up, till he sees all things thro' narrow chinks of his cavern.[1]

Plato argues that we need to replace or dispel the shadows of our cavern in favor of some more transcendent reality. As a matter of fact, Blake argues that this does not lead us to a reality in which the orders of the material and spiritual are related and interdependent; rather, it keeps us in a cave in which our senses are imprisoned. Worse yet, in this cave we imprison our senses when we struggle for an elevated perception of reality as spiritual, as if the spiritual is split away from the material. A restored humanity, Blake asserts, sees reality aright, that is, everything as it is—an infinite sky. The purpose of *Marriage* is to help us recognize our condition of bondage, "cleanse" our "perception," and participate in the infinite; in other words, we see reality anew.

1. Blake, *The Marriage*, xxii.

PREFACE

From 1938 to 1939, Tolkien wrote a short fictional story titled "Leaf by Niggle." This story precedes the initial work on *The Lord of the Rings* by only a few months. Niggle is an artist, or at least he would like to be an artist, but is distracted by his neighbors Mr. and Mrs. Parish, who believe Niggle would be better dedicating himself to gardening rather than painting. He is also distracted by himself, maniacally focusing on detail and never progressing. Self-absorbed and resented, he is afraid that his project will go nowhere. One day, Niggle is asked to help Mrs. Parish, who is sick. It turns out that she is not so sick, but in the meantime, Niggle resists the impulse to help. Then, he changes his mind, tries to help, gets a fever, and dies. Niggle is brought to purgatory. Tolkien describes purgatory as a sort of hospital, or a prison. During his "first century or so" there, Niggle is cured with bitter medicine and spends most of his time regretting. Finally, when he drops his regrets, he just wants to be useful. "He has no 'time of his own,'" and he does what he can when asked. Obedience replaces self-centeredness, and when he paints, he paints, but he is always ready to interrupt his work the moment the bell rings. Time for painting is no longer unlimited like his obsession for perfection; time is a gift, and he makes the best of it. With no sense of rush, Niggle finds peace inwardly. Purgatory turns into a monastery.

One night, Niggle hears two voices. The First Voice represents God the Father and the second, God the Son. The First Voice is more judgmental of Niggle; the Second Voice pushes mercy. Then the First Voice asks Niggle if he has anything to say, and Niggle immediately asks about Parish. At that point, even the First Voice agrees with the Second: Niggle is ready and should move on. Niggle is now in a country that is nothing else than his own painting made real. The painting, that is, the country, is still unfinished, but Niggle recognized that it is his, only more fully developed. Moreover, Niggle acknowledges Parish's influence on his work.

> Some of the most beautiful [...] examples of Niggle's style—were seen to have been produced in collaboration with Mr. Parish.[2]

Disdainful neighbors and distracting intrusions mysteriously contributed to his work and fed his creativity as a painter. As Niggle walks about his country and plans completion of it, he realizes that he needs Parish. Niggle's prayer for Parish's help, which Niggle doesn't recognize as a prayer, is instantly granted. As they work on the painting together, Niggle becomes

---

2. Tolkien, "Leaf by Niggle," 54.

more like Parish by gardening, and Parish becomes more like Niggle by contemplating. The country they have worked on together becomes a place of consolation for those to come, including Mrs. Parish.

This is not the end of the story. Two people who knew Niggle share their opinion on him after his death. The first, a minor bureaucrat, dismisses Niggle as "a useless person," a sentimental artist who missed the point. The second, a school teacher, replies that Niggle really painted leaves quite well. "I can't get it out of my mind," he says. "Out of what?" the bureaucrat replies, incredulous, for the human mind—like anything else in this world—does not have creative powers.

When Niggle relinquishes his obsession for grandeur to live a smaller life in purgatory, he is redeemed and his project with him, only his project is now a communal project, inspired by God and coming out of love between neighbors. Artistic imagination *is* creation (despite what bureaucrats can think) when it is conceived not as a romantic journey in isolation, but as a collective work infused with God's grace and dependent on love.

Blake's and Tolkien's works are pieces of poetry and fiction, not theology. Nonetheless, they help point out at the start of this study that there are ontological frameworks that amend Plato and yet can take us in the direction of the Holy (Blake), and that when artists are not estranged from God and their neighbors, they possess the faculty to imitate divine creation (Tolkien). Their prose reveals a mythopoetic ingredient, the creative power of artists to generate a world that is not only meaningful but grace-full. Their scope is nothing less than awakening the reader's imaginative sensibility so that the reader realizes that we all live, the authors and the readers, in a sacramental world. Their texts belong to a quite distinct variety of literature, in which the world is not assumed to be rationally understood but rather is re-enchanted. This, I hope to show, is part of what it means to show and share and re-enact a "sacramental imagination."[3]

---

3. As a matter of curiosity, Thomas Merton's master's thesis at Columbia University, written in 1938, was on William Blake's poetry. Merton later said that it was through Blake that he had come to the church and to Christ. "As mystic," Merton argues, "Blake belongs to the Christian tradition of the Augustinians and the Franciscans." Quoted from Bailey, *Thomas Merton on Mysticism*, 44. Tolkien was a Roman Catholic novelist.

INTRODUCTION

"You are ... a symbol."

—Panikkar, 2005[1]

Introduction

WHILE THERE ARE NO doubts that Abhishiktānanda's life was dedicated to the quest for the absolute, the idea at the center of his thinking and the coherence of his work still require definitive interpretation. A focus on Abhishiktānanda's contemplative and ascetic vocation gives insight into one of the deepest motivations permeating his life; however, merely observing the centrality of the monastic life in Abhishiktānanda's life is not sufficient. Questions remain: is there an element within his thought that gives insight into his overall intellectual concerns? Is there a particular discernible link between his monastic vocation and his overall intellectual contributions? The purpose of this study is to identify a central key to unlock the guiding theological intuition of Abhishiktānanda's thought and to explain why the search for such a focal point has remained elusive. This introduction provides a brief profile of Abhishiktānanda and the basic assumption of this work and its implications. I will also present the main output in a synthetic summary. A brief look at methodology and structure will end this section.

---

1. *Letter 2*, xiv. Panikkar argued the same in his *Letter*. Panikkar also uses the same definition for Jules Monchanin. See Panikkar, "The Symbol He Is," in *Memorial*, 127. It is well known that articles and books were signed Raimund, Raimoundo, Raymond, and Raymound as well as Pàniker, Panikker, and Panikkar, before the choice Raimond Panikkar became definitive.

PASSAGE TO INDIA

State of the Art

Swami Abhishiktānanda (1910–73) is widely considered to be a spiritual seeker and a pioneer of monastic interreligious dialogue. He was born in 1910 in St. Briac, a small town on the north coast of Brittany. He was the first child of Alfred Le Saux and Louise Sonnerfaud, who named him Henri Briac Marie. In 1921, his parents sent him to the minor seminary at Châteaugiron; in 1925, he moved on to the major seminary at Rennes. He entered St. Anne's Abbey in Kergonan in 1929 and there was known as Dom Henri Le Saux (also Henri Le Saux, OSB). In 1948 he joined Father Jules Monchanin (1895–1957) in India to establish Shantivanam, a Christian ashram near Trichinopoly. The two men were inspired by the ideal of inculturation, as envisioned by Pius XI and Pius XII: the fusing of Christian faith with the cultures of every land. Hence, the distinctive goal of Shantivanam was to incorporate the customs of *samnyāsa*, Hindu renunciation, with Benedictine monasticism to whatever degree possible without compromising the Christian faith. However, Abhishiktānanda's interaction with Hinduism would go far beyond these original plans, for he would seek not just to follow the customs of *samnyāsa*, but to immerse himself in the spirituality of the associated school of mysticism and philosophy, Advaita Vedanta. Abhishiktānanda's immersion into this spirituality led to both deep dialogue and deep tension for him between Advaita and Christianity, although he claimed to have found peace in his final years.

Abhishiktānanda spent his first ten years in India in the southern state of Tamil Nadu founding the Benedictine ashram with Monchanin. During those years, Abhishiktānanda studied Sanskrit, Tamil, and English (adding to his knowledge of Hebrew, Greek, and Latin). He also encountered several masters of Advaita Vedanta (the two most significant being Sri Ramana Maharshi and Sri Gnānānanda) and adopted the Indian monastic ideal of *samnyāsa* (signified in the name Abhishiktānanda, or "Bliss of the Anointed One [Christ]"), all while still a practicing Roman Catholic priest and Benedictine monk.

After Monchanin's premature death, Abhishiktānanda spent another decade between his Saccidananda Ashram and a small hermitage in the Himalayas. When English Benedictine Bede Griffiths (1906–93) assumed responsibility for the ashram in 1968, Abhishiktānanda moved to Griffiths's hermitage in the north, a hut near Uttarkashi along the Ganges, from which he would continue to travel throughout India until the end of his life. While he never gave up his commitment to a contemplative vocation,

INTRODUCTION

Abhishiktānanda was in increasing demand as a partner in dialogue, a retreat leader, and a spokesperson for liturgical reform in the Indian church. In the decade of Vatican II and *Nostra Aetate*, he organized and participated in several groups, primarily convening with other Christians, which explored the potential dialogue with Hindu spiritualities. This brought him into contact with younger theologians whose lives and thought he would influence. In 1969, he played an influential role in the Catholic Church's All-India Seminar in Bangalore, contributing a book-length memorandum on how the Indian church should be renewed through contact with Hindu sources, through liturgical reform (inculturation), and through contemplation. Abhishiktānanda died of heart failure at Indore in December 1973. Between his childhood and his final days lies a remarkable pilgrimage that took Abhishiktānanda deep into the spiritual treasure-hold of one of the world's primordial traditions. He learned the Hindu tradition on an experiential basis, though he remained Christian.

Abhishiktānanda's complexities make him a difficult subject. In the last half century, scholars have attempted to unveil the essential characteristics of his identity, concluding that such core characteristics are an unrepentant spiritual search and an unapologetic acceptance of the inherent truthiness of Hinduism. Scholars have also addressed the meaning of his unique life and writings and articulated at least three sequential interpretations of Abhishiktānanda: the contemplative monk, the inculturated missionary, and the theologian. While his search for God remains the mark of his life, initially the central feature of his life and thought was identified by his dramatic search for God and by his spiritual writings. Then, his acceptance of Hinduism as a true religion elevated him as a champion of pluralism in the theology of religions. More recently, his intellectual views have received intense scrutiny and his theological orthodoxy has been reviewed more carefully.[2] Panikkar called him "a symbol," but Abhishiktānanda symbolizes different things to different people.

A common trait of these interpretations is a representation of Abhishiktānanda as a divided and troubled man: an acosmic monk with cosmic concerns, namely, an acosmic monk not courageous enough to go all the way toward becoming a total acosmic; a missionary who went to India to convert and was converted to Hinduism; and an unfit theologian—an

---

2. Beltramini, "Abhishiktānanda: A Reception History." Part of the bibliography included in this book is addressed in that article.

intellectual who maintains passion and interest in theological issues despite his evident shortcomings.

While the numerous studies seeking a central key to unlock the identity of Abhishiktānanda have yielded many insights into his life and work, the quest for a central or focal *intellectual* point has nonetheless remained elusive. Undoubtedly, one reason is simply the monumental and unique life of inculturation he lived. Another reason is the doubt surrounding the orthodoxy of his work, introduced by several professional theologians. Abhishiktānanda has been applauded as a man who took the ideas and intellectual project of Monchanin and stretched them far beyond anything their first author had imagined. He has been criticized as a spiritual author and theological thinker with no appetite for academic precision and doctrinal rigor. Yet, if we see his works exclusively as an episode in the history of Christian spirituality and interreligious dialogue, one significant feature of Abhishiktānanda's thought remains totally mysterious. If the years Abhishiktānanda spent in France and the influence of Monchanin on Abhishiktānanda in the first period at Saccidananda Ashram are taken at face value, the overall perspective changes. When one makes the geographical shift from India to France, one finds that his story is part of a larger narrative to recover the supernatural (or "the sacramental order of reality") for the sake of Catholicism.

This Study

Abhishiktānanda is best known as a Christian spiritual seeker and Hindu-Christian dialogue pioneer. Yet, quite apart from his spiritual search and his exploration of Hinduism, Abhishiktānanda was also a remarkable man who grew up in a remarkable milieu. He spent his childhood and youth in a family and a seminary in France in the years between 1910 and 1928. Then from 1928 to 1948, the first part of his adult life, he lived and worked at the Abbey of Sainte Anne de Kergonan (a member of the Solesmes Congregation), during what was one of the most fertile, original, and intellectually creative periods ever in French Catholicism. When he left France for India, he was a thirty-eight-year-old man, a Breton, a Frenchman. And anyone who had the chance to know Abhishiktānanda personally in India soon found that he was a product of that milieu and that era. In this research, I paint a picture of French Catholicism and its intellectual life; I believe that

INTRODUCTION

in presenting this picture I shall have helped make Abhishiktānanda's own intellectual preoccupations and achievements more intelligible.

Previous studies assume that it is unnecessary to survey his life in France in order to understand fully the life and thought of a man like Abhishiktānanda (who became notorious, even legendary, for his asceticism and spiritual life in India), while assessing his direct intellectual contributions to the Catholic theological and spiritual debate. Meanwhile, when considering his intellectual contribution from the point of view of spirituality or theology of religions, scholarship points out that we must begin at his encounter with Sri Ramana Maharshi and Sri Gnånånanda, who were the explicit objects of Abhishiktānanda's admiration; then, we must ask how far Abhishiktānanda's own spiritual experience enabled him to overcome the theological and cultural obstacles left unsolved by other Western missionaries in India. The appropriate course would be to focus on Abhishiktānanda's period in India, on the assumption that the existing scholarship on Abhishiktānanda is an indication of the correct course of action. This present account, by contrast, rests—methodologically speaking—on a contrary assumption: namely, that Abhishiktānanda's life in France and the distinctive features of the religious and spiritual situation in Catholicism of the early 1900s provide valuable insights. This contrary assumption takes into consideration the intellectual and cultural situation in French Catholicism of the early 1900s, the dogmatic mentality of that period, the efforts of a generation of Catholic intellectuals to oppose such a mentality, and how these efforts were understood and framed. This contrary assumption provides insights about the principal intellectual problems as Abhishiktānanda himself presumably conceived them when embarking on the explorations that resulted in his theological and spiritual writings.

The existing scholarship on Abhishiktānanda adds to our detailed knowledge of his life in France, before his move to India: his birth in St. Briac, a small town on the north coast of Brittany; his time at the seminaries in Châteaugiron and Rennes; and his monastic life at Sainte-Anne de Kergonan. But these surveys tend only to distract from the larger framework of Abhishiktānanda's intellectual attitudes and spiritual aspirations, within which all those steps took place and on whose character they were necessarily dependent. These attitudes and aspirations had a direct impact on the immediate course of Abhishiktānanda's intellectual development and personal choices.

A survey of the early twentieth-century French Catholic theological landscape, the landscape in which Abhishiktānanda became a priest and a monk, reveals that it was dominated by the ultimate dilemma between supernatural extrinsicism and historical immanentism. The options can be listed as follows: (1) the supernatural is extrinsic to nature, or (2) everything is natural. With the former, one can mean the addition of the supernatural to an essential, autonomous nature; with the latter, one takes account only of the realm of nature. This is a convenient manner of schematizing intellectual positions in relation to the matter in question. In this respect, a specific stream of philosophers and theologians, who can be labeled *nuovelle theologians* for lack of a better term, mounted a legitimate attempt to confront Catholic doctrine, opposing the fixed dogmatic theology of scholastic extrinsicism without embracing the exigencies of science and modern intellectual culture (modernists). This group of Catholic intellectuals envisioned a form of Catholicism that, in its own autonomous movement, would spontaneously open up and out toward a more dynamic, paradoxical, and ultimately rigorous relationship between nature and the supernatural. The heroes of this book, Blondel, de Lubac, and Monchanin, successfully escaped both the Scylla of extrinsicism and the Charybdis of historicism by way of a return to authentic Christian discourse.

When Abhishiktānanda reached Monchanin, he entered into contact with this influential circle of French intellectuals. Driven by the concern that Roman Catholics had lost sight of the fundamental unity—in distinction—of nature and the supernatural, this group of active, opinionated, and self-willed men had made a gigantic effort to challenge the philosophical dualism that opposes the supernatural dimension against the natural. In a mundane reality saturated with secularism, coupled with an ecclesiastical world saturated with dogmatism, this circle of Catholic intellectuals became convinced that the problem with the Roman Catholic Church that needed solving was the recovery of a perspective of the natural order and the supernatural as interrelated elements that make a unified whole. In this study, *supernatural* stands for transcending the powers of natural order and refers to God or the Holy Spirit in His self-communication or relation with creatures, not to greater than natural powers that do not come from God ("preternatural"). Also, it is not an entity but a *relationship*. It is, to borrow de Lubac's words, "the divine order understood in its relationship of . . . union with the human order."[3] On the other hand, *natural order* can

3. De Lubac, *A Brief Catechesis*, 17.

mean human nature and/or cosmos (physical nature), depending upon the context. Nature is more than the modern definition of "nature": it implies a blending of nature and the supernatural.

It is important to draft some basic analytical distinctions between "the supernatural" as a central theological category, "the supernatural argument" (or "thesis," "theory," "question," or "debate"), the "retrieval of the supernatural," and the "sacramental" as a worldview. The supernatural is a concept that has assumed multiple meanings, including that of opposition or union between the divine order and the natural order. The supernatural argument is an analytical conceptualization of theological-historical process (only briefly mentioned in this book) through which the supernatural has come to mean the opposition between the divine order and the natural order. The retrieval of the supernatural is the conceptual alternative to such opposition and the blending of the divine order and the natural order. Finally, the sacramental is the worldview emerging from such reunion. The "recovery of sacramental view" is a shortcut for the recovery of a unified view of the whole in which the blending of nature and the supernatural is a matter of obligation or necessity.

De Lubac, Monchanin, and other Catholic theologians and philosophers, mostly based in France, were involved in defining the supernatural, developing the supernatural argument, and promoting the recovery of the supernatural through a return to the original patristic sources. In his life in France, Abhishiktānanda became painfully aware of the existential implications of the opposition between the divine order and the natural order; during his period in India, he tried to articulate a conceptual solution to such opposition through engagement with Advaita Vedanta. He failed. He was much more successful in his attempt to empower a sacramental view.

In this book, the "retrieval of the supernatural" is sometimes used as a synonym of the "retrieval of sacramental ontology," in the sense that the supernatural is no longer conceived as unrelated to the natural: the recovery of the supernatural, therefore, is the recovery of the supernatural in unity with nature, that is, a sacramental order of reality. In fact, the fundamental character of the recovery was its belief in connaturality, a connection between the order of the natural and the supernatural. In this book I use the terms "connaturality," "participation" (of the natural in the supernatural, of creation in God), and "blending" as synonyms, more or less. Moreover, the very idea of sacramental ontology rested precisely on a specific connection between the natural order and the supernatural.

In the course of the narrative, I use "the supernatural" as a shortcut for Abhishiktānanda's engagement with the question and the retrieval (or "recovery") of the supernatural, and "the sacramental" for the sacramental tendency expressed in his writings.

Here I tell the story of pre-Vatican French Catholicism and its intellectual issues; in presenting this narrative, I help make Abhishiktānanda's own intellectual preoccupations and achievements more intelligible. If I am correct, the crisis regarding the dogmatic extrinsicism of the Catholic Church, manifested in the French Catholicism of the first half of the century, struck deep into Abhishiktānanda's mind, shaping and conditioning the central preoccupation of his thought and writings; in return, his encounter with Indian spirituality raised the question of a Catholic supernatural religion, shedding light on certain characteristic features at work in the Western Catholic historical consciousness. In turn, these features forced Abhishiktānanda to embed a sacramental component into his writing.

The aim of this study is to identify a central key to unlock the guiding theological intuition of Abhishiktānanda's intellectual project, and to explain why the search for such a focal point has remained elusive. The identification of the pre-Vatican era in French Catholicism as the correct historical and theological landscape to explore in order to identify the sources of Abhishiktānanda's intellectual concern covers the first part of this project; the investigation of the literary form taken by his guiding theological intuition covers the second.

This work focuses on a specific trait of Abhishiktānanda's thought: his understanding of the supernatural as a necessary complement to the order of nature. Moreover, this book investigates his ideas about the experiential as an alternative to the intellectual as the proper way to recover the original unity of nature and the supernatural. From this author's perspective, Abhishiktānanda's story is not a story of the ultimate triumph of Christian spirituality or of interreligious dialogue. Rather, it is a story of a correction of Western Christian ontology and of an empowerment of Catholic imagination.

The sacramental view is a prism through which to view his writings in terms of literary theology, a literature with deep theological roots and ecclesial implications. In light of his engagement with the sacramental, in this work Abhishiktānanda is seen primarily as an artist—a poet, with a theological concern. In a nutshell, he fell short as a theologian; as an artist, however, he powerfully re-enacted the sacramental imagination of Catholicism. He was not a theologian and his writings resist an overly

INTRODUCTION

systematic or analytical theological scrutiny. The literary approach is a better way to investigate Abhishiktānanda's thought and embrace the richness of imaginative resources in his theological reflection. When placed in the context of the sacramental view, Abhishiktānanda can be better understood as an artist who applied his imagination to a theological problem that he thought crucial for Catholicism. Moreover, his entire spiritual journey maintained an ecclesial character.

As a matter of fact, one contribution of this work consists of a correction to the current interpretations of Abhishiktānanda, a correction that resolves some of the inconsistencies in the existing literature and cements the relevance of his contribution to the current state of World Christianity. The current literature portrays Abhishiktānanda as an intellectual with theological acumen; this study depicts him as an artist with a sacramental imagination. Abhishiktānanda was immersed in the world of the image, of lively imagination and beauty, which appealed to his heart far more than theology and the abstract. Although Abhishiktānanda failed to articulate a relationship between the order of nature and the supernatural, he developed a creative sacramental imagination that reflected a distinct understanding of creation and that still powerfully resonates with his readers' sensibilities.

Another contribution of this work is a correction to the current interpretations of Abhishiktānanda as an "acosmic." I argue that Abhishiktānanda's entire spiritual journey maintains an ecclesial character, that is, a social concern. In an attempt to mitigate the interpretation of Abhishiktānanda as an acosmic, who was engaged in an individualistic yet heroic journey to salvation, I point out his priestly mindset. He was a contemplative who maintained "social" concerns, where *social* can be understood in the light of de Lubac's *Catholicism*, that is, in organic unity with the church and all humankind.[4] Of course, Abhishiktānanda was at times tempted to leave everything behind and simply penetrate the mystery of *advaita*. But, as he pointed out, a priest needs to penetrate the mystery (as a monk) in order to reveal it.[5] He was a priest and a monk, and his spiritual search was the result of the combination of these two vocations.

In summary, this book seeks to reintroduce Abhishiktānanda and reposition his legacy. In this regard, the study proposes a reinterpretation of Abhishiktānanda based on the assumption that pre-Vatican French Catholicism is the best context in which to understand Abhishiktānanda's

---

4. De Lubac, *Catholicisme*.
5. *Diary*, 335 (December 21, 1971).

intellectual concerns. While this study is a new assessment of his life and thought, I must make it clear at the outset that this work is in no sense a biography of Abhishiktānanda. Instead, I am concerned here with one specific topic, that is, the engagement of Abhishiktānanda with the supernatural, which, if well-founded, will serve to re-establish the significance of links between Abhishiktānanda and the Catholic French thought of his time, links that have been obscured as a result of his later associations with Hindu-Christian dialogue. To deal effectively with this subject, I was compelled—in the nature of the case—to assemble a substantial body of circumstantial evidence, especially about Abhishiktānanda's time in France. Rather than present the whole picture, in all its richness and complexity, I have decided to sacrifice much of the resulting detail so as to keep the focus on Abhishiktānanda alone, in a way that makes him a crucial figure, although not the only man on stage.

I attempt to see important aspects of Abhishiktānanda's literary work in relation to his life and to how he saw himself. I do not attempt to cover all aspects of his life or his work, but to identify ways in which they fit together. I take at face value Abhishiktānanda's commitment to recover the supernatural through the experiential rather than through the intellectual. I also take seriously his sacerdotal consecration and Eucharist devotion as well as his priestly inclination that resisted the seduction of total acosmism. Finally, I embrace Abhishiktānanda's self-identification as an artist and the literary style he adopted. His attempts to frame his findings in professional form, in the precise and serious style considered more acceptable by specialists, by his own admission eventually failed. In his writings, a tone that may sound too "romantic" for theologians eventually ends up creating a text in which the Catholic element re-enhances the dormant sacramental imagination of many Christians. This work does not present the whole story of Abhishiktānanda's commitment to the supernatural: the intention is simply to assemble some ideas for those who would attempt such an investigation.

As said, this study is varied in content, combining biography and intellectual history with theology. To make my case, I resort on the one hand to assembling a substantial body of circumstantial evidence, especially when it comes to investigating Abhishiktānanda's time in Brittany. Many of the crucial sources are not available for study, leaving certain things to conjecture. This study thus has to fall back on circumstantial evidence of what we thought the seminary and the monastery would look

INTRODUCTION

like to someone with Abhishiktānanda's concerns. On the other hand, I discuss features of Abhishiktānanda's literary work that may invoke the way he thought about himself and his theological concern. Thus, in this book I have tried to establish a narrative of the early twentieth-century Catholic theological and monastic milieu; I believe that in presenting this picture I have helped make Abhishiktānanda's theological preoccupations and subsequent literary achievements more intelligible. This work does not pose anything that casts doubt on the importance of India in the development of Abhishiktānanda's life and thought; on the contrary, once his engagement with the Indian spiritual landscape is put back into context, its rule and significance become more apparent with regards to Abhishiktānanda's own intellectual and spiritual path.

While I made use of official translations by scholars such as du Boulay, Panikkar, and Stuart, I always preferred to study the original texts in French, when relevant. I translated many relevant passages myself. I used passages from Abhishiktānanda that were written in French and, wherever possible, I quote the source. When I made use of secondary literature in Italian, Latin, and other languages, I translated the content into English and quote sources. In the case of quotations from other authors like Bergson, Blondel, de Lubac, and Monchanin, I worked from the French original and the translations are my own; references are to the French edition, not the English authorized translation of that work. In most cases, the English translation is immediately followed by the original French passage, in brackets (if a short quotation) or in the corresponding footnote (if a long quotation).

Although I am sensitive to gender-inclusive language in religious discourse, I made no attempt to change Abhishiktānanda's formulations in this regard. A few explanatory remarks should be added about the structure of the manuscript and the nature of the claims I would make for its argument. This study, *Passage to India: Abhishiktānanda and the Retrieval of the Supernatural in Roman Catholicism*, recasts the discussion on Abhishiktānanda in terms of the supernatural and examines his literary efforts in India to recover a sacramental understanding of reality through the image of a sacramental Being. The study is divided into eight chapters, an introduction, and a conclusion. The eight chapters present the arguments in sequence: Chapter 1 frames the French Catholic intellectual context and introduces the notion of the supernatural. Chapter 2 retells the story of Abhishiktānanda's move to India. Chapter 3 clarifies what he learned from Monchanin. Chapter 4 identifies the centrality of the supernatural in Abhishiktānanda's thought. Chapters 5 and 6 reframe Abhishiktānanda as an artist and a priest. Chapters 7 and 8 investigate the engagement of Abhishiktānanda with the supernatural (or "sacramental ontology") and his sacramental vision.

Conclusion

Over the past four decades, research on Abhishiktānanda has focused on his time in India and on his spiritual search and pioneering work as a bridge between Christianity and Hinduism. In this research, I suggest that a correction to this interpretation of Abhishiktānanda is not only possible but necessary. To revitalize the studies on Abhishiktānanda, I introduce a new assumption—that Abhishiktānanda matured his existential preoccupation in France and that his intellectual interests and theological concerns mainly depend on this preoccupation. The main outcome of this assumption is a reinterpretation of Abhishiktānanda in terms of his engagement with the supernatural, which he addressed in literary form.

1

THE RECOVERY OF THE SUPERNATURAL

"This mystery of the supernatural [...]
is the mystery of our divine destiny."

—Henri de Lubac, 1965[1]

Introduction

When Abhishiktānanda met Jules Monchanin in India, in 1948, he not only became acquainted with a sophisticated, dense, precise Catholic intellectual with a decisive appetite for philosophy of religions, he also met a passionate, uncompromised follower of Marcel Blondel and a close, personal friend of Henri de Lubac. Blondel and de Lubac were the two Catholic intellectuals at the forefront of re-establishing the relationship between the order of nature and the supernatural in Catholicism. This chapter explores their ideas in the context of the intellectual landscape of the Third Republic, in which the uncompromised secularism of the state matched the equally dogmatic religiosity of the Catholic Church. This chapter functions as an introduction to the subsequent two chapters, in which the existential problem that Abhishiktānanda experienced at Kergonan and Monchanin's theological ideas and methods are explored.

---

1. De Lubac, *The Mystery of the Supernatural*, 167.

France

In the literature on the first thirty years of his life, between his birth in Saint Briac and the beginning of World War II (1910–40), Abhishiktānanda is depicted as a man growing up in a serene Catholic environment: a religious family, a seminary, and a monastery in a placid and enchanted region. Brittany is an exemplary case of rural beauty, punctuated by rolling hills, winding rivers, and thousands of acres of lush forest—a fascinating mix of spectacular coastline, sandy beaches, and the fastest tides in all of Europe. But it is also home to Roman Catholic abbeys and churches, and annual fêtes, celebrating the local saints and showing devotion to a particular saint (such as Saint Fiacre [gardeners], Saint Jacques [sailors], and Sainte Barbe [fire fighters]), from whom grace or a pardon was requested. The large number of sacred fountains, pilgrimages, votive offerings, and chapels that play a real part in Breton consciousness are an expression of the faith of the Breton people. To anyone who has even slightly scratched the surface of the late Third Republic (between the two World Wars), however, a very different-picture emerges, for all those things that made up the image of Brittany and its Catholic heritage were simultaneously facets of another, darker side of Brittany's life. Brittany was a Catholic enclave under attack.

The Third Republic was established in the wake of the demoralizing defeat in the Franco-Prussian War (1870–71) and the overthrow of the Second French Empire with the capture of Napoleon III at Sedan. The new Republic was devastated by the long siege of Paris and terrified by what most of the bourgeoisie saw as seventy-three days of anarchy under the radical socialism of the Commune. Much of the new Republic's effort at spiritual restoration was driven by a rejection of the traditional values of institutional religion, which it aimed to replace with an enlightened secular worldview. The rejection was particularly concentrated against the monarchy and religion. The monarchy was definitively abolished, while the Catholic Church in France was politically attacked and the law of the separation between Church and State was ultimately passed in 1905. In the period between 1882 and 1905, religious instruction in all schools was forbidden, and religious orders were denied to teach in them. Civil marriage became compulsory, divorce was introduced, chaplains were removed from the army, and nuns substituted in many hospitals. An anticlerical sentiment fuelled the closure of all parochial schools and the prohibition of all fifty-four religious orders, which were dissolved, after which about 20,000 members immediately left France. Then in 1905, all church property was confiscated. The religious personnel no longer were paid by the State and the Church lost half its priests. Public worship was given over to associations of Catholic laymen who controlled access to churches.

On the other hand, the Third Republic was committed to spiritual restoration through a nationalistic ideology and an imperialistic foreign policy. France was rapidly transformed from a rural nation with the peasant (Catholic and monarchic) farmer the typical citizen to a network of urban (secularized and republican) communities that became connected by way of railroads, public schools (*école républicaine*), and universal military conscription. The accelerated modernization of France also affected Brittany, particularly the cities of Nantes, Fougères, and Châteaubriant, which were rapidly industrialized and linked directly to Paris by railroad lines. Federally funded public works, and the growth of military and maritime industries, combined with the emergence of private businesses, enhanced the economic and social life of Western Brittany. The impact of industrialization on the landscape of Brittany not only altered the physical appearance of the region but also affected the people socially, since in Brittany the myths and legends that surrounded the forests and lakes were deeply rooted within society. Then, a more drastic project of cultural eradication was conceived and conducted to the Bretons (and other minorities across France) for the sake of the Third Republic's Francization policy: Bretons were forbidden to speak the Breton language at school. Breton (like Latin) was considered a language that kept Brittany in the hands of the Roman Catholic Church, sufficiently so that Brittany has sometimes been called the "French Ireland."[2] Famously, in the 1920s signs in schools read, "Il est interdit de parler Breton et de cracher par terre" [it is forbidden to speak Breton and to spit on the floor].[3] As a result, a generation of native Breton speakers was made to feel ashamed of their language and avoided speaking it or teaching it to their children. This generation is Abhishiktānanda's generation.

In the highly polarized Breton society before and after World War I, being a young Catholic Breton was like being part of a communal struggle

---

2. Le Gars, *Les Bretons par eux-mêmes*, 25.

3. Planson and Koshaneg, *Histoire de la nation bretonne*, 110. The original source of this detail is contained in Hélias, *Le Cheval d'orgueil*, 22. When Hélias (1914–95), *nom de plume* Pierre-Jakez Hélias, went to school in his native town of Pouldreuzic (Finistère), only a two-hour drive from Saint-Brieuc, four years after Abhishiktānanda, French was still considered a foreign language. An autobiographical remark on this can be listened to here: http://www.ina.fr/video/I04343670.

for cultural and religious survival. The psycho-sociological effect of this constant, profound war of words for or against the state and future of Brittany's language and culture to a generation of young Bretons equally loyal to their nation and their region, produced a spiritual *malaise*. With the centenarian tradition of bilingual schools (French and Gallo in Upper Brittany, French and Breton in Lower Brittany) in disarray and Breton cultural distinctiveness at risk, a wide spectrum of reactions—from cultural autonomy to political decentralization, from Breton nationalism to political autonomy—arose, showing the crisis of identity of an entire region. A sense of alienation, from Brittany or France, or both, dominated that era. Breton Catholicism was tormented by the secularized attack of the Third Republic and dreamed of restoring the integrity of the church, liberating it from the rule of the State. On the other hand, it tried to maintain distance from the neo-paganism inherent to the Celtic revival ignited by Breton regionalism. Probably nobody reflects the complexity of this spiritual struggle better than Jean-Pierre Calloc'h (1888–1917), a Breton Catholic poet who considered himself politically neutral but religiously an autonomist, a member of not simply a minority, but a "minoritized" one.[4] A "prophet of the Celtic-Christian resurrection," as he was called decades later, he died near St. Quentin on the Western Front during World War I while fighting a war that decimated the young male population of Brittany.[5]

Blondel

At the beginning of the twentieth century, the intellectual life of Catholicism in France was dominated by the problem of the reintegration of Christianity within an anti-clerical society. The pioneer of this original intellectual investigation was Maurice Blondel. Historians have framed the crisis as a moral anxiety in the face of the Third Republic's materialism, "the

---

4. His main work, *Ar en deulin* (On our Knees), was published posthumously by his friend Pierre Mocaer; see Calloc'h, *Ar en deulin* (à *genoux*). The term "minoritized" is borrowed from Lainé, *Le droit à la parole*, 42. The quotation "prophète de la résurrection celto-chrétienne" is from Concernat, "Calloc'h," 9–23.

5. A figure of 240,000 losses is often mentioned, which would mean a mortality rate of 1 in 10 for Brittany as a whole (2,600,000 in 1911). We can deduce a mortality rate of 1 in 5 for Brittany's male population and 1 in 3 for the male population in the age range for conscription. See Chardronnet, *Histoire de Bretagne*, 201 and Caron, *An Economic History*, 124.

discrepancy between material progress and spiritual dejection."[6] A Roman Catholic philosopher, Blondel articulated ideas such as moral anxiety as an effect of the rupture between life and religion. In his personal reflections, Blondel succinctly lays out the problem:

> We no longer know how to suffer in order to act and produce. We lack heart. We know, we understand, we refine, we contemplate, we enjoy—we do not live.[7]

He believed that behind the French *malaise* lay a succession of disparate searches for fulfillment, futilities that leave human beings so weary of themselves they can only cry out: human beings, who pretend to be self-sufficient without God, can only find fulfillment in their Creator.

At that time, Christian intellectuals lived in a world where the secular and the religious, the human and the divine, the natural and the supernatural, were not only distinct but also separated from one another. Catholic intellectuals were entrapped between secular modernism and religious traditionalism. Blondel called the former "historicism"—that is, the idea that everything comes from history and what can be documented, without any room left for Christian mysteries—and he characterized the latter as dogmatic extrinsicism—namely, that truth should be satisfied with merely abstract deductions that impose dogmas to be believed in blindly and without any reference to history. Christian mysteries were taken as granted, without any attempt to include them in serious, reasonable investigations, believing that such investigations would be irrelevant to the transcendent truths of religion. There was no reason to relate the incommensurate supernatural order of the Christian mysteries to anything in the natural order of reason and historical consciousness.

Blondel framed this problem of the ultimate meaning of life and of human action in world history as an existential problem, and he

---

6. Quotation from Weber, *France, Fin de siècle*, 3.

7. Blondel, *Carnets intimes*, 85. The date of the notation was October 10, 1886. Other works of Blondel that are quoted in this study are: *L'Action*, hereinafter referred to as *L'Action*; "Histoire et dogme: Les lacunes philosophiques de l'exégèse moderne," hereinafter referred to as *Histoire*; "La Semaine Sociale de Bordeaux et le Monophorisme," hereinafter referred to as *Semaine*; Maurice Blondel and Auguste Valensin, *Correspondence (1899–1912)*; Maurice Blondel and Joannes Wehrlé, *Correspondance 1*; *Lettre sur les exigences de la pensée contemporaine en matière d'apologétique et sur la méthode philosophique dans l'étude du problème religieux*, hereinafter referred to as *Lettre*. Page references to the sources are to the texts in the French edition or the English translation, as indicated.

addressed this problem as a philosopher. As a philosopher, and as a Christian, Blondel recognized that in the early twentieth century, a lucid distinction between the natural and the supernatural was required. He pointed out that the problem of the supernatural stands as the very condition of philosophy itself, as the latter is incomplete without the former. Blondel showed that philosophy needs a supernatural religion to answer the ultimate question or questions about the ultimate meaning of life and of human action in world history.

Blondel's doctoral dissertation, "Action: Essai d'une critique de la vie et d'une science de la pratique," defended in 1893 at the Sorbonne, is a rigorous and meticulous phenomenology to draw limits to the sphere of human action from the inside, so as to disclose its ultimate insufficiency. "Action" begins with a simple question: "Yes or no, does life have a meaning and does man [sic] have a destiny?" And it ends with a simple affirmation: "It does." However, the author claims that this answer goes beyond the domain of philosophy.[8] By claiming that philosophy is not self-sufficient, he paved the way for hypothesizing the necessity for a religious completion. In the highly polarized intellectual landscape of the Third Republic, the very notion of a Christian philosophy was problematic for both secular philosophers, who identified religion with superstition, and Catholic theologians, who maintained the autonomy of Christian revelation. The notion of Catholic philosophy was problematic also because of Blondel's specific view of Catholicism as a supernatural religion: how could a supernatural religion be relevant to the domain of reason? How could philosophy as a rational enterprise be capable of investigating the supernatural claims of the Catholic religion? Yet, this was exactly the point of fracture between the intransigence of secular thinking and the dogmatism of traditional religious faith that Blondel aimed to mend.

He answered his secular critics in his 1896 Lettre.[9] At the very center of Blondel's philosophy is a renegotiation of the relationship between immanence and the transcendent according to which secular philosophy and Catholic faith can progress in union. Rebutting the view of an immanent order rationally self-justified, or of a transcendent addendum to the immanent order, Blondel suggested recognizing such an immanent order as

---

8. L'Action (1893), vii and 492.

9. Lettre sur les exigences de la pensée contemporaine en matière d'apologétique et sur la méthode philosophique dans l'étude du problème religieux, Annales de Philosophie Chrétienne, January-July 1896.

insufficient to itself and conserved and affirmed as an integral part of the larger structure. In this regard, Hans Urs von Balthasar said that Blondel attempted to recover the ancient intuition that the transcendent is already contained in the immanent.

> [Blondel's goal] was to burst the bonds of the whole sphere of nature to reach that of revelation—which had already occurred in fact and which indeed was the very foundation of the whole sphere of nature in the first place.[10]

Blondel's goal consisted of recovering an outlook on life that brings together natural philosophy and supernatural religion. Implied in this argument was the adoption of an integrated view on the relationship between philosophy and faith, and the consequent rejection of the alternative view in which a sphere of nature, dominated by philosophy, is separated from the supernatural, left to theological investigation. He repeatedly insisted that there is an essential heterogeneity, with real continuity, between the natural and supernatural orders. Accordingly, his aim was to articulate a Catholic philosophy that can operate at the intersection between philosophy and supernatural religion, without reducing either one to the other. To put it differently, Blonde claimed that to end the crisis between reason and faith, or the secular state and Catholic religion, we need to keep the immanent order and the transcendent together as one in their irreducible and inseparable distinction from one another.

Written primarily for the philosophical community, Blondel's *Lettre* is a defense of *Action* in strictly philosophical terms, and the philosophical community was more or less satisfied with Blondel's clarifications. In thus resolving the problem on the side of philosophy, however, Blondel only found himself immersed in a more serious crisis with religious authorities. For Blondel, it was of critical importance that religion be conceived as supernatural, "coming from God as transcendent," quoting philosopher Oliva Blanchette, "as offered from on high and as having to be accepted freely and responsibly."[11] At the same time, the supernatural needs to be seen as touching base with the concreteness of the very reality of human life (in Blondel's term, "method of immanence"). Yet this touching, this graceful touch of grace, does not belong to the realm of human life creation but is always the gratuitous gift of God. Blondel was cautious in protecting the idea of a

---

10. Balthasar, *The Theology of Karl Barth*, 341.
11. Blanchette, "Why We Need Maurice Blondel," 160.

total incommensurability between the supernatural order of mystery and the natural order, but ready to be open to the inquiry of reason. Blondel proposed this idea of incommensurability between the natural order and the supernatural order but without denying the possibility of interpenetration from either side. His critics inside Catholicism, especially the anti-modernist encyclical *Pascendi* (1907), understood Blondel as proposing a sort of naturalization of the supernatural. In order to appreciate how close to condemnation he was, one must recall the words of Pope Pius X in *Pascendi* that caused Blondel so much grief in 1907 and thereafter:

> We cannot but deplore once more, and grievously, that there are Catholics who, while rejecting *immanence* as a doctrine, employ it as a method of apologetics, and who do this so imprudently that they seem to admit that there is in human nature a true and rigorous necessity with regard to the supernatural order—and not merely a capacity and a suitability for the supernatural, such as has at all times been emphasized by Catholic apologists. (Paragraph 37)[12]

Since the time of his doctoral dissertation, Blondel had identified the gap between the infinite power of willing and the finite willed action as the problem of life (or of action), and he searched for a solution, a religious solution, that was not only based on abstract ideas but on a kind of religion by no means incompatible with reason, though surpassing it. The problem of life needs to be resolved here and now, in this immanent order of the universe, and philosophically, with respect to the critical exigencies of modern thought. It could only be resolved from the side of immanence, where the affirmation of transcendence takes place and where the hypothesis of a supernatural gift must be conceived as necessary for the completion of human nature. The problem can be resolved through a supernatural religion that justifies itself as a necessary hypothesis, not through a merely abstract deduction that would only impose dogmas. In arguing for the necessity of a religion open to reason, Blondel barely survived the modernist crisis, which was an attempt by Catholic doctrine to confront and suppress the exigencies of science and modern intellectual culture within Catholicism.

In the aftermath of *Pascendi*, Blondel achieved a certain paradigmatic stature in discussions of philosophy and theology. First, he clarified the terms of his way of immanence, by connecting it to the chief representative of the Christian tradition of interiority. Blondel made a point of showing

---

12. Pope Pius X, Encyclical *Pascendi dominici gregis*, paragraph 37. The Encyclical defined and condemned "modernism."

how Augustine's philosophy was in sync with the notion of a supernatural gift added to nature. He recognized in Augustine an antecedent in a philosophy of the effect the supernatural power of grace can have in human life, when its truth is freely and voluntarily accepted. Blondel found in Augustine an inspiration for the more interior way God has for communicating with souls through reason rather than only in an external way through formal documents. He also detects a sort of path, from the world to his soul, and from his soul to God, a restless human aspiration toward the divine as transcendent and supernatural, from which one could recognize the notion of a supernatural gift added to nature.

In his pre-*Pascendi* writings, Blondel had given the impression that he meant a gift "from below and, so to speak, from the depths of nature." His critics inside Catholicism, and especially the anti-modernist encyclical *Pascendi*, understood Blondel as saying that a supernatural fulfillment, divinely revealed, is added from the outside to a "natural" fulfillment operating on the inside, as if Christianity "emerges from nature by a subconscious and spontaneous evolution."[13] No, Blondel replied, "Christianity is not an emanation of the religious conscience of humanity," it is not an answer to human urgencies.[14] Under pressure to clarify his position during the modernist crisis, Blondel defined his idea of the double *afference* of the supernatural: one internal as well as one external. Here is how Blondel summarized his position and that of his critics:

> They speak only of the *afference* of the external gift; whereas I equally take in account the *afference* of the internal gift.

He said that the "external gift of the teaching and precepts of Christ, which, confided to the apostles, is communicated to us by the church and her infallible head" performs together with the internal one, which operates on the basis of the immanence of the supernatural order to the natural.[15] The "internal fact" of hidden grace at work in the depths of the human spirit that Blondel recovered from the Great Tradition is an "internal gift of grace that feeds the Christian life." In other words, the interior fact of soliciting grace is ultimately immanent.[16] When he argued for the necessity of raising the idea of a second gift from God, he meant an "internal fact" of a real

---

13. Blondel, "L'Encyclique 'Pascendi dominici gregis,'" 7.
14. Blondel, "L'Encyclique 'Pascendi dominici gregis,'" 7.
15. Blondel and Wehrlé, *Correspondance* 1, 283–84.
16. Blondel, "L'Encyclique 'Pascendi dominici gregis,'" 7.

interior gift that works in man—but is brought to man by God—in cooperation with the "external fact" of the revealed supernatural.

The implications of Blondel's theory of "double afference" are monumental: first, there is no such thing as pure nature; second, there is no such thing as a revelation from outside with little connection between what God reveals and our deepest dynamism. In other words, there is not a revelation from outside without the interior fact of soliciting grace. The interior fact of soliciting grace and the external fact of revelation, together, make up Christianity.

Blondel saw the misinterpretation of his notion of double *afference* as a consequence of the current tendency of Catholicism to "extrinsicism." An extrinsicist approach in religion tends to be dogmatic in character to the point that it considers the supernatural order of Christianity to be self-enclosed and purely extrinsic to the order of nature and reason. Blondel characterized this approach as *dogmatic* extrinsicism because it sees God as communicating with people only in an external way through formal documents.[17] Blondel wrote in 1910

> One must even say, that in so far as monophorism (*intégrisme*) [i.e., extrinsicism] triumphed, the Catholic apostolate would be sterilized, the religious sense perverted, Christian piety falsified.[18]

However, he also rejected the opposite option, historicism, the idea that there is nothing in "the historical Jesus" except what could be documented through observation of documents according to the canons of modern historical research. Blondel rejected what he saw as a fierce polarization of opinion between rigid traditionalists, whom he characterizes as dogmatic extrinsicists, because they took little or no account of history in their interpretation of the Christian fact, and the historicists, whom he characterized as immanent modernists, because they exclusively rely on historical research to establish the truth of the Christian faith. Blondel's thesis is that

> *Extrinsicism* and *historicism* [. . .] are opposite extremes, but of the same kind, based on similar habits of mind, suffering from analogous philosophical lacunae, and aggravating one another by their conflict.[19]

---

17. Blondel, *Histoire*.
18. Blondel, *Semaine* (French edition), 93.
19. Blondel, *Histoire* (French edition 1904), 224.

The tradition of the church properly understood, maintained Blondel, allowed one to escape both the Scylla of extrinsicism and the Charybdis of historicism. Tradition, for Blondel, is a living reality through which dogma developed. It is in developing the dogma (in history) that the church became aware of the supernatural truth of his dogma.

De Lubac

Enter Henri de Lubac. Blondel had a great impact specifically on Henri de Lubac and a group of French Jesuits at La Fourvière, the Jesuit theologate in Lyon, to the point that Étienne Fouilloux goes so far as to describe de Lubac's work as, "in large measure, the theological extension of the philosophy of action" that Blondel had advocated.[20] De Lubac marked the transition from a philosophy of the supernatural to a theology of the supernatural. De Lubac's debt to Blondel is enormous. As a matter of fact, de Lubac cited Blondel, along with Joseph Mar'echal and Pierre Rousselot, as contemporaries to whom he owed "a particular debt."[21] In his *Petite catéchèse sur nature et grace* (1980), de Lubac looked back to his early discovery of Blondel. Blondel, de Lubac explained,

> is the one who launched the decisive attack on the dualist theory which was destroying Christian thought. Time after time Blondel demonstrated the deficiencies of the thesis of the "extrinsicist" school, which recognized no other link between nature and supernature than an ideal juxtaposition of elements which [...] were impenetrable to each other, and which were brought together by our intellectual obedience, so that the supernatural can subsist only if it remains extrinsic to the natural and if it is proposed from without as something important only in so far as it is a supernature.[22]

First, Blondel helped de Lubac recognize the mortal peril of dualistic thought, in which philosophy is self-contained in its own natural order,

---

20. Fouilloux, *Une Église en quête de liberté*, 178.

21. De Lubac, *At the Service of the Church*, 19.

22. The doubly indented paragraph gives de Lubac's quotation of *Histoire* (1904), 67. De Lubac, *A Brief Catechesis*, 37. Other works of de Lubac that are quoted in this book and not already mentioned are: *Sur les Chemins de Dieu*, hereinafter referred to as *Chemins*; *Corpus Mysticum: The Eucharist and the Church in the Middle Ages*, hereinafter referred to as *Corpus*; *The Splendor of the Church*, hereinafter referred to as *The Splendor*; *At the Service of the Church: Henri de Lubac Reflects on the Circumstances That Occasioned His Writings*, hereinafter referred to as *At the Service*; and, *The Mystery of the Supernatural*.

separate from the religious order, and without any need or necessity for supernatural aid to bring it to its completion. This idea of separation between the two orders allowed Christians to think of the supernatural order of Christianity as self-enclosed and as purely extrinsic to the order of nature and reason, also taken to be self-enclosed in rationalist fashion, without a relation of any kind to a supernatural order. On the contrary, the recovery of the supernatural was seen as an ontological antidote to the incumbent dualism that, in the words of de Lubac, "was destroying Christian thought."[23]

Second, de Lubac borrowed from Blondel the fundamental intuition of a supernatural gift from God to complement the gift of nature and freedom already granted in the creation of a human being, so that he could articulate a picture of Christianity as an inspiration from the inside out, and not merely as an imposition from the outside in. The very idea of the supernatural assumes an account of a grace that is doubly "afferent," entering into the human both from "without" and from "within," both from "above" and from "below." The recovery of the supernatural recognizes both the "external fact" of the revealed supernatural and the "internal fact" of hidden grace at work in the depths of the human spirit, that is, the desire for the supernatural: quoting Augustine: *Ab exterioribus ad interiora, ab interioribus ad superiora*.[24] The supernatural working of grace within human nature—material nature as well as spiritual nature—allows human beings to recognize external revelation. This triadic feature, outside, inside, and higher, from the outside to the inside, from the inside to the higher, identifies a movement within an ever-greater interiorization. Given this situation, once grace and spirit are understood as inseparable, and actually operative interiorly in human beings, the idea of a supernatural truth imposed on man from the outside—and solely through a church authority—became ambiguous.

Third, De Lubac expanded Blondel's original claim of an insufficiency of philosophy in dealing with the problem of human destiny and the requirement of an aid of some supernatural grace, which human reason and will can freely accept or reject. More precisely, he investigated from a theological standpoint Blondel's call for another way of conceiving the relationship between these two incommensurate orders, the supernatural order of mystery and the natural order open to the inquiry of reason. Implied in this argument was the idea of a total incommensurability and heterogeneity

---

23. De Lubac, *A Brief Catechesis*, 37.

24. This is an almost unanimous scholarly interpretation of Augustine, *Confessions*, VII.17.23.

between the supernatural and the natural, but not in the sense of a separation between the two orders: while the order of the supernatural is unnaturalizable, the order of nature is open to the supernatural. In other words, there is no separation between the two orders, rather a necessary participation (on the side of nature), without nature transgressing into the supernatural mystery. The very idea of a sacramental order of reality rests precisely on the relation between the natural order and the supernatural as a matter of *necessary* connection of the latter in the life of the former. A synonym of "sacramental order of reality" is "sacramental ontology." According to the sacramental ontology of much of the Christian tradition, the created order participates in a greater reality, from which it derives its being and its value. Here we have a unique Catholic use of the term *supernatural*, to speak of a divine raising of humanity, not simply to refer to a realm above the natural. In his 1965 reprise of *Surnaturel* (1946), entitled *The Mystery of the Supernatural*, de Lubac asserted that

> this mystery of the supernatural, which is the mystery of our divine destiny, appears rather like the framework within which all the other mysteries of revelation have their place. It can be envisaged under many aspects; it poses many problems to the mind.[25]

To put it differently, the problem is to replace a vision of the supernatural as a separated order in a kind of two-storey view of the world, with a self-sufficient "natural" world on the one side and an added "supernatural" world on the other. The replacement strategy is to bring the order of nature and the supernatural together, without confusing them with one another, much less reducing either one to the other, in an original sacramental order of reality.

The relation between the natural and the supernatural is a matter of necessity, because of the insufficiency of the former, and required a certain penetration of the latter into the order of nature. Accordingly, the relationship between nature and the supernatural is neither in the sense of the metaphysical touch of something imposed on human thought and will with its very being nor of harmony between aspirations, on one side and the other. This is a main point of controversy with contemporary neothomists, who fear that de Lubac's theology fails to respect the relative autonomy of nature and undermines the gratuity of grace.[26] For de Lubac, that which is natural

---

25. De Lubac, *The Mystery of the Supernatural*, 167.

26. See McInerny, *Praeambula fidei*; Feingold, *The Natural Desire*; Braine, "The Debate," 543–90; Portier, "Thomist Resurgence," 494–504; Mulcahy, *Aquinas's Notion of Pure Nature*; Bonino, ed., *Surnaturel: A Controversy*.

already contains spiritual realities, so any division between natural and supernatural is a philosophical and theological fiction. Yet, the natural is not already supernatural in character. Balthasar himself points out that de Lubac never made this move: for de Lubac, there is "no trace yet of supernatural grace" in created spiritual nature.[27] Grace does not come to reshape nature into something other than nature; grace reshapes fallen nature into genuine nature, which is nature in communion with God. As he had already said in a 1932 letter to Maurice Blondel, grace brings natural abilities and natural inclinations and natural desires to their fulfillment.[28]

De Lubac's primary theological contribution was the replacement of the dualistic ontology hidden within much of modern Catholic theology and recovery of the "Platonic-Christian ontology" inspired by the patristic period. He pursued a reappropriation of the supernatural as a divine elevation (deification in the East and grace in the West) of humanity. With "elevation" we refer to an "ontological transformation into as close a likeness with God" that is possible without merging the division between creator and creation.[29] He focused his attention on a replacement of the notion of "pure nature" with the question of the natural desire for supernatural fulfillment. As de Lubac said in a 1932 letter to Maurice Blondel, the problem with pure nature is "how can a conscious spirit be anything other than an absolute desire for God." Instead of grace being an "extrinsic" addition to nature, grace brings natural abilities and natural inclinations and natural desires to their fulfillment.[30] The relation between the natural order and the supernatural, in de Lubac's theology, is the place of human nature, which occupies a suspended middle, a non-ontological space that is neither in the sphere of natural theology nor in that of doctrine. "Human nature," Teilhard de Chardin pointed out, "is completely and essentially suspended to the divine attraction."[31]

More recently, theologian Hans Boersma has offered a more nuanced definition of "sacramental ontology." According to Boersma, de Lubac developed a link between the theology of nature and the supernatural and his

---

27. Balthasar, *The Theology of Henri de Lubac*, 71.

28. De Lubac, *At the Service*, 183–85.

29. Milbank, *The Suspended Middle*, 16. Other works on the same topic: Mulcahy, OP, *Aquinas's Notion of Pure Nature* and Portier, "Thomist Resurgence," 494–504.

30. De Lubac, *At the Service*, 183–85.

31. Letter by Pierre Teilhard de Chardin to Henri de Lubac, June 27, 1934, in *Lettres intimes*, 277–78.

theology of the church. Boersma calls this link "sacramental ontology."[32] In his view, de Lubac developed an understanding of the unitary nature of the dual-aspect church. There are two aspects, the visible (temporal, terrestrial, social, institutional, structural, external, hierarchical, juridical, historical) and the invisible (atemporal, interior, spiritual, theoretical, and mystical) as it relates to the nature–supernatural relationship, and they are two aspects of the *one* church. One hears echoes in ecclesiology of the nature–supernatural relationship paradox where the two are united in order to better distinguish them. De Lubac, according to Boersma, also articulated an interpretation of the bond between the two aspects of the one church, as sacramental (and not soteriological). The sacramental has a two-fold characteristic: it is the sign (of the invisible) and the reality (of the visible). In other words, the sacrament is a qualification of the church in terms of reality and sign.

For de Lubac, the church is a sacrament and a mystery: "If Christ is the sacrament of God," Henri de Lubac pointed out, "the Church is for us the sacrament of Christ."[33] The church is a sacrament; that is to say, she is also a mystery. The mystery of the church to which it refers above is the two aspects of the church, visible and invisible, taken together. The church participates of the nature–supernatural dynamic itself. Moreover, the Eucharist and the church are intrinsically linked, that is, the Eucharist corresponds to the church as cause and effect. De Lubac investigates the connection between Eucharist and church. He argued that the first millenium, and especially the era of the fathers of the early church, was characterized by the idea that "the Eucharist makes the Church," whereas the second millennium, the era of scholasticism, held more to the idea that

32. Hans Boersma has popularized the term *sacramental ontology*, which was initially articulated by Dennis Doyle. Doyle writes that de Lubac's doctrine of the supernatural "provides an ontology that allows for speaking of knowledge of God in an historical and critical framework," which assumes that the historical nature of God's revelation does not occlude knowledge of God, but is a means to knowledge of God's self. Doyle, "Henri de Lubac and the Roots," 209–27. In Boersma's view, however, de Lubac recovered a metaphysics—which he calls "sacramental ontology"—that functioned as a common systematic method. Accordingly, sacramental ontology concerns an underlying sacramental view of reality. Boersma closely relates this sacramental view of reality with Neoplatonic ontology. See Boersma, *Nouvelle Theologie*. See also: Boersma, *Heavenly Participation*; Flipper, *Between Apocalypse and Eschaton*; Flynn and Murray, eds., *Ressourcement: A Movement*; Mettepenningen, *Nouvelle Theologie*; Milbank, *The Suspended Middle*; Boersma, "Sacramental Ontology: Nature and the Supernatural," 242–73; Daley, "The Nouvelle Theologie," 362–82.

33. De Lubac, *Catholicisme*, 76.

"the Church makes the Eucharist."[34] The two statements eventually identify two rather different images of the church. If we say that the Eucharist makes the church then we will readily understand that the church is itself a family of eucharistic communities, a communion of local churches, which was the patristic model. De Lubac noted that, at its origins, *corpus mysticum* referred to the eucharistic body of Christ in closest relation with the ecclesial body associated with Him, so that there is no distinction in meaning between the two forms of Christ's flesh, the mystical body of Christ, the church, and sacramental body of Christ, the Eucharist. Both are intrinsically united and depend on one another to exist. If we say that the church makes the Eucharist, then we will recognize the damage the eucharistic controversy at the start of the second millennium had on the original community dimension of the Eucharist. Juridical factors then began to shape the church, and the standard picture of the church in the scholastic era is that of an institutional pyramid, with the pope at the top. The Eucharist ceased to shape the church and became one of seven sacraments that the church celebrates. Hence, the church makes the Eucharist. Clearly, de Lubac was suggesting a nexus between the eucharistic body and the ecclesial body as a way, among other results, to recover "a 'mystical identification' between Christ and the Church" and therefore a conception of the church in which nature and the supernatural can be integrated again.[35] In other words, he advocated for a returning to the sacramental origins of the mystical body in an attempt to demonstrate that the church and the Eucharist are intrinsically united.

In Boersma's view, sacramental ontology is in de Lubac's theology the point of unity between Eucharist ecclesiology and a correct understanding of the relationship between the orders of natural and supernatural. In a nutshell, "sacramental ontology" is a term to describe de Lubac's theological vision of the sacramental realities of the created order as shaped by a sacramental correlation of the Eucharist and the church. To put it differently, there is an overall unifying vision that links the main works of de Lubac, in particular his seminal *Catholicisme* (1938), in which he presented an initial exposition of the Eucharist and the church, subsequently outlined in detail in his *Corpus mysticum* (1944) and in *Surnaturel*, published in 1946 (but ready in 1941, according to de Lubac), his historical study on the supernatural. First, he affirmed the "social" character of the church, that is,

---

34. De Lubac, *The Splendor*, 134.
35. De Lubac, *The Splendor*, 110.

the church is the social embodiment of God's grace. Then he entangled this idea of the church with the concept of a supernatural end:

> Christianity alone continues to assert the transcendent destiny of man and the common destiny of mankind.[36]

Here de Lubac affirmed the unity of the human race as created with a view to the supernatural end of human life in fellowship with the triune God. Catholicism is not concerned with the salvation of individuals—quite the contrary, de Lubac claimed. Catholicism is social because of the unity of all humanity, both in its origin and in its ultimate goal, its common destiny.

> The human race is one. By our fundamental nature and still more in virtue of our common destiny we are members of the same body.[37]

Of course, it is the church's mission to reveal to the world its original, organic unity, as well as to restore and complete this unity.

In their work, Blondel and De Lubac reflected a reality in which the life of Christians in their parish church, their faith and their believing in the Catholic tradition, their reading of the Scriptures, remained separated from their life in their society, workplace, and country. Thus, the question of a supernatural religion was nothing less, and nothing more, than the question of an integrated faith and life, of making a connection between two orders, one rational and natural and the other religious and supernatural, to unify the order of the natural and the supernatural without confusing them with one another, much less reducing either one to the other. The larger idea of Blondel and De Lubac was to recover the supernatural and make it available to amend a "rupture between theology and life."[38] The fundamental character of the recovery was its belief in connaturality, a connection between the order of the natural and the supernatural. The recovery from the patristic heritage of the idea of a unity of the supernatural and nature was a wealth of themes and vibrations that turned Catholicism's attention inward and rejected a notion of a supernatural order that exists in complete isolation from its historical context.

---

36. De Lubac, *Catholicisme*, 140–41.
37. De Lubac, *Catholicisme*, 222.
38. Daniélou, "Les orientations," 6.

Conclusion

With a driving concern that Roman Catholics had lost sign of fundamental unity—in distinction—of nature and the supernatural, due to secularization (on one side) and extrinsicism (on the other side), a gigantic effort was put in place to challenge the philosophical dualism that opposes the supernatural dimension against the natural. A generation of philosophers and theologians in the early twentieth century became convinced that the problem with the Roman Catholic Church was to recover a perspective of the natural order and the supernatural as interrelated elements that make a unified whole. In this chapter I have focused on the problem of extrinsicism in Blondel and de Lubac, because—this is the operating assumption—that was an existential problem to Abhishiktānanda and an intellectual concern to Jules Monchanin, too.

2

ESCAPING EXTRINSICISM

"It was in my deep dissatisfaction [with the life in the monastery] that my desire to come to India was born."

—Abhishiktānanda, 1967[1]

Introduction

The reason that Abhishiktānanda moved to India has been always a question for further investigation. Was he seeking an added calling to the monastic vocation, or did he have an interest that was born in the library of the monastery, reading missionary bulletins? This chapter takes a second look at Abhishiktānanda's relocation to India and considers what motivated him to leave France. Did Abhishiktānanda himself already experience an existential problem, before he ever got in touch with Monchanin and the Indian *sadhu*? Can we identify this existential problem as a main cause that prompted him to leave France? In this chapter, I am compelled—in the nature of the case—to assemble a body of circumstantial evidence and to take a different approach. If well-founded, this chapter's content will serve to sustain my hypothesis that a problem at St. Anne's Abbey in Kergonan preoccupied Abhishiktānanda to the extent that he left France for India. I address this problem as the reason why Abhishiktānanda left France, and I suggest that such a reason concerns moving away from a devotional understanding of monastic charisma.

---

1. Letter to J. Lemarié, March 13, 1967. See *Diary*, 12.

A Scholarly Problem

An initial understanding of Abhishiktānanda emerged during his time in India from a generation of friends and acquaintances who constantly resisted the idea that Abhishiktānanda had developed a second vocation in India. In their memoirs, Panikkar and Rogers made absolutely clear that he remained French in mindset—an indisputable product of Cartesianism. In these friends' views, there is no rupture between the monk at St. Anne's Abbey in Kergonan and the *sannyāsī* in orange, only a kind of evolution or an eventual radicalization of the initial vocation. A successive generation of scholars—more concerned with Abhishiktānanda's experience at the border between Christianity and Hinduism—was able to make Abhishiktānanda a founding father of Hindu-Christian dialogue, developing a mainstream description of his life that differs from the previous in a key point: at some point Abhishiktānanda fell in love with India and made India his ultimate home. The new scholarship needed to explain how a monk from Brittany found himself in dialogue with Advaita Vedanta. Should a Benedictine monk be interested in Hinduism? Or should he collect rice on the streets? Should he sleep in caves? Scholars scrutinized Abhishiktānanda's life in India, both the period of spiritual search and his encounter with a Hindu *sadhu*, in search of the origins of this new trajectory—an unequivocal turning point. A classic example of this narrative identifies Abhishiktānanda's retreats as a hermit in the caves of the holy mountain Arunachala between 1949 and 1955. Another example of this narrative is the encounter with Sri Ramana Maharshi as the turning point. Until then, Abhishiktānanda seems to be following a peculiar but linear path, from contemplation in a monastery to contemplation in mission. After the meeting with the Hindu saint, as this interpretation goes, Abhishiktānanda initiated the disengagement from the original plan that drove him to Hindu-Christian dialogue at an experiential level.

As the center of gravity of Abhishiktānanda's interest shifts in scholarship from contemplation to dialogue, also the relationship between Abhishiktānanda and Monchanin assumes a new meaning. While Panikkar never stopped referring to Monchanin as Abhishiktānanda's "first guru (master)" and traced the enduring influence of the former on the latter, a generation of scholars tended to dissociate Monchanin from Abhishiktānanda, more at ease with the pluralistic approach of the latter than with the inclusivist strategy of the former.² Accordingly, that scholarship would probably summarize the story of Abhishiktānanda as follows: a French monk (Abhishiktānanda) who becomes increasingly engaged in a peculiar call for contemplation in mission asks to be packed off from France and sent to India to a Christian theologian (Jacques Monchanin). There the encounter with a Hindu *sadhu* (Sri Ramana Maharshi) awakens in him a wild passion for deeper spirituality, as well as a peculiarly intense fascination with the religion that actually produced the *sadhu*. The monk grows close to another Hindu *sadhu* (Sri Gnånånanda), becoming a regular visitor to the solitary caves and silent temples of South India. The monk is troubled by his encounter with Hinduism and attracted by its spiritual treasures, putting his loyalty to Christianity at risk. Nonetheless, he successfully completed the quest before the end of his life, articulating his experience and ultimately opening the gates to further dialogue between his religion and the local one. It is not clear how it happened, but at a certain point, the narrative above became the running thesis. A great deal of scholarship on the intellectual, spiritual, and experiential dimensions of Abhishiktānanda's engagement with Hindu-Christian dialogue emerges from this new framework.

Authoritative works on Abhishiktānanda still invite scholars to assume that his spiritual interests and experiential preoccupations date from after his relocation in India—that his contact with Sri Ramana Maharshi awakened his concern with Advaita. Yet there also exists a strong presumption against this point of view. The belief of the first generation of scholars was that there is continuity to the hidden stream of interests that had been crossing Abhishiktānanda's mind. Despite some scholars' valiant efforts to purify Abhishiktānanda's spiritual search of Western dress and reframe its questions in a kind of born-again form, Abhishiktānanda's theological ideas and existential problems were already embedded like geological specimens. In the process of inculturating Abhishiktānanda in his new and deliberately chosen location, scholars can too easily forget the historical origin and cultural matrix in which ideas and problems took shape. This conclusion is also in line with a remark that Abhishiktānanda's own friend and literary executor, Raimon Panikkar, once made: that among the most important facts to remember about Abhishiktānanda was that he was French, a Breton.

---

2. Panikkar supposes that Monchanin suggested Abhishiktānanda to be prudent in his approach to Hinduism. See *Diary*, xvii.

Brittany

Monk, priest, and pioneer of Hindu-Christian dialogue, writer and poet Henri Le Saux was a French-Indian Catholic. But this French-Indian Catholic was also a Breton. He was born on August 30, 1910, in Saint Briac, within the historical bishopric (then diocese) of Saint-Brieuc, named after the Welsh monk Brioc, who Christianized the region in the sixth century and established an oratory there. Saint Briac is a small town in the region of Ille-et-Vilaine, corresponding to the eastern half of the region (also know as Upper Brittany), where Gallo is traditionally spoken. In the early twentieth century, Upper Brittany was the half of the peninsula in which the impetus of modernization that affected different parts of Brittany was less powerful, to the point that in the period between the two world wars it remained largely rural and agricultural. Despite many changes in social and economic life experienced by Bretons toward the turn of the twentieth century, it was in Upper Brittany that Breton culture continued to flourish in the traditions of local people in their households, neighborhoods, fields, fishing boats, cafés, and markets.

The imagination of Lower Brittany, on the verge of accelerated modernization, was mirrored by the science fiction of writer Jules Verne (1828–1903), a native of the Breton seaport of Nantes whose stories seamlessly merged science and tradition. The consciousness of the eastern half relied instead on the life and work of François-René, vicomte de Chateaubriand (1768–1848), born at Saint-Malo, only ten miles away from Saint Briac: Chateaubriand was a royalist in the Napoleonic era, an apologist of the Catholic faith, and the founder of French romanticism. An adventurous man who lived an adventurous life, he lost and then successfully recovered the faith of his childhood, as he explains in his *Mémoires d'Outre-Tombe* ("Memoirs from Beyond the Grave"), an autobiography in which he recounts his childhood spent in the seacoast town of Saint-Malo. The memoirs, particularly those focusing on his early years in Combourg, the remote and forbidding château where he was raised, abound in instances of poetic prose with such melancholy and tenderness that they helped establish Chateaubriand as the hero and the idol of the French romantics.[3] His two novellas—*Atala* and *René* are his two best-known works—about the comforts of Christianity and tortured souls in conflict with society inspired the early romantic writers. Perhaps even more than *Atala*, *René*

---

3. De Chateaubriand, *Mémoires d'outre-tombe*.

embodies the romantic hero: solitary, mysterious, ardent, and poetic, he is in open revolt against a society whose values he rejects. René is the man who flees in search of something that cannot be defined, perhaps a utopian happiness is all that was left to seek, a man constantly choked and pushed by unnamed anxieties. Chateaubriand's sense of the world's futility and his inclination for experience are well summarized in a memorable definition of the Christian soul:

> The more nations advance in civilization, the more this unsettled state of the passions predominates; for then [. . .] the multitude of books we possess, give us knowledge without experience. [. . .] One's imagination is rich, abundant, full of wonders; life is dry and disenchanted; one lives with a full heart in an empty world.[4]

Les Chrétiens habite avec un cœur plein un monde vide. Christians live with a full heart in an empty world. Chateaubriand's request to be buried on the tidal island Grand Bé, near Saint-Malo, accessible only when the tide is out, meant that he ended his life in the spirit of the Romantic epoch.[5]

The romantic turn, the Celtic heritage, and the natural beauty of the region began attracting the attention of Parisian artists during the latter half of the nineteenth century, attention that was augmented in the twentieth. Initially, poets and novelists such as Honoré de Balzac (1799–1850) and Victor Hugo (1802–85), Gustave Flaubert (1821–80) and Guy de Maupassant (1850–93) became inspired by Brittany. Then graphic artists such as Marc Chagall (1887–1985), Paul Gauguin (1824–98), and Claude Monet (1840–1926) moved temporarily to Brittany to paint its scenic and mysterious coastlines. These artists came from different backgrounds and aesthetics and gave this landscape its full reality and significance through a variety of themes and viewpoints. The artistic interpretation of Brittany as the land of romanticism, of idyllic nature and infinite coastlines, and its impressive storms (like the *Storm on the Coast of Belle-Ile* by Théodore Gudin) are some of the countless and timeless visions that Brittany summoned in all these artists. Faraway and mysterious lands, often still barely accessible, unchanged by secular traditions, dominated by legends and myths, cradled by stormy oceans and associated with a lifestyle often no longer in tune with modern advances in the rest of France: nothing could seduce, intrigue, and

---

4. De Chateaubriand, *Le Génie Du Christianisme*, 221.

5. The title probably came out of a specific episode of de Chateaubriand's biography. His financial troubles forced him to yield the rights to his work to a society that published it until his death, paying him accordingly. In his words, "to mortgage [his] tomb."

inspire artists more than the magic of Upper Brittany. The attraction, even fascination, that Upper Brittany's landscapes exerted over several generations of artists is well testified by the picturesque views of the cities, the stone alignments, the dark forest interiors, the distant horizons, and this unique encounter with the sky, the sea, the landscapes.[6]

Chateaubriand's romantic view of medieval Christianity deeply influenced a teenager of Sablé-sur-Sarthe, at that time a small town at the very border with Bretagne: Prosper Guéranger was to become a secular priest and pioneer of the liturgical revival within Catholicism in the first half of the nineteenth century. He articulated a fusion of ultramontainism—the primacy of the papal authority over the indigenous French Church—and traditionalism, especially in the realm of liturgy. His main idea was the restoration of the Roman liturgy in its medieval form. In his writings, Guéranger proposed a liturgy in Latin, saturated with scriptural passages, veneration of the Virgin and the saints, and prayers for the pope, while re-establishing the dignity and role of the priesthood. He insisted that liturgy and apostolic authority are intertwined, for Christ gave his apostles power to dispense the mysteries; Christ bestowed liturgical power. Guéranger's multi-volume works, *l'Année liturgique* and *Institutions liturgiques*, were devoted not only to the revival of monastic chant but more broadly to exploring the historical and theological grounds for a recovery of the Roman liturgy. He emphasized mysticism in terms of interior sanctification that comes by participating in the mysteries. The celebration of the mysteries, an exterior element, serves as the means to encounter Christ interiorly, in the soul, ultimately igniting an increase in feeling. The liturgical renewal that would be celebrated in the twentieth century by the highly influential Bavarian priest and scholar Romano Guardini, as well as his liturgical theology, finds its roots in Guéranger's pioneering work.

In the 1830s, Guéranger received permission from Pope Gregory XVI, a Camaldolese monk, to re-establish monastic life in France (after it had been wiped out by the French Revolution) at the abandoned priory of Solesmes, not far from Le Mans. In 1837, Gregory XVI erected Solesmes as an Abbey and it became the mother house of a Congregation that showed an absolute devotion to the church and to the pope. The Congregation restored Gregorian chant in the careful observance of prescribed rubrics,

---

6. Two years before he died, Abhishiktānanda wrote to a friend from Brittany, Anne-Marie Stokes, that "The Himalayas are splendid, and Arunachala is greater still; yet what can be compared to the sea of my Emerald Coast . . . ?" Letter to Anne-Marie Stokes, August 3, 1971; see *Letters*, 250.

a kind of Benedictine monastic liturgy of the Romantic era. In 1897, the Congregation founded the Kergonan monastery, which inherited the Solesmes spirit to cultivate a solemn, public liturgical office, and understood the Catholic liturgical revival as awaking the interior fervor of believers by increasing their feeling. The monks of Kergonan celebrated God's glory in Latin, so appropriate to communicating God's majesty and their sense of the sacred, and embraced the enclosed life with its round of liturgical prayer performed with great precision and splendor.

A Devotional Life

Abhishiktānanda's parents had a grocery in this small town. He went to the local primary school, l'Ecole de Sait-Anne, and made his first communion in 1920. As a young man he expressed a desire to become a priest, and when he was eleven his parents sent him to the Petit Séminaire (minor seminary) in Châteaugiron, near Rennes. Noting his great intellectual gifts, his superiors wanted to send him to Rome to continue his studies. On October 15, 1929, Abhishiktānanda instead entered the Benedictine Abbey of St. Anne Kergonan, located in the Morbihan department, at the entrance of the Quiberon peninsula. This monastery belonged to the congregation of Solesmes. He was nineteen years old at that time. Abhishiktānanda entered monastic life to find "the presence of God immediately." How he framed his call for monastic life and for God is evident in a letter from the young seminarian to the Novice Master of the Abbey of Saint Anne de Kergonan:

> What has drawn me from the beginning and what still leads me on, is the hope of finding there the presence of God more immediately than anywhere else. I have a very ambitious spirit—and this is permissible, is it not? when it is a matter of seeking God—and I hope I shall not be disappointed [...] I feel an irresistible call.[7]

The letter is dated 1926, and Abhishiktānanda entered the Abbey three years later. He was committed "to aim high," to become more than "a common place monk," in order to aim at "holiness," and to live "a life perfectly suited to the pursuit of holiness."[8] He was a devoted Catholic, a diligent monk, and an obedient priest. We have no evidence that he complained about

---

7. Letter to the novice-master, Abbey of St. Anne de Kergonan, December 4, 1928; see *Letters*, 2–3.

8. Letters to R. Macé, October 27, 1929, and May 9, 1935; see *Letters*, 6–7.

anything; rather, he was militant in exploiting his duties as senior ceremoniary, librarian, and teacher of the novices in canon law and church history. This behavior aligns with his understanding of his Benedictine vocation as a "sacrifice, a holocaust to the Good Lord." The very facts that he was an impeccable monk and that in his first complete (and yet unpublished) manuscript, *Amour and Sagesse*, written in 1942, he showed a great command of Scripture, tradition, and theology have given the whole subsequent interpretation of Abhishiktānanda at Kergonan the stamp of complete satisfaction. Yet the question needs now to be raised, in retrospect, whether the monastic life at Kergonan delivered the Presence—whether Abhishiktānanda would have left the Abbey if he thought there was nowhere else he would more immediately find the presence of God.

When Abhishiktānanda first made contact with the novice master of the Abbey of Saint Anne de Kergonan he was entering into a cultural situation and into a group of monks having well-marked spiritual imprinting and a definite ultramontane spirit and devotional style. A devotional style is based on the assumption that an increase in external devotional practices tends toward a development in spirituality. As a novice, he attended a program of monastic and theological studies under the control of the novice director and oriented to monasticism and liturgy. Which books did he receive because he was nurtured during the novitiate? Certainly, he had on hand the Book of Psalms and probably the Bible. And what else? He also likely had the Rule of St. Benedict—not from its source but rather through the commentary of Paul Delatte (the third abbot of Solesmes), *Commentaire sur la Règle de st Benoît*. Monastic history was covered through two seventeenth-century texts, the *Concordantia Regularum*, a work of government and observance ascribed to Benedict Bibcop (b. about 654, d. 690)—not the original text, but rather the 1638 edition—and the *Monasticarum Disquisitionum Libri XII*, a great folio volume of 1,400 pages published in 1644 by Benedictus Van Haeften (1588–1648). Monastic spirituality was addresses through *Le Christ, ideal du moine: Conférences spirituelles sur la vie monastique et religieuse*, a book of Christocentric spirituality by Columba Marmion published in 1922, a collection of retreat lectures (*conférences*) to monks for edification. The genre is that of devotional literature, saturated with Scriptural passages in Latin but without theological criticism and historical exegesis. Marmion was a follower of Guéranger, the founder of Solesmes and the author of *l'Année liturgique* and *Institutions liturgiques*, two indispensable books on liturgy for a novice at Kergonan.[9] The texts of Basil and Cassia, Augustine, and Gregory the Great were in Latin or Greek, available to the novice for consultation. An introduction to Christian mysticism was covered mostly through the writings of the Carmelite mystics of the Catholic Reform, John of the Cross, and Teresa of Avila; the French school of mysticism focused the devotional life of the Catholic faithful on a personal experience of the person of Jesus and the quest for personal holiness; and Thérèse of Lisieux, Frederick William Faber (1814–63), and Mgr Gay (Charles Louis Gay). Thus, Thérèse of Lisieux's Little Way, Faber's Marian Devotion, and Mgr Gay's interior path of Marie and her perfect transparency were among the examples of sentimental mysticism offered to a novice such as Abhishiktānanda.

A good example of the devotional style of these texts can be found in a set of images suggested by Benedictus van Haeften: Christ is depicted in separate emblems—with blood dropping from his pierced hand and bloody forehead into the heart of man; the cherub Christ and man grasping each other's right hands, with their left hands holding the twine that joins their hearts. Man imagines his heart being nailed to the cross instead of Christ's, but it is instead being stretched and twisted out of shape, suggesting that it can never completely be crucified. The perfection of the monks of the Solesmes Congregation was to be traced in their imaginations and through the timely and scrupulous observance of a precise schedule and a myriad of small, everyday minutiae. Every moment of the monk's life, day and night, was governed by some particular devotion, including the eucharistic adoration, the devotion to the Real Presence. Before falling asleep, the good novice was supposed to pursue an internal scrutiny and to make sure that all the required practices of devotion and asceticism had been exploited. The so-called active orders, such as Jesuits, Salesians, and so on, identified asceticism with the total commitment to the other; contemplative orders, including the Benedictine, characterized asceticism in terms of penance and mortification (vigils, fasting, silence). The perfect monks were those who were able to live faithfully and heroically a life of penance, those able to show the greater zeal for daily practices of piety. Monastic formulae are few and simple: deny self to follow Christ. Be a stranger to what the world does. Give up self-will. The path of perfection

---

9. Delatte, *Commentaire sur la Règle*; Marmion, *Le Christ, ideal du moine*. For the list of monastic and theological sources of the novitiate, see Euverte et al., *Henri le Saux*, 36.

was essentially a path of self-perfection through *pondus diei et aestus* (the burden and the heat of the day) (Matthew 20:12).

It is highly improbable that Abhishiktānanda had a keen awareness in his adolescence of the intellectual crisis and spiritual malaise that was gripping French society. We can be quite sure that the monks were ignorant of the main intellectual discussions of the age, historical modernism and dogmatic extrinsicism in Catholicism, and the *nouvelle théologie* or *ressourcement*. Most monks were local, from the villages and small towns of Brittany, and were not inclined to intellectual disputes. In general, the monks had little interest in abstract or conceptual learning; they left this to those teaching at the schools. Monks were instructed that at its best monasticism pursues theognosis, the knowing of God, which is a means for a unity in love which transcends all knowledge. This ultimate end is union with God or, partaking in the nature of God, the theosis of church fathers Ireneus and Athanasius. The Eastern tradition, whose masters were Origen, Evagrius, and Pseudo-Dionysius the Areopagite, has never made a definite distinction between theology and mysticism, the personal experience of the divine mysteries. At its worst, monasticism was against knowledge *tout court*. In the monastery, simplicity was supreme. Monks were encouraged to demonstrate a cautious attitude toward intellectual activity and frequently remembered the widely cited passage of St. Paul, *Scientia inflat, caritas vero ædificat* (knowledge puffs up, but love builds up) from 1 Corinthians 8:1. Monks were warned that knowledge was eventually irrelevant for their ascetic path, or eventually a distraction if not a corrupting factor for humility. They maintained an indisputable loyalty to the church and her tradition, accustomed to *jurare in verba magistri* (swear in the words of master), that is, to blindly trust the words of another (such as a teacher/master).

Leaving France

By now, we have a good deal of evidence about Abhishiktānanda's experience at the monastery. He apparently accepted without reservation the heroism of total obedience, believing that obedience is the highest form of renouncement, since it pursues the denial of man's self will. We also know that the rigid, disciplined schedule at Kergonan was never a problem for Abhishiktānanda. When he lived in the monastery—a place for radical choices—his asceticism took the usual forms. He had aspirations of being a perfect monk, to go beyond, to see God Himself, not just His gifts.[10] Abhishiktānanda would maintain a self-disciplined life in India that soon attracted the admiration of Panikkar. So, why did Abhishiktānanda leave?

Virtually the whole recent corpus of literature on Abhishiktānanda interprets his life in light of his embrace of Indian *sannyāsa* and Hindu spirituality, while his decision to leave France and his monastery and move to India is usually explained as a response to a "call." However, no clear traces of this supposed call have been identified. Shirley du Boulay suggests that the call to go to India was "another vocation" to be added to the monastic one, although she has to concede that about the origin of this call to move to India, "no firm conclusion can be drawn."[11] Gispert-Sauch suggests that the origin of this call might be found in the reading available in the Abbey of Kergonan.[12] This is an interesting insight. Hardly anything exists in the library that might localize, concretize, and dynamize the desire he eventually held for the monastic life in India. We know that manuscripts mentioning India and Hinduism were quite rare in the monastery library, limited to the 1928–37 volumes of *Xaveriana*, the mission studies journal of the Jesuits of Louvain.[13] *Xaveriana* did not investigate spirituality or non-Christian forms of monasticism; it was instead a collection of monographs dealing with socio-cultural problems encountered by missionaries. The *Xaveriana* series was the journal of the so-called Louvain school of missiology, led by Pierre Charles and promoting the thesis that salvation is collective—non-individual—and therefore that missions are about converting nations and civilizations. Moreover, Charles was the proponent of the indigenous church, the "planting" of the church in non-Christian countries. Charles was not specifically concerned with the conversion of India, although he visited the subcontinent.[14]

Another interesting insight is the visit that Abhishiktānanda paid to Clervaux Abbey, established in 1890 by the Congregation of Solesmes, in

---

10. Le Saux, "Amour et Sagesse." Quoted in *Letters*, 7.

11. *Life*, 40.

12. In *Life*, du Boulay mentions an email received from Canon Lemarié, who became a monk at Kergonan and a friend of Abhishiktānanda. Farther Lemarié sustains that there was absolutely nothing on India in the library of the monastery. So, the question is not yet settled. *Cave*, 39.

13. Euverte et al., *Henri le Saux* 43.

14. Shirley du Boulay mentions "an American scholar" who compiled the list of the books and articles believed to be in the library at the time, including a few reviews of the missions to the East. See Boulay, Abhishiktānanda Centenary, 7.

Luxembourg. In 1937, he went to Clervaux with regards to his task as librarian at Kergonan. There he met Jacques Winandy, who after the Second World War would become abbot of the Clervaux community. Winardy was part of the thread in twentieth-century Christian monasticism of rediscovering eremitism. At that time, only a few dozen Camaldolese monks in the entire Catholic Church were allowed to live as hermits. Coenobitic life—a form of monasticism based on "life in common"—was the norm of the Benedictine order while the solitary life of the hermit was the exception. Candidates for eremitism, who were (are) under the Canon and required formal authorization, were regularly discouraged from leaving their community. Some monks, however, wanted more solitude than could be found in the coenobitic orders and felt a call to return to this third-century AD eremitic life with its simplicity and monastic integrity, where they could enter into radical asceticism and constant prayer. Thomas Merton is the most famous case; he was allowed to live a semi-solitary (eremitic) life after twenty-three years of community (coenobitic) life, but it was Winandy who provided the opportunity for aspiring monks to live the hermit life in the 1960s. Winandy would become an advocate of Abhishiktānanda's Indian project within the Congregation of Solesmes.[15]

At this point it should be clear that canonical rules existed within the Benedictine institution that made it difficult for Abhishiktānanda—or anyone in his position—to leave the monastery. These rules can be summarized as follows: the community eventually grants the monk permission to leave; the congregation confirms that his special vocation (to move to India) is compatible with the congregation's constitutions; and finally, the Church in Rome provides the permission of exclaustration, that is, permission to leave the monastery. In other words, a monastic community has the right to let one of its members go to consecrate himself to a special vocation under certain conditions, eventually going through a chapter (community) vote, while the congregation's constitutions might allow (or not) a monk to become a *sannyāsī*. Moreover, a community can grant different degrees of approval, that is, permission to leave and support to a monk's request for exclaustration to Rome, without giving the exiting monk a mandate to go to India in the name of the congregation or committing itself to financially support him.

This canonical rule, though, was only part of a greater problem, which is related to the vow of stability. The Benedictine community is a family

---

15. Euverte et al., *Henri le Saux*, 41.

because the abbot is a father and the monks are brothers. Usually, the abbot remains in place until his death, and it is until his passing that the monks promise to remain in the monastery of their profession. This stability gives the monastic community solidarity, security, and peace; that stability is visible in the monastery as a whole and is reflected on every face. Perseverance in work, respect for tradition, unity of minds, love of the common good—all these are the natural fruits of Benedictine life. Benedictine monks are well aware of *acedia*, "the noonday demon," the false notion that spiritual search improves by leaving the monastery for another place. Monks know the temptation of the noonday demon who meets them at various times of the journey; this is why the vow of stability as a spiritual discipline is a pillar of monastic vocation. The monastic vow of stability is a retaining wall against the temptation to demonize the monastery and the community in which the monk lives as a place of frustration and disappointment, and to idealize and romanticize the place one might go. When a monk enters the monastic life, not only himself, but the entire community believes that the monastery is the very place God is working in him to transform him. Accordingly, leaving the monastery not only fosters the false notion that by leaving situation and place, the problem would be solved; moreover, it interrupts the process of deification at work in that particular situation and place. In other words, to leave a community could be seen as an infidelity, an escape, or an act of unfaithfulness to one's vow of stability.

Benedictine monks are usually left free to develop their own vocation. They are allowed to change monasteries if one can no longer accomplish the promises made to God in the place of one's profession. Abhishiktānanda was a monk in spiritual maturity and intellectual clarity, and his desire to move to India seemed sincere, the expression of a deep aspiration and desire for a different ascetic life with respect to temporal things. Of course, stability is an authentic monastic value, although it is not the last word on monastic perfection. We can only guess that the community at the Abbey of Kergonan granted Abhishiktānanda an approval like that of Pontius Pilate: do what you believe to be your vocation—we do not prevent you from pursuing his, but expect no approval, no blessing, no sponsorship. Certainly, Abhishiktānanda's mission was not officially sustained with a canonical affiliation. His request for exclaustration canonically forbade him access to the community and, in the absence of a *nihil obstat*, denied him the privilege of considering himself a Benedictine monk.

While no conclusive evidence can be found in the library of the Abbey of Kergonan about a potential "call" to India, the connection with Winandy opens up another option. If we follow this line of thought—namely, that Abhishiktānanda had to leave Kergonan in order to be himself, that is, a hermit—we might locate Abhishiktānanda in the so-called new hermitical movement. This brings us to the highly influential comment of his friend Panikkar that Abhishiktānanda was an acosmic. However, Abhishiktānanda did not ask permission to leave the monastery to pursue a more radical asceticism. The desire of a more radical life, a greater need for asceticism, could be resolved by asking permission to lead an eremitical life in the monastery or in Europe. This is Merton's option. Abhishiktānanda asked permission to leave and join Monchanin in a project of contemplative mission. More precisely, Abhishiktānanda was allowed to withdraw his vow of stability, not to find more solitude within the monastic life but to join a missionary project, which he rapidly dismissed when in India.

The very fact that Abhishiktānanda showed a great deal of interest in going to India and joining Monchanin in his project of contemplative mission, and then—only a few years later—expressed his disengagement from such a project has been a further hindrance for scholars. The spiritual awakening that Abhishiktānanda experienced in India at Sri Ramana Maharshi ashram has been used as an explanation. It is understandable that scholars thought of Abhishiktānanda as a highly talented monk who went through a spiritual awakening in India. And it is pardonable, also, that Abhishiktānanda's later abandonment of a contemplative form of mission in favor of a spiritual search should have struck his fellow monk Monchanin as a defection. As a by-product of this fact, a gulf has opened up between our views of Abhishiktānanda the monk at Kergonan and Abhishiktānanda the *sadhu* in India.

His friends Stuart, Baumer-Despeigne, and Panikkar believed that there was no rupture between the monk at St. Anne's Abbey in Kergonan and the *sannyāsī* in orange. His friends considered Kergonan as an obstacle for Abhishiktānanda, who found himself in need of another place to continue his spiritual quest. Odette Baumer-Despeigne establishes a link between Abhishiktānanda's vocation to India and his intuition—by reading Gregory Nazianzen's Hymn to God beyond All Names—of the apophatic way to God.[16] She does not elaborate further, but she seems to imply that Abhishiktānanda realized that he had to go to India to find

---

16. Coff, *Abhishiktananda: An Interview*, 51.

God beyond all names and forms. Panikkar makes a similar remark: Abhishiktānanda had to go to India to be able to reach "the total experience" in the terms of à Kempis: *quiquid Deus non est: nihil est* (whatever is not God is nothing).[17] His biographer Stuart writes that Abhishiktānanda was dissatisfied at Kergonan—not with community life, but with something much deeper, which apparently prevented his aspiration for "total monasticism."[18] In an important remark, Panikkar mentions Abhishiktānanda's opinion that a theologically based "sociological impossibility" in the current Christian tradition of reaching the total experience was Abhishiktānanda's main motivation to move to India.[19]

Surely, there is a strong presumption that Abhishiktānanda faced a particular problem in France and hoped to find a solution for it by moving to India. What kind of problem? In the absence of more direct evidence, we can hope to answer the question only if we are prepared to look first at the situation in which he grew up. To capture the complex picture of Abhishiktānanda's involvement in Hinduism, one must consider it as emerging from a particular spiritual milieu, the milieu with the religious environment in which Abhishiktānanda grew to maturity in France. For a brilliant man of great sensitivity, born into a serious Catholic family, who grew up in seminaries and monasteries and was exposed to a rigorous training in the spiritual and theological tradition of the patristic and medieval fathers, what "sociological impossibility" in the current Christian tradition might reasonably be expected to present itself as an existential problem to which the move to India became the final solution? In the climate of the times, for a man born in France who was raised in a strict, traditional, pre-Vatican II Catholicism, for a man with a passion for spiritual quests, for a monk of the cloistered Solesmes Congregation, what might the problem be? In answering that question, we must look directly at the Roman Catholic Church of Abhishiktānanda's childhood, at its theological and spiritual preoccupations, its doctrinal extrinsicism, and above all at that devotional framework that was the common possession of priests, monks, and clergy of all kinds, especially in the Solesmes Congregation. And, to the extent that we see more clearly the character of the Catholic environment that was the cradle for so much of Abhishiktānanda's life and

---

17. *Letter*, 446. For the quotation, see Kempis, *The Imitation of Christ*, 161.
18. Letter to J. Lemarié, March 13, 1967; see *Letters*, 12.
19. *Letter*, 446.

thought, we can hope that this investigation will help in reappraising our view of Abhishiktānanda and his existential problem.

What problem did Abhishiktānanda face in Kergonan? The problem likely had something to do with his perceived inability to progress in his search for God within the parameters of the monastic life at Kergonan. Abhishiktānanda's move to India can be seen properly in relation to his "deep dissatisfaction" with his life in Kergonan. In his words, at the end of his life, "it was in my deep dissatisfaction [with the life in the monastery] that my desire to come to India was born."[20] This dissatisfaction was a vital concern. Accordingly, his move to India can be better understood in relation to his lack of spiritual progress in France; his desire to move to India was ultimately a desire to flee from his condition as a monk in Kergonan.

Given the theological, spiritual, cultural, and institutional situation I have depicted here, and given also Abhishiktānanda's radicalism in terms of spiritual search, we can suppose that he was uniquely placed to feel the full force of the devotional framework at work in Kergonan, and to recognize that the only possibility of continuing his quest was by leaving. Now that we have at least a broad idea of the kind of devotional theology and sentimental spirituality he found at Kergonan, it is easier to see the possible source of his deep dissatisfaction. After almost two decades at Kergonan, we have no knowledge that anything extraordinary happened there. There was no decisive enlightenment, no awareness of the "naked will of God."[21] It has been said that "the original aim of monasticism was to provide a setting in which the mystical life could be lived."[22] The more time Abhishiktānanda spent at the monastery, the less he came to see the monastery as some separate vehicle for sanctity and an island of deeper realities.

We can also recall a comment from Monchanin, a comment that has traditionally been seen as part of the increasing tension between the two founders of Shantivanam. In the context of the traditionalist spirit of the Solesmes Congregation, on one side, and Blondel and de Lubac's criticism on the inherent extrinsicism of such a tradition on the other, however, Monchanin's words sound like a confirmation of our hypothesis. In 1955, Monchanin explained in a letter to his friend Eduard Dupperray that "He [Abhishiktānanda] comes from a *rigorist* and even *integrist* theology." In Blondelian terms, "integrism" is a form of extrinsicism. If Monchanin is

---

20. Letter to J. Lemarié, March 13, 1967; see *Letters*, 12.
21. See references in *Letters*, 4.
22. Underhill, "The Essentials of Mysticism," 34.

a trustworthy observer of the movement of thought of his companion, Abhishiktānanda became aware of his devotional mentality when he moved to India and clashed with Indian *sannyāsa* and its spirituality. At that point, he realized that he suffered from the institutional church's narrowness. Monchanin could not miss the ironic circumstance: "The institutional Church is a burden to him [Abhishiktānanda] (to him who was earlier devoted to Canon Law and Liturgy)." The sophisticated priest of Lyon, who was de Lubac's friend and an acquaintance of Teilhard de Chardin, was simply horrified at Abhishiktānanda's forms of "muddled thinking." He blamed his companion for his inability to manage the transition from "its [institutional church] narrowness" to "his contact with Hinduism." "The change is too sudden," he concluded.[23]

Monchanin claims that Abhishiktānanda, who was an integral part of the institutional church that Abhishiktānanda now rejected, realized through his contact with Hinduism the narrowness of the institutional church. Monchanin did not see Abhishiktānanda's move to India as an intentional escape from this kind of narrowness, but rather as a commitment to his project of contemplative mission. According to Monchanin, Abhishiktānanda committed to Monchanin's project and brought the narrowness of Kergonan and its monastic tradition with him to India, where he became aware of such narrowness; he then overreacted as a consequence. If we are ready to accept both statements—Abhishiktānanda's statement of his "deep dissatisfaction" with his life in Kergonan, and Monchanin's statement on Abhishiktānanda's "*integrist* theology"—we are well positioned to deal with the possibility that the narrowness of Kergonan was a reality, and that Abhishiktānanda experienced it directly.

The reason behind Abhishiktānanda's move to India has been called a "mystery"; however, the "mystery" is no longer a mystery if we hypothesize his increasing estrangement from the supposed contemplative context of French monasticism (or at least of Kergonan), although this feeling was initially not recognized as such.[24] A monk who is increasingly estranged from the religious and spiritual atmosphere in his monastery develops the idea to leave, an idea that will take the form of a call to missionary work in India. This missionary call is a matter of spiritual discernment and such

---

23. Letter to Edouard Duperray, December 14, 1955; see *Letters*, 80.

24. "There are quite a few mysteries about Henri Le Saux. One of them is how, after nearly 20 years in the monastery, he was overcome by a passionate desire to go to India." Du Boulay, *Abhishiktananda Centenary*, 6.

discernment can be summarized as follows: Was his move to India compatible with his vocation, his profession, his vow of stability? Was the move really a matter of a second vocation, a desire for a more radical life, a thirst for the absolute, or was it an escape, an infatuation with a fad, or a thirst for personal adventure? Monchanin's project seemed to be the providential answer, as leaving the monastery was like letting go of something solid to grasp a shadow. Monchanin could remove all the obstacles, that is, the Lord himself was directing Abhishiktānanda's footsteps and his superiors could give him permission. Monchanin was providential also for another reason—that is, because the request for exclaustration needed to be backed up by a letter from the bishop of the diocese where he would settle, and Monchanin could provide that letter. A project of contemplation in mission seemed to satisfy the monk, the institution, and his Christian companion and teacher in India, Monchanin, who offered a concrete opportunity.

Abhishiktānanda was sincere in his request to leave France for a project of contemplative mission, yet he misread his deeper motivation. After the encounter with the first Hindu *sadhu* and related spiritual awakening, the monk deciphered the character of his dissatisfaction at the monastery and established a link between his experiential problem at Kergonan and the extrinsicism of the church. For the next twenty years Abhishiktānanda's self would be divided: his call to a true search for God and his attempt to distance himself from a perceived dogmatic institution, on the one hand and on the other, his gratitude to his Christian teacher and his loyalty to the project of contemplation in mission that granted him the opportunity to move to India. He accomplished the former with growing militancy and the latter without passion. He increasingly recognized that the root cause of his move to India was a spiritual need that he was unable to satisfy in France. He recognized that—for a long time—he had a problem, an existential problem. Only in India was he able to frame his problem intellectually: in France, at Kergonan, he suffered from church narrowness. When he arrived in India, he learned to distinguish between the need for unconditional contemplation that is at the core of his vocation, the sense of incompleteness of the monastic life that he experienced in Kergonan, and the convenient form that his move from France to India eventually assumed.

There is no reason to assume a break between Abhishiktānanda's life in France and in India. Surely in India he was a curious, touchy, and eccentric figure, with un-Indian habits and idiosyncrasies. Yet scholars ignore these foreign oddities on account of the unique contribution he made to the development of Indian Christian theology. By labeling Abhishiktānanda a foreigner of odd personal habits, with an extraordinary, phenomenal, possibly unique talent for spiritual search, scholars have neutralized his nostalgia for France, Gregorian chant, and all the rest. Abhishiktānanda himself did nothing to cut himself off from the wider theological and cultural traditions with which he was familiar in his youth. His comparative ignorance of the older theological classics was counterbalanced by a rich and varied familiarity with the main contributions of the pre-Council theology. No doubt, something in his intellectual background and upbringing would explain his personal peculiarities—the neo-scholastic background, the "rigoristic and even fundamentalist theology," and all that, but it scarcely seems to have occurred to scholars that there might be more than a chance connection between this "narrowness" and the man who rejected all these aspects of the traditional life of a monk, who eventually escaped the Abbey of Saint Anne.

Conclusion

This chapter gave a second look at Abhishiktānanda's move to India and argued that the decision had less to do with his desire to move to India than his urgent desire to leave France. The question is not why he headed *to* India, but why he moved *from* France. He moved from France because the reality of a "sociological impossibility" was an insuperable limit at Kergonan to his radical search for God. In the next chapter, I will explain how the meeting with Monchanin helped Abhishiktānanda link his personal experience with an ecclesial concern—how a sociological impossibility in a monastery could become paradigmatic of a much bigger story, that is, the extrinsicist character of Western Christianity.

3

MEETING MONCHANIN

"It is from him [Monchanin] that I learnt."

—Abhishiktānanda, 1956[1]

Introduction

CERTAIN AUTHORITATIVE AND SCHOLARLY books about Abhishiktānanda still invite us to assume that Abhishiktānanda's theological interests and preoccupations date from after his meeting with Monchanin—that Abhishiktānanda's concern with a Christian-Advaitic synthesis was awakened by his contact with the "fulfillment" theology of Jules Monchanin, and subsequently with the doctrine of Advaita Vedanta of Sankara. In this chapter I consider instead the possibility that the meeting in question was important for a different reason: Monchanin's theological ideas and methods helped Abhishiktānanda reframe into theological terms what was a personal preoccupation.

Monchanin

When Abhishiktānanda met Monchanin, on August 16, 1948, the former was a much less learned and intellectually sophisticated monk than his companion. His studies were limited to what he gained at the seminary and then at the abbey. On the contrary, Monchanin was, according to Abhishiktānanda,

---

1. *Diary*, 138 (January 12, 1956).

one of the most brilliant intellects among the French clergy, a remarkable conversationalist, at home on every subject, a brilliant lecturer, and a theologian who opened before his hearers marvellous and ever new horizons.[2]

So what kind of theologian was he?

Though Monchanin has often been painted as a brilliant and genial intellectual, he preferred the humble and practical life of a parish priest, first in France, then in India, over a splendid academic career.[3] He favored the intellectual freedom of a parish over an academic life of notional and abstract theology under the jurisdiction of the ecclesiastic authority. Monchanin's opinion on the church was certainly acute, but also unusually critical:

> I am not surprised that the services of the Church, distorted that way, become despised. Some serious reforms must be carried out.[4]

He expressed a dispirited vision of a non-dogmatic, social, and mystical character of the church, and he showed sympathy for those Catholic intellectuals rejected by the church or marginalized from her (like Laberthonnière and Blondel, respectively, both of whom remained faithful to the church).[5]

Monchanin was intellectually close to both Blondel and de Lubac. Monchanin read *Action* in 1921, receiving a copy probably from Laurent Rémilleaux, when he was at the seminary of St. Irenée and before his ordination and oath against modernism. He immediately expressed his admiration in a letter to friend Eduard Duperray. The same year, Monchanin held long conversations with Louis Richard, one of his seminary professors,

---

2. *Memorial*, 2.

3. Monchanin reads *Action*: Letter to Duperray, s.d. Conversations with Richard on Blondel as Monchanin's maître à penser. Included in Jacquin, *Une amitié Sacerdotale Jules Monchanin*, 24 and 30.

4. "Je ne m'étonne pas que les rites d'Église, ainsi défigurés, tombent Dans le mépris. Il y aurait de profondes réformes à faire." Monchanin, *Lettres à Ma Mère, 1913–1957*, 93, hereinafter referred to as *Mère*. Other works of Monchanin quoted in this volume are: Monchanin, *De l'Esthétique à la Mystique*, hereinafter referred to as *Esthétique*; Monchanin, *Ecrits Spirituels*, hereinafter referred to as *Ecrits*; Monchanin, *Mystique de l'Inde, mystère chrétien: Ecrits et Inédits*, hereinafter referred to as *Mystique*; Monchanin, *Lettres au Père Le Saux (1947–1957)*, hereinafter referred to as *Père Le Saux*; Monchanin et al, *Jules Monchanin: Théologie et spiritualité missionnaire*, hereinafter referred to as *Théologie*.

5. Petit, *La Jeunesse De Monchanin*, 189 (Laberthnnière, Blondel). For the non-dogmatic character, see, "nowadays, there is no more Christian thinking than Christian art, than Christian action, than Christian love. All that is left is mysticism. But are there still mystics in the Church, now that Saint John of the Cross is dead?"

on the religious problems introduced by Blondel.[6] Monchanin considered Blondel (and Blondel's colleague Laberthonnière) his *maîtres à penser*, particularly because they addressed what Monchanin considered to be an essential question: "how to adapt Christianity to modern civilization."[7] In the years to come at the faculty of theology, he extended his studies to include Bergson, Nietzsche, and a disciple of Blondel, Auguste Valensin, among others. As a matter of fact, Monchanin joined the Blondelian philosophical-scientific circle of Lyon, *Le Groupe*, as a theological associate. Monchanin shows a Blondellian inclination in his understanding of conscience in terms of "existence (concrete, dynamic, tragic, scattered, turn, but trying to unify itself);" in his philosophy of time, including the Bergsonian notion of duration but with an interesting addendum on the change of status that brings the encounter with the supernatural; in his claims that "the person is a spiritual movement [. . .] centred on consciousness, oriented by love," and that "the human being is a substantial movement toward God." The notion of "movement toward" is the cornerstone of his missionary vocation—a movement toward another (*esse ad alterum*)—and his Trinitarian vision, in which "each Person is constituted in relation to two Others by being in movement toward the two Others."[8] Skilled commentators easily recognize the influence of both Bergson and Blondel on Monchanin.

Monchanin first met Henri de Lubac in 1930 in Lyon when both lived there. The friendship spanned three decades and eventually outlasted even Monchanin's own life, for, in 1967, de Lubac published a book of recollections about his friend and consistently refuted his friend's critics. They belonged to the same generation, hardly a year apart, and to the same Lyonese

---

6. Petit, *La Jeunesse De Monchanin*, 143.

7. Petit, *La Jeunesse De Monchanin*, 148 (maitres à penser), 149 (modern civilization). As for the decision to turn his back on the academic career that his teachers had planned for him, an undated manuscript about a certain "Bernard" was found among his manuscripts. Bernard—alias Monchanin—attempts to make "a marriage of dogma, thought, and life" but then regards the task as difficult, painful, futile, and artificial, and declares that he wants "to be free and to live." Black folder, s.d. Monchanin sources. In the same letter in which he informed his friend Duperray of the imminent dropping, he mentions his tiredness of "theological ratiocinations with syllogisms constructing God." Letter to Duperray, March 16, 1924, in Archives Municipales de Lyon: see Jacquin, "The Spiritual Journey of Jules Monchanin" 133. These remarks can also work to describe his criticism toward the church.

8. Monchanin, Letter to Lullima (remark on coscience), July 18, 1955: see Gadille, "Jules Monchanin, a Prophet," 24; Monchanin, Letter to Duperray (time), July 3, 1957: see Jacquin, *Une amitié Sacerdotale Jules Monchanin*, 253–55; see also: Monchanin, *Esthétique*, 55 (spiritual) and 70 (movement), and see Monchanin, *Théologie*, 37 (Trinity).

milieu; their intellectual orientation was the same, with a decisive inclination toward the mystical in Monchanin's case. They shared confidences and tragedies: they were both affected directly by the encyclical *Humani Generis* (1950), as de Lubac was disbarred from teaching in Lyon and Monchanin was kicked out of Shembaganur, the Jesuit theological college in India. Theologian Grummett credits Teilhard de Chardin and Monchanin for their distinct vision of nature and its dependence on divine action: while de Lubac usually identified nature with human nature, de Charden and Monchanin extended the notion to the entire natural order, which depends on God for its creation, preservation, and redemption.[9]

In 1938, on the eve of Monchanin's departure for India, the men held a meeting in the streets of Lyon. De Lubac shared with Monchanin details about how, since his seminary days, a vision for a grand project had been taking shape in his mind:

> to rethink everything in the light of theology and to rethink theology through mysticism, freeing it from everything incidental and regaining, through spirituality alone, everything essential.

At the same meeting, de Lubac suggested that Monchanin embrace such a vision, and Monchanin obliged.

> He [de Lubac] believes that it is in colliding with India that I will be able to rework theology much better than by going into theological problems in themselves.[10]

These quotations merit three additional points. First, de Lubac suggested Monchanin approach theology in the same way he did, responding to immediate circumstances rather than proceeding systematically through issues. As a matter of fact, Monchanin was an intuitive thinker with a dense prose style and a unique gift for amazing strokes of genius; he was not a systematic theologian. Second, de Lubac proposed to Monchanin a missionary project of audacious radicalism, asking him to rethink everything in light of theology à la Blondel, that is, according to the deepest sense of incarnation, and to rethink theology through a filter of mysticism, as de Lubac did in his own research. Finally, de Lubac invited Monchanin to be cautious and to maintain a prudent distinction between the essential from the incidental in Christian doctrine. This last point is particularly important because it brings to light what ultimately united the circle of theologians,

9. Grumett, "Eucharist, Matter and the Supernatural," 165–78.
10. Monchanin, *Mystique*, 21–22.

including Monchanin, around de Lubac: the conviction that the goal to engage Catholic theology in dialogue with contemporary thought is limited, in the words of de Lubac, to "whatever can be assimilated."[11] In a similar fashion, the task to engage Hinduism and Indian thought in dialogue is limited to whatever can be assimilated.

Monchanin's Project

Monchanin's project, the establishment of a Roman Catholic ashram in India, aimed to reach the very core of the Indian soul and to Christianize it from within. As monasticism has been the primary form of spiritual quest and religious commitment in India since the Vedic era, the raison d'être of an Indian Benedictine ashram was an attempt to integrate into the church the vocation of the Indian *sannyāsa*. *Sannyāsa* is a distinct and rare form of monasticism that avoids any sort of social and ritual engagement for the sake of the absolute, transcendent, and ineffable Divine. *Sannyāsa* in Sanskrit means "renunciation of the world," renunciation of all, including identity. The Indian *sannyāsa* embraces acosmism and renounces one's own self. "Who is the seer?," monks like to repeat to distinguish the speaking "I" (the phenomenological ego) from the true "I" (the interior Self). In Monchanin's mind, "la vie missionnaire" and "la vie contemplative," mission and monasticism, were finally entangled for the first time since the Middle Ages. As a result, India, the most precious gem of Asia, the timeless country of sages and holy men, and the tradition of such spiritual treasures, seemed at hand.

Monchanin's project of a Roman Catholic ashram in India was a turning point, an attempt to overcome the counterfeits and shortcomings of the previous waves of Christianization. It marked a dramatic shift in the missionary strategy: from colonialism to inculturation. Inculturation in Monchanin's view maintains the priority of the faith over culture, so that Christian missionaries embrace Indian cultural forms as long as the specificity and the integrity of Christian faith are not compromised. The central point of Indianization was that Monchanin and his fellow monk Abhishiktānanda would "become" Indian without ceasing to be Christians and would formulate their faith in Indian terms. Monchanin's plan was to adopt Indian philosophy with a certain discernment in order to give expression to the Christian deposit of faith in the Indian context. I offer a definition of the main terms used here:

11. De Lubac, *Catholicisme*, 148.

identity is cultural identity; *deposit of faith* stands for the body of saving truth revealed by Christ to the apostles. *Tradition* stands for the articulation of the deposit of faith, that is, the transmission of revelation for the belief of the faithful. Finally, *essential* stands for unconditioned.

In pursuing his inculturation project, Monchanin adopted an "indigenization from above" strategy. He was aware of the capacity within Christianity to reproduce its constructions and then refashion them as indigenous, that is, to generate Christian reproductions of indigenous structures as a means of mission. However, the identity strategy at work within mission was always related to Christianity and therefore, despite the intent, inculturation recreated Christian structures. To put it differently, Monchanin's inculturation project proposed a hybrid identity that was constrained by a semi-essentialist tradition—a tradition that assimilates Indian components—and an essentialist faith. In fact, Monchanin's inculturation strategy was not really an attempt to negotiate French priesthood in exchange for Indian monasticism, but rather an implication of his understanding of Christianity as superior to Hinduism. Monchanin's concentration of an essentialist faith, characterized by purity and perfection, functions as an anchor within the inculturation strategy, where identity can be understood as complementary. With Monchanin, inculturation is cultural hybridity that includes—with a certain discernment—tradition.

He made clear that "Our task [. . .] is [. . .] to accept [in Hinduism] that which is compatible, to reject that which is incompatible with Christianity."[12] At the level of religious traditions, the meeting with Hinduism would happen on Christianity's terms. Monchanin was careful to frame his project not as a combination of Catholic faith and Hindu thought, but rather of Catholic faith and Indian thought. In this context, he made clear that identity can be negotiated, while faith cannot.

In addressing how Christian religious tradition—that is, theological concepts and patterns of thought that have been elaborated in the European dogmatic tradition—can be negotiated in the Indian context, Monchanin proceeded with caution. In methodology, he aimed to collude with Indian thought in order to uncover the primitive expression of Christian faith. He believed that in coming into contact with India, he would be able to "recapture Christianity in its original vigour."[13] In terms of principle, Monchanin seemed to see tradition as composed of two parts: an "infrangible core of

---

12. Monchanin, *Mère*, 542.
13. Monchanin, *Théologie*, 85.

the Revelation itself," the dogma in its pristine state, and several "constellations" formed around this nucleus, the subsequent development that began in the times of the apostolic fathers and carried on through the course of the European history of Christianity. He argued that "no medieval summa and no critical history of dogmas can surpass the theology of Paul and John."[14]

The dual movement of Monchanin's theological enterprise is clear. On one side, he clashed with India to reach the essence of Christianity. Not accidentally de Lubac pointed out that a move to Indian will help Monchanin

> rethink everything in the light of theology and to rethink theology through mysticism, freeing it from everything incidental and regaining, through spirituality alone, everything essential.[15]

This essential core, once freed "from everything incidental," would become the irreducible, non-negotiable pure state of Christian dogmas, the criteria presiding over the replacement of a European set of terms with Indian ones deemed more fitting to the Indian mind. In theorizing this semi-essentialist character of tradition, Moncahnin created an anti-assimilation stance against the risk of misrepresentation of the revealed mystery, and he protected faith from any sort of hybridity. For him, the fundamental essence of faith and tradition is pure and authentic and autonomous from its cultural clothes: if the path of inculturation were reversed and Christian missionaries were to liberate themselves from indigenous customs, if they plumbed the depths of their faith, then they would locate something fundamentally Christian.

The meeting with India did not pose the greatest threat to Monchanin's identity, while his encounter with Hinduism forced him to reconsider the possibility of a hybrid tradition. In fact, once Monchanin clashed with Hinduism, he rediscovered his European Christian roots. He called himself "Greek" as a short-cut for the Christian mindset that emerged from the synthesis between biblical narrative and Greek philosophy in the Classic era. European-based tradition, for Monchanin, paradoxically

---

14. Monchanin, *Théologie*, 86.

15. Monchanin described his farewell meeting with de Lubac, just before he left for India (April–May 1939) in a letter to Duperray: "J'ai revu le P. de L [...], seul, longuement. Il m'a redit toute son amitié, étant celui qu'il cherchait, réalisant l'intuition qu'il avait eue, dès séminaire: repenser tout à la lumière de la théologie et celle-ci par la mystique, la dégageant de tout l'accessoire et retrouvant, par la seule spiritualité, tout l'essentiel [...] Il a surtout aimé mes notes sur l'amour et celles sur l'Inde. Il pense que c'est en me heurtant à l'Inde que je pourrai refaire la théologie, beaucoup mieux qu'en creusant les problèmes théologiques pour eux-memes." *Ecrits*, 21–22.

was reinforced in the process of inculturation, as defined as a difference from Indian thought. Monchanin's original notion of a "gravitational centre" and successive synthesis of Christian thought in Europe and beyond was replaced by the notion that Greek metaphysics can claim exclusive privilege for interpreting Christian faith. In his mind, Christianity was unencumbered and unaffected by the cultural collision birthed by the encounter with Greek philosophy.

Monchanin arrived in India in 1939; he loved India and felt at home there. He left only in 1945, soon after the end of World War II, to be the secretary to his Indian bishop in Rome. Monchanin then returned to India at the beginning of 1947, but left again in September 1957, when it was discovered that he had a tumor in his abdomen; He died one month later in Paris. Monchanin reacted in a distinct way to the process of inculturation to forge a true transnational identity. In his encounter with Indian religious tradition, however, he experienced an absolute rejection. Monchanin considered Hinduism, fundamentally different from Christianity, to be homogeneous in its radical heterogeneity. He reacted by rejecting the entire indigenous religion tradition *en bloc* and recovering his European Christian tradition. He declared to a friend, "I react in a contrary direction; never have I felt myself intellectually more *Christian* and also, I must say, more *Greek*."[16] Monchanin argued the absolute truth of Christianity and the parallel fallacy of Hinduism; he also claimed that tradition is not subject to hybridization. In the end, Monchanin resolved to add an Indian facet to his French identity, while maintaining his native-born characteristics as far as his Christian faith and faith articulation were concerned.

Meeting Monchanin

Panikkar persistently referred to Monchanin as Abhishiktānanda's guru and traced his consistent and enduring influence on Abhishiktānanda. But what specifically did Abhishiktānanda learn from Monchanin? When Abhishiktānanda met Monchanin, the latter was charming, intense, and intellectually gifted; it was gratifying and flattering for Monchanin to come in contact with this brilliant younger monk, who shared his project of contemplative mission and apparently was poised to contribute with his own personal experience of asceticism and monasticism. So, it is highly possible that Monchanin himself thought of Abhishiktānanda as a highly talented friend

16. Quoted in Rodhe, *Jules Monchanin, Pioneer*, 47.

and pupil and viewed Abhishiktānanda's expectations and purposes entirely from Monchanin's own problems in Christian mission. It is also possible that scholars have seen the relationship between Abhishiktānanda and Monchanin in light of Monchanin's project of contemplative mission. Another option to consider is that what Abhishiktānanda learned from Monchanin concerns rather the renewal of the Western Church.

When Abhishiktānanda first made contact with Monchanin and was drawn into the circle of his academic companions and *les amis* who so influenced his life between 1948 and 1958, he was entering into a cultural situation and a group of active, opinionated, and self-motivated people having distinct preoccupations and a definite history.[17] From the synthetic portrait of these intellectuals and of the cultural atmosphere of Catholicism in France at large, dominated in the early twentieth century by a conflict of faith and reason, we recognize their main preoccupation. One consequence of the dominant tendency that arose from considering reason and faith as two completely separate worlds was that Catholics in France felt somehow like an alienated people. Catholic intellectuals like Blondel and de Lubac feared for the future of the church, under attack by the secularized government and academy, and suffered from the enforced imposition of an authoritarian, didactic, and dispassionate inclination of the church. They were torn between a world of historical secularism freed from all traces of the transcendent and one of dogmatic statements imposed authoritatively on the passive believer, as if they were from the outside; indeed, this spiritual malaise was worse for clergy, who languished from a speculative mentality that encompassed a vast network of areas—spirituality, education, clerical administration, theology—in which personal experience, creativity, and imagination were simply banned. Catholic clergy were asked to adopt a notion of the supernatural in complete isolation from human experience. Moreover, Blondel and de Lubac articulated a view of Catholicism as a supernatural religion, including a notion of a sacramental ontology, a synthesis of communion ecclesiology and the recovery of the supernatural. Monchanin was completely aligned with this intellectual framework.

Monchanin's missionary enterprise naturally emerged from de Lubac's rejection of a "modern, non-sacramental world," and his rediscovery of the mystical and contemplative dimension of Christian theology. De Lubac's intention was to infuse into the consciousness of humanity the forgotten Christian truth that the supernatural—the presence of God's

---

17. The expression *les amis* is used by Abhishiktānanda in his *Memorial*, 41.

saving activity—is not an otherworldly reality detached from the mundane, secular world. He suggested Monchanin should "rethink Christianity in an Indian way and to rethink India in a Christian way," which seems to be a two-way movement. On the one hand, Monchanin was asked to "Christianize" India, that is, to fulfill the unexpressed desire of India for unity beyond all forms and names, such as correcting the latent temptation of Indian spirituality to pluralism. On the other hand, he was supposed to "Indianize" Christianity, or help the church absorb and exalt the "uncommon gift" that "India has received from the Almighty [. . .] an unquenchable thirst for whatever is spiritual." By engaging Indian religions, Monchanin supported the return of Catholic theology to its mystical sources and rediscovered its original connection with God. Hinduism was instrumental in achieving this goal. Monchanin was committed to two tasks: a task of mission in his goal of Christianizing India, and a task of Western Christian renewal in Indianizing Christianity.

The resacramentalization of the church remained one of Monchanin's major concerns until the end of his life. A critical study by Hans Urs von Balthasar of Georges Barnanos (*Le Chretien Barnanos*) was one of the last books Monchanin read in the summer of 1957 at Kodaikanal.[18] Barnanos was considered by many to be the greatest French Catholic creative writer of the twentieth century. Balthasar's goal was simply to convey Bernanos's thesis of his country's "spiritual exhaustion." A lack of conviction and the absence of a sense of the mystery, indispensable to the vitality of Christianity, were in Bernanos's view the chief causes of this demise, which, as Balthasar pointed out with Barnanos, the church contributed to. In fact, both authors agreed that the very problem lies in the fact that Christians themselves have lost sight of the mystery at the heart of Christianity. As an antidote, Barnanos created in his writings an ecclesial existence "derived not merely from an abstract, individual faith, but from a faith of the Church," which contains a *sacramental* dimension.[19] Balthasar noted that

> The use of the word "sacramental" in Bernanos is highly peculiar. Not infrequently it uses it to refer to human experiences that have nothing to do externally with the sacraments of the Church but [. . .] are received and celebrated like holy actions, states, and realities. This can sometime occur [. . .] as a reference—over and

---

18. Balthasar, *Bernanos: An Ecclesial Existence*. For the remark on Monchanin, see de Lubac, "A Witness of Christ."

19. Balthasar, *Bernanos*, Foreword.

beyond the individual sacraments—to the wholly sacramental character of ecclesial and human existence.[20]

This sacramental character of ecclesial and human existence refers to the notion of natural sacraments such as the handshake of friendship and the kiss of love. This wider sense of sacramentality is, in fact, a celebration of the finite. This finite world is the immediate scene of a strange, mysterious sense of wholeness, of an unbroken worldview.

For Blondel, as for de Lubac, a middle way between modern intellectual methodologies and traditional church doctrines was available, a path that confronts the key question of human existence without diluting devotion and loyalty to the church. To achieve their goal, these Catholic intellectuals recovered an Augustinian orientation—a language of heart and passion, desire for God and inner divine presence—that offers a compelling way out of the intellectual morass of the day. As we saw, however, de Lubac went beyond this by arguing on the sacramental relationship between nature and the supernatural that he believed constituted a truly patristic and Catholic understanding of reality. And, to the extent that Monchanin was deeply aligned with de Lubac's project of resacramentalization of the Christian consciousness, we shall come to see more clearly the interaction between Monchanin and Abhishiktānanda: on the one hand, the intellectual priest of Lyon whose brilliant variations on the philosophical theories of Blondel and de Lubac were doing so much to carry forward Catholic theological arguments in India; on the other, the man who rejected all his traditional privileges as a monk of Abbey Sainte-Anne de Kergonan in order to seek God.

So, what specifically did Abhishiktānanda learn from Monchanin? In their last years, the two hermits rarely were at the ashram together. Before that, intricate and painful discussions about practical problems and theological concerns occurred more and more often between the two companions. In the first years, however, Abhishiktānanda was manifestly courteous and recognized the authority of Monchanin as chief and founder of the project that he was joining. When together, their time was divided among prayer in common, silent meditation, light domestic work, and long conversations. It was during those first years that we can imagine Monchanin, "one of the most brilliant intellects among the French clergy, a remarkable conversationalist," spending long quiet afternoons talking with Abhishiktānanda under the mango trees. We can imagine Monchanin talking

20. Balthasar, *Bernanos*, 128.

freely, as he was known to unabashedly share his encyclopedic theological knowledge with anyone willing to listen, likely opening up for his companion "marvelous and ever new horizons." Did these horizons include Blondel, de Lubac, and the recovery of the supernatural? The possibility that Monchanin introduced Abhishiktānanda to the theology of Blondel and de Lubac has never been scrutinized.

By assuming that Abhishiktānanda learned from Monchanin, I do not mean to imply a traditional disciple-master relationship. Monchanin has been called Abhishiktānanda's master and he himself likely would have accepted this title, at least in the earliest period of their friendship. Yet, there is something generally implausible about any picture of Abhishiktānanda as a theological "disciple" or "follower" of Monchanin. For all of Abhishiktānanda's later indebtedness to "one of the most brilliant intellects among the French clergy," we must remember that he himself took the initiative to approach Monchanin.[21] We know that Monchanin was quite at a loss in dealing with Abhishiktānanda's manuscript of *Guhantara* and passed it on to de Lubac in the hopes that he might do better; however, judging from de Lubac's reaction to the manuscript, the intellectual gap remained relevant. If there was an intellectual gulf between Monchanin and Abhishiktānanda, it was not only because Monchanin's philosophical methods, style of exposition, and target subject matter were unique and unparalleled. The gap was a sign, too, of a culture clash: the clash between a gifted priest whose intellectual problems and personal attitudes alike had been formed in the *nouvelle theologie* environment of Lyon, in which supernatural and nature were essentially bound up with each other without absorption and fusion, and a traditionalist monk from Brittany whose intellectual preoccupations had been shaped by the existential problems he experienced at his monastery. Nevertheless, in the absence of more direct evidence, we shall do much better to treat Abhishiktānanda as an entirely independent thinker and see him as someone who picked up ideas and methods from Monchanin only to put them to use for his own intellectual concerns.

Abhishiktānanda did, however, recognize his debt to Monchanin. In 1956, he noted in his *Diary* that "It is from him that I learnt that Scriptures and Christian doctrines are relatives: once I understood it, thanks to him, I just applied logic."[22] This is a fascinating insight. First, we have a glimpse of the private conversations between the two founders of Shantivanam.

21. *Memorial*, 2.
22. *Diary*, 138 (January 12, 1956).

Second, we have rare, more direct evidence that Blondel, de Lubac, and the whole discussion on the sacramental were part of these conversations. Of course, it is highly unlikely that Monchanin had invited Abhishiktānanda to consider *sic et simpliciter* that Scriptures and Christian doctrines are relative. Monchanin was considered by Jean Guitton as someone who "flies higher than Teilhard." He was an intellectual whose prose was so dense and precise to reframe sacramental ontology as follows:

> The Unity of the Mystical Body is participation in the Unity of the Trinity. The missions of the Word and the Spirit constitute the mystical Body, which itself depends on the Unity of the Trinity. There again, the Unity is communion, the unity of *co-esse* that is the foundation for the communion of the saints.

Is it possible that Abhishiktānanda learned from such a sophisticated intellectual that Scriptures and Christian doctrines are relative and then he just applied logic? Is this reconstruction of Monchanin's contribution to Abhishiktānanda's intellectual development reliable? It is much more possible that Monchanin taught Abhishiktānanda the lesson of Blondel, that is, tradition, as a connection between history and dogma, as a labor of penetration of the truth, is a work in progress. Monchanin's writings translate Blondel's lesson on tradition in terms of doctrinal deposit of faith in Christian history that has universal validity, although such deposit assumes different cultural variations.[23] What Abhishiktānanda might have learned, rather, is that extrinsicism's "fixism" (doctrine never changed or developed) is unsustainable.

In this context, I suggest that we consider how Abhishiktānanda might look at his devotional preoccupations, and above all at the general theological framework that was the common background of the priests, monks, and clergy he knew in Brittany, when he finally placed such a framework in the greater theological terms set out by Monchanin. I also suggest that we consider how his exposition to Monchanin helped him see more clearly the extrinsic character of the Catholic environment that was the cradle for so much of his "sociological impossibility" to pursue a spiritual quest at Kergonan. His expositions to Monchanin's theological ideas and methods might have encouraged him to re-evaluate his devotional preoccupation in terms of desacramentalized Christianity.

---

23. Monchanin understood tradition in terms of "the infrangible core of Revelation" and several "constellations: Origenist, Augustinian, [. . .] formed around this nucleus." See Monchanin, *Théologie*, 86.

In a previous chapter, I reconstructed the situation in the early twentieth-century French Third Republic and indicated the importance of the fracture between secularism and Catholicism for the educated people of that milieu—not just for academic philosophers and theologians, but for all laity and clergy. Although the whole intellectual and cultural picture, in all its richness and complexity, has been sacrificed to narrow the focus to two thinkers, Maurice Blondel and Henri de Lubac, the connection between the extrinsicism of French Catholicism, on one side, and the "sociological impossibility" Abhishiktānanda faced at St. Anne's Abbey in Kergonan, on the other, seems highly possible. Can we claim that the "sociological impossibility" at Kergonan was—ontologically speaking—the same as the fracture between the order of the natural and the supernatural as schematized by de Lubac? Can we argue that the extrinsicism mentioned by Blondel was effectively at work at Kergonan? Can we at least argue that the connection was direct and obvious to Monchanin, considering, "He [Abhishiktānanda] comes from a *rigorist* and even *integrist* theology," in which "integrism" stands for extrinsicism? If we believe that for Monchanin, the connection was direct, then we may argue that it was also evident to Abhishiktānanda himself. Thus, Abhishiktānanda realized through his contact with Hinduism that he suffered from the church's narrowness. In this context, I suggest that the encounter with India and Monchanin's theology might have enabled Abhishiktānanda to see as unassailable the connection between his existential problem at the monastery and the extrinsicism of the church. He experienced an epiphany at personal and ecclesial levels: the extrinsicism he suffered was the same extrinsicism that affected the entire church. Thus, extrinsicism—in all its ramifications—and the supernatural, as a form of remedy, are what Abhishiktānanda learned from Monchanin.

The effects of reframing the personal story in terms of general meaning can be seen in Abhishiktānanda's *Diary*. After hundreds of pages dedicated to crafting a theological synthesis between Advaita and Christianity, across twelve books and several articles, a constant effort devoted to theological synthesis, theologians are faced with few concluding statements in Abhishiktānanda's letters and diary. They remain confused while facing a string of dogmatic statements about the effects of a devotional theism, a devotionalist vision of God, and the rejection of the inherent dualism of ascetic perfectionism.[24] Abhishiktānanda used the final pages and his writing skills to take his own experience, the spiritual poverty

---

24. *Diary*, 367–72 (February 2, 1973).

he experienced in France and the richness he encountered in India, and transformed that into a call for the renewal of the church. I will address this topic in a later chapter.

Conclusion

In this chapter we discussed how Abhishiktānanda's existential problem, the devotional preoccupation, the "sociological impossibility" he faced in France, was redefined as an *intellectual* problem after he was exposed to Monchanin's theology in India. In India, Abhishiktānanda realized that he moved from France because the reality of an extrinsicist church was an insuperable limit to his radical search for God. This connection between his personal search and the more general destiny of the church affected Abhishiktānanda's life and thought from that point on, forcing him to reconsider his views on Christianity and Hinduism and to frame his search in the larger context of the renewal of the church.

4

A THEOLOGIAN?

"In committing myself totally to *advaita*, if Christianity is true,
I risk committing myself to a false path for eternity."

—Abhishiktānanda, 1953[1]

Introduction

THE PURPOSE OF THE previous chapter was to identify a central key to unlock the guiding theological intuition of Abhishiktānanda's intellectual project. For this purpose, I rewrote the history of Abhishiktānanda's move to India: he wanted to escape the devotional and despiritualized landscape of his monastery in Brittany. After clashing with Hinduism, Abhishiktānanda reframed intellectually his experience at Kergonan once he learned from Monchanin. From this point on, Abhishiktānanda's awareness of the narrowness manifested in the institution of the church struck deep into his mind, conditioning the central intellectual preoccupation of his life and thought in India. Now it is time to unveil his theological intuition.

In this study, I have dealt with two notions, the extrinsicist tendency and the recovery of the supernatural, which have deeply affected the trajectory of French Catholicism in the twentieth century. In this polarity, the former is the problem, and the latter is the solution. In this chapter I consider the notion of the supernatural, that is, the unity in distinction of supernatural and nature, as central to unlocking the theological intuition that shaped Abhishiktānanda's thought. This theological intuition,

---

1. *Diary*, 73–74 (September 25, 1953).

if well-founded, will illuminate the central point of his thought that has nonetheless remained somewhat elusive. Merely observing the centrality of the supernatural in Abhishiktānanda's thought, in fact, is not sufficient. The notion of the supernatural is a particular link that we can discern between his overall concern for the destiny of the church and his personal search for God. On the one hand, the supernatural is a remedy to the extrinsicist character of the church; on the other, it is the overall horizon of his personal search for God.

So far, our inquiry has been progressively narrowed down from a broad study of the Third Republic and its structural problems, by way of certain general preoccupations of the *fin-de-siècle* French Catholic intellectual milieu, to the specific problem that Abhishiktānanda experienced at the monastery and which precipitated his move to India. I will now move in the reverse direction by subsequently exploring the wider ramifications of the supernatural as a concept and an experience in Abhishiktānanda's life and thought.

Preliminary Remarks

Abhishiktānanda has been studied as a great spiritual seeker and pioneer of Hindu-Christian dialogue. Indeed, he was a seeker of God. In almost all his writings the reader can find fascinating accounts of his spiritual search. At the beginning of his life at the Abbey of Saint Anne de Kergonan in Brittany, he provided a sketch of his vocation:

> What has drawn me from the beginning, and what still leads me on, is the hope of finding there the presence of God more immediately than anywhere else. I have a very ambitious spirit—and this is permissible, is it not? When it is a matter of seeking God—and I hope I shall not be disappointed.[2]

For the rest of his life, he offered a description of his experiences:

> He who receives this overwhelming Light is both petrified and torn apart; he is unable to speak or to think anymore; he remains there, beyond time and space, alone in the very solitude of the

---

2. Letter to the novice-master, Abbey of St. Anne de Kergonan, December 4, 1928; see *Letters*, 2.

alone. It is a fantastic experience, this sudden irruption of the fire and light of Arunachala.[3]

While there is no doubt that Abhishiktānanda's life was dedicated to the quest for the absolute, the idea at the center of his thinking and the coherence of his work still need definitive interpretation. Abhishiktānanda worked tirelessly on articulating a living synthesis between Hinduism and Christianity. From the unfortunate attempt of *Guhantara* in 1955 to the last weeks of his life in 1973, his search for reconciliation between two polarities—experience and dogma, Advaita and Trinity, mysticism and revelation—was endless. His inability to reach such a synthesis until the very end of his life caused him immense anguish and interior pain. A focus on Abhishiktānanda's contemplative life and Hindu-Christian synthesis gives insight into one of the deepest motivations permeating his life; however, merely observing the centrality of the monastic life in Abhishiktānanda's life and his commitment to Hinduism is not sufficient. Questions remain: Is there an element within his thought that gives insight into his overall intellectual concerns? Is there a particular discernible link between his monastic vocation and Hindu-Christian synthesis, on the one side, and his overall intellectual contributions, on the other? The purpose of this chapter is to identify the supernatural as a central key to unlock the guiding theological intuition of Abhishiktānanda's thought.

In this chapter, Abhishiktānanda's spiritual search and Hindu-Christian synthesis are considered as part of a larger story in light of his understanding of the Christian supernatural, that is, the retrieval of a sacramental order of reality in which the supernatural stands in unity, although in distinction, with nature. The dynamics of the supernatural were conceived as an operation, which includes both external authoritative revelation and the supernatural working of grace within human nature that allows man to recognize external revelation. Abhishiktānanda's spirituality and Christian faith are investigated in this chapter through the lens of this operation, which Abhishiktānanda named the "path for eternity."

The working assumption is that Abhishiktānanda assimilated from Jules Monchanin, Shantivanam co-founder, the double-afference theory. Early in the twentieth century, as stated in a previous chapter, French philosopher Maurice Blondel had reintroduced Augustine to Catholic thought; he refined the notion of a double afference of the Christian supernatural, which recognizes that both the "external fact" of the revealed

3. Quoted in Baumer-Despeigne, "The Spiritual Journey of Henri Le Saux," 315.

supernatural and the "internal fact" of hidden grace of God are at work in the depths of the human spirit.[4] Monchanin then embraced Blondel's philosophy, early in his life and without reservation. Here I assume that Blondel's double-afference theory is at work in Abhishiktānanda's mind as a valuable "path for eternity." Supporting evidence can be found in Abhishiktānanda's letters and articles, particularly those from the final phase of his life.[5] Moreover, in the translator's note to Abhishiktānanda's *Hindu-Christian Meeting Point*, Sister Sara Grant portrays Abhishiktānanda's theological framework in a way that ultimately seems to sustain the above assumption.[6]

If this supposition is valid, the movement of the double afference, both coming from God and proceeding from and to the higher, became the framework that gives shape to his alleged theological synthesis. If the assumption is met, Abhishiktānanda's torment in light of the apparent incompatibility between Advaita and Christianity can be better seen as his struggle to conciliate an "internal fact" perceived in its Hindu forms and an "external fact" received in Christian forms. If the hypothesis is well founded, the social (ecclesial) character of Abhishiktānanda's quest would be validated. Not coincidentally, in his first open letter to his friend Abhishiktānanda, Raimundo Panikkar called Abhishiktānanda's quest one "for life and death on a cosmic level," somehow confirming the cosmic, and therefore social and ecclesial character of the quest.[7]

This chapter is divided into two parts: first, I briefly re-introduce Marcel Blondel and his theory of double afference, the necessity of an external afference (external revelation) and of an internal afference (an interior contribution of grace); second, I apply such a theory to Abhishiktānanda's spiritual search and Hindu-Christian synthesis. I limit this study to three episodes of Abhishiktānanda's life in India: *Guhantara*, his first (and unsuccessful) literary project, together with his twin literary project, *The Secret of Arunachala*; *Sagesse*, his more advanced Advaita-Trinitarian synthesis and his preparatory work, *Hindu-Christian Meeting Point*; and the "awakening."

---

4. Blondel, *Semaine*, 268–71.

5. Letter to Fr. Vachon, February 27, 1970, *Letters*, 226, and letter to Sr. Thérèse, March 18, 1970, *Letters*, 230–31. See also Abhishiktānanda, "Le chrétien en verité," in Abhishiktānanda, *Eveil à soi—éveil à Dieu: essai sur la prière*.

6. *Hindu*, vii.

7. See *Letter*, 438.

I offer a definition of the main terms used here: *mystic* (or *spiritual*) means: (1) supernatural mysticism—that is, an *afference* of the supernatural, an interior gift of grace that feeds the Christian life, or (2) natural mysticism—that is, an *efference* of the supernatural arising from man or by human means, from below; *supernatural* stands for an ontological order that is gratuitous and transcendent, and *natural* for "human nature," an ontological order that is naturally oriented to be penetrated by the supernatural without becoming confused with it. *Divine* (as the opposite of *human*) is a synonym for "supernatural." *Grace* is God's gift to human beings that is necessary for attaining communion with God. Finally, *revelation* stands for the articulation of the deposit of faith enjoying authoritative status, that is, approved by institutionalized church authority.

Theory of Double Afference

We have already seen that Blondel (1861–1949) exerted significant influence on his contemporaries and during the Second Vatican Council. Hans Urs von Balthasar called Blondel "the greatest Catholic philosopher of modern times."[8] Blondel's philosophy can be assumed as canonical—his thought has been magisterially sanctioned by the encyclical *Fides et ratio*,[9] but because most of this work has not been translated into English, Blondel remains relatively unknown today.

Blondel coined two neologisms, "extrinsicism" and "monophorism" (*monophorisme*). In a series of papers from 1904 to 1905, he identified a middle path for the living Christian tradition as the way to avoid the opposite extremes of extrinsicism in dogmatic theology on one hand and historicism on the other in historical research. An extrinsicist approach tends to be dogmatic in character to the point that it considers the supernatural order of Christianity as self-enclosed and as purely extrinsic to the order of nature and reason. Blondel characterizes this approach as *dogmatic* extrinsicism because it sees God as communicating with people only in an external way through formal documents. However, he also rejects the opposite option, historicism, the idea carried by historicists, whom he characterized as immanent modernists, because they relied exclusively on historical research to establish the truth. Blondel's thesis is that

---

8. Balthasar, *Dare We Hope*, 114.

9. Pope John Paul II, *Fides et Ratio*. The Encyclical addresses the relationship between faith and reason. Allusions to Blondel can be found in paragraphs 26, 59, and 76.

> *Extrinsicism* and *historicism* [. . .] are opposite extremes, but of the same kind, based on similar habits of mind, suffering from analogous philosophical lacunae, and aggravating one another by their conflict.[10]

He pointed to the living Christian tradition as the way of uniting the elements of truth inherent in both positions.

Between 1909 and 1913, Blondel wrote a series of articles in the *Annales de philosophie chrétienne* which he signed "Testis" or "Witness." In this series he investigated some ramification of extrinsicism, especially the notion that tradition is all about a revelation from outside, with little connection between what God reveals and the course of time and the flow of history. This is a supernatural revelation superadded to a relatively autonomous philosophical account that can freely operate without the superaddition. In eight articles in the *Annales*, Blondel used the label *monophorists* for those who saw God as communicating with people only in an external way through formal documents. In the footsteps of the nineteenth-century Belgian Cardinal Victor Dechamps (1810–83) and his apologetic "method of Providence," Blondel mentioned the hypothesis of a "double afference." In his interventions at Vatican I, Dechamps suggested a method of Providence in which operates the "interior fact" as well as the "exterior fact." This corresponds to Blondel's notion of a "double afference" of God's supernatural gift as coming "from both inside and outside human consciousness." *Monophorisme* is then a single "afference," or the afference from the outside. Here is how Blondel summarizes his position: "They [the authors of the Encyclical *Pascendi*] speak only of the *afference* of the external gift; whereas I equally take in account the *afference* of the internal gift."[11] In arguing for the idea of a second gift from God, Blondel meant a real interior gift that works in man, but is brought to man by God, in cooperation with the "external fact" of the revealed supernatural.

This concept of the double *afference* of the supernatural, one internal as well as external, assumes that the "external gift of the teaching and precepts of Christ, which, confided to the apostles, is communicated to us by the church and her infallible head" performs together with the internal one, which operates on the basis of the immanence of the supernatural order to the natural. The "internal fact" of hidden grace at work in the depths of the human spirit that Blondel recovered from the Great Tradition is an

---

10. Blondel, *Histoire* (French edition 1904), 224.
11. Blondel, *Blondel-Auguste*, 360.

"internal gift of grace that feeds the Christian life." In other words, the interior fact of soliciting grace is ultimately immanent.[12] Blondel found in Augustine an inspiration for a more interior way that God has for communicating with souls through reason, rather than just an external path via formal documents. Blondel detected a sort of path, from the world to his soul and from his soul to God, a restless human aspiration toward the divine as transcendent and supernatural, from which one could recognize the notion of a supernatural gift added to nature.

It is important to identify the implications of Blondel's double-afference theory: one implication is that there is no such thing as pure nature. Another implication is, however, equally important: there is no such thing as a revelation from outside with little connection between what God reveals and our deepest human dynamism—or, a revelation from the outside without the interior fact of soliciting grace.

Implicit in Blondel's double-afference theory is the notion of movement. The cooperation of the interior fact of soliciting grace and the external fact of revelation takes form in the flux of time. Human nature, in its own autonomous movement, in its freedom, spontaneously opens up toward Christianity, maintaining the fixity of orientation toward the supernatural.

Abhishiktānanda

In his first years in India, Abhishiktānanda was already experiencing a vibrant spiritual life, details of which were mirrored in both his more formal writings, destined for a larger audience, and in his *Diary*. It is in his *Diary* that we find a revealing note. In a moment of overwhelming tension in his life, he reflected on the question that caused him the greatest anguish:

> What gnaws away at my body as well as my mind is this: after having found in *advaita* a peace and a bliss never experienced before, to live with the dread that perhaps, most probably, all that my latent Christianity suggests to me is none the less true, and that therefore *advaita* must be sacrificed to it. [. . .] In committing myself totally to *advaita*, if Christianity is true, I risk committing myself to a false path for eternity.

The *Diary* note continues:

---

12. Blondel and Wehrlé, *Correspondance* 1, 283–84.

> All my customary explanations of hell and the rest are powerless against a reality that exists in a way unknown to me. [...] Supposing in *advaita* I was only finding myself and not God? And yet, it is only since I made the personal discovery of *advaita* at Arunachala that I have recovered peace and a zest for life.

All the customary "explanations of hell"—namely that Hinduism, and consequently Advaita, leads to hell—are powerless against the experience. Perhaps the best explanation of this sentence is that Abhishiktānanda was exploring the opposition between self-validating experience and the unappealable verdict of the doctrinal. At this particular point of his note, however, Abhishiktānanda asked himself if Advaita is a path to find himself or to find God. Here he was exploring the relationship between experience and salvation: if Christianity is the community that has the exclusive truth of the true God, if Christianity is the community that knows about the way of salvation, then committing himself to Advaita was the same as committing to a false path for eternity. By breaking away from Christianity, Abhishiktānanda may deprive himself of the possibility of God's gift of salvation. The whole interpretation is complicated by the editorial work done to the text.[13]

In the last years of his life, Monchanin became skeptical about the whole project of assimilation of Hinduism into Christianity. He confessed his view in a letter to his mother:

> It seems to me more and more doubtful that the essence of Christianity can be found by going through Advaita (the non-dualism of Sankara). Advaita, like yoga and more than yoga, is an abyss.

Then he seems to move his attention to Abhishiktānanda:

> Whoever dizzily plunges into it [Advaita] cannot know what he will find in its depths. I fear it may be himself rather than the living, triune God.[14]

Abhishiktānanda echoes Monchanin's remark and mirrors his fear in several notes. Here is one of many tormented cries from his journal: "Therefore I am full of fear, plunged in an ocean of anguish whichever way I turn. [...] And I fear risking my eternity for a delusion. And yet you are no delusion,

---

13. The editors have lightly edited this entry in his *Diary*, 73–74 (September 25, 1953).

14. Mondhanin, *Ecrits*, 127.

O Arunachala."[15] On one side is the spiritual experience of Arunachala, on the other, the eternity as promised by revelation. In the middle stands the abyss to be filled.

A Blondelian reading of Abhishiktānanda's notes identifies two different orders at work: the order of the experience, the spiritual experience, mysticism; and the order of the doctrine, the Christian revelation, faith. At the crossroad is human consciousness, where the two orders intersect. From a Blondelian perspective, experience and revelation operate within the articulation of this radical union. Blondel continually argues for union without confusion, as one cannot legitimately and with impunity enclose oneself in any one order. Paraphrasing Pierre Teilhard de Chardin, one is totally and essentially suspended between experience and divine attraction.[16]

Guhantara

Monchanin explained in a letter to his friend Eduard Dupperray in 1955 that "He [Abhishiktānanda] comes from a *rigorist* and even *integrist* theology." In Blondelian terms, as we know, "integrist" is synonymous of "monophorist."[17] If Monchanin is a reliable observer of the movement of thought of his companion, Abhishiktānanda became aware of his monophorist mentality when he moved to India and clashed with Indian *sannyāsa* and its spirituality. At that point, Abhishiktānanda realized that he suffered from the institutional church's narrowness. I have already pointed out that Monchanin could not miss the ironic circumstance: "The institutional Church is a burden to him [Abhishiktānanda] (to him who was earlier devoted to Canon Law and Liturgy)."[18]

In India, Abhishiktānanda framed this condition of extrinsicism in terms of a "contemplative deficit" of the Roman Catholic Church, pointing to Hinduism as a way to fill the contemplative deficit of the Western Church. Abhishiktānanda showed no patience for the institutional church's

---

15. Abhishiktānanda, *Diary*, 180 (November 27, 1956). See also: Panikkar, *Letter*, 348.

16. Here is the original quote: "Nous sommes totalement et essentiellement *suspendus à l'attraction Divine.*" See Letter from Pierre Teilhard de Chardin to Henri de Lubac, 27 June 1934, in *Lettres intimes*, 277–78.

17. Blondel, *Semaine*, 93.

18. Monchanin, *Mystique*, 211–12.

deficiencies, which seemed impenetrable to the action of the spirit. However, he recognized the operation of the supernatural at the level of Christian revelation according to the church as the sole authority responsible for the custody and teaching of such revelation. "Christian theology had [...] revealed to me," points out Abhishiktānanda, "the eternity of the mystery of Jesus in the bosom of the Father."[19] While Abhishiktānanda had no problem identifying the church with institution and dogma, he struggled to align the church with the interior initiative of spirit:

> If only the Church was spiritually radiant, if it was not so firmly attached to the formulations of transient philosophies, if it did not obstruct the freedom of the spirit [...] with such niggling regulations, it would not be long before we reached an understanding.[20]

In his early years in India, Abhishiktānanda moved from a distinct form of unconscious monophorism from the outside to an opposite—probably conscious—pervasive form of monophorism from the inside as a result of the clash with "these powerful new experiences" he was living in India.[21] As a matter of fact, in his early writings he downplayed the importance of words and concepts. Signs of Abhishiktānanda's growing awareness of the power of silence as a means to communicate beyond notions can be found in *The Secret of Arunachala*, a sister project to *Guhantara*. He mentioned his meeting with a silent *sadhu* and his encounters with renunciants who could neither read nor write, but preferred carrying only one book, "a book not written by human hands," the book of the interior of their heart.[22] He recorded his first dialogue with Shri Harilal Ponja, a man who will exercise some influence on Abhishiktānanda's life, who suggested that the atman has nothing to do even with Scripture: "The Truth is the Truth, and cannot be passed on to others by anyone."[23] What can be said, Abhishiktānanda argued at that point, between two human beings that cannot be communicated more effectively by silence?[24]

With the Blondelian framework of a double afference of the Christian supernatural in mind, we can see how the negation of notions and

---

19. *Diary*, 331–32 (July 23, 1971).

20. Letter to Canon J. Lemarié, October 24, 1960; see *Letters*, 132.

21. Quote from *Arunachala*, 9. For an example of the original monophorism, see letter to his family, September 16, 1949, in *Letters*, 28.

22. *Arunachala*, 68.

23. *Arunachala*, 82 and 84.

24. *Arunachala*, 32.

concepts in Abhishiktānanda's life was matched with the rising of the essential reality of the spirit. Clearly, his main challenge was to identify a form of internal operation of grace that could legitimately be considered as operating inside the church. During these years, the result of some precise theological distinctions and the merging of several theological influences coalesced into the infamous project *Guhantara*.

In *Guhantara*, Abhishiktānanda recognized the spiritual nature of his experience in India and proposed a first attempt to reconcile the mystical and the doctrinal. In this work, three assumptions are at work. The core assumption of the manuscript is that mysticism tends by its very nature toward Christianity. To put it differently, Abhishiktānanda initially assumed that every mystical experience is in itself, in essence, a supernatural experience. Henri de Lubac recognized Abhishiktānanda's assumption when commenting Abhishiktānanda's draft version of *Guhantara*. De Lubac read the manuscript and sent a letter to Abhishiktānanda with his comments.

> For you the mystical breath of India is all ordered toward Christ and the Church, the mystical spark is perfect and the experience there is basically the same as in Christian mysticism [. . . ,] from that, one will conclude [the] essential unity of mysticism.[25]

Abhishiktānanda's second assumption, notably, is an attempt to neutralize the relationship between the experience and revelation. Here he sought to demonstrate the truth of experience as distinct from purely conceptual truth, demonstrate that this truth is autonomous in its own method, and maintain the unity of truth within the distinction of their experiential and conceptual characters. According to de Lubac, Abhishiktānanda operates as if the experience is sufficient unto itself or it at least possesses a "suitability" with respect to the supernatural that makes unnecessary a synthesis between experience and revelation. As a matter of fact, Abhishiktānanda proceeded as if it were unnecessary to trace a precise line of contact, as if it is possible to assume a commensurability of elements that unites the experience and the formulation, without further investigation or articulation. This commensurability will become a trademark of Abhishiktānanda's thought: the integration of the experience of interiority, so relevant in Hinduism, into a Christian life of faith, is in Abhishiktānanda's view unproblematic.

---

25. De Lubac to Henri le Saux, January 23, 1955; see Monchanin, *Père Le Saux*, 253.

Abhishiktānanda's third assumption works like this: a total acceptance of mysticism reveals that mystical experience surpasses the confusion of ideas necessarily present in ordinary knowledge, including conceptualization and formulation. De Lubac commented on this point:

> You take no account of the metaphysical synthesis that serves to underpin it [i.e., mysticism]; according to you, there is partial error only in the conceptualization and formulation.

De Lubac's criticism, of course, is based on the Blondelian premises that God's embrace elevates and perfects the dynamism of *both* mysticism and the life of faith that constitutes human existence. In such dynamism, the heterogeneity of mysticism and Christian faith operates in distinction (without confusion) within the articulation of this union. "This dichotomy," continues de Lubac, "appears on the one hand too simple and on the other, in many passages, the second term is depreciated in relation to the first." According to de Lubac, revelation is for Abhishiktānanda treated as an external overlay. Revelation is a superfluous superimposition by purely extrinsic command that relates to a highly active potency, without the internal gift being able or having to entail the help of an external contribution. De Lubac claimed the formulation simply could not be denied. Consequently, a Christian account cannot unilaterally exclude formulation from reflection. Rather, the duty of adhering to the goals and methods of tradition places the responsibility on the theologian to examine and critique the mystical phenomenon, including the epistemological relationship of natural and mystical consciousness.

As a Benedictine monk and co-founder of a Christian ashram, Abhishiktānanda was aware that contemplation had been mainly lost in modern Christianity, and he aimed to renew the church by means of assimilating Indian spirituality. Nevertheless, in the same period that Abhishiktānanda wrote *Guhantara*, he had trouble reconciling the overwhelming spiritual experience with his monastic institution, his priesthood, and his monastic vocation. "Shantivanam henceforth interests me so little. Arunachala has caught me."[26]

Although deemed a failed project (parts of the original manuscript were published in other books and as fragments), *Guhantara* set up three major themes that would run through Abhishiktānanda's writings for the rest of his life: a persisting emphasis on the latent extrinsicism of the

---

26. Quoted in Rogers and Barton, *Abhishiktānanda: A Memory*, 2.

church; an invincible conviction that his spiritual experience in the form of Hinduism was true; and a struggle to reconcile his spiritual experience with Christian revelation. *Sagesse* would emerge as a possible recipe that includes these components.

Sagesse

In the 1960s, Abhishiktānanda maintained his conviction on the truthful character of his spiritual experience. The Advaita is true. "In its own sphere [i.e., the sphere of the experience], the truth of Advaita is unassailable."[27] However, this time Abhishiktānanda could benefit of the theological innovations and the church's more relaxed attitudes toward other religions. At the Second Vatican Council, Catholicism was invited to recognize "the seeds of the Word" present and active in the various religions (*Ad Gentes*, 11; *Lumen Gentium*, 17), particularly the elements "of truth and grace" that can be found among the nations (*Ad Gentes*, 9) and "true and holy" elements in non-Christian religions (*Nostra Aetate*, 2). This overall vision of the nations and religions in which God's grace is operating outside the boundaries of the church was built on the Blondelian intuition that although the routes taken may be different, all human beings, Christians and non-Christians, have a natural desire (*desiderium naturale*) for the eternal vision of God. Simply as a creature, not merely as a redeemed creature, a human being is completely affected by the realm of grace and, as a result, has a natural, built-in longing for supernatural fulfillment; that is, he or she aims to be united to God: "in the design of God, Hinduism tends of its very nature towards Christianity as its escato-logical fulfilment."[28] To put it differently, human is not "purely natural." Since human is created, the "supernatural" is already present within ordinary creation.

The point can be narrowed: human is, in the terms of theologian Milbank, created nature and created spirit, and the latter is free and intellectually reflexive ("personal").[29] As de Lubac said in a 1932 letter to Blondel, the problem with pure nature is "how can a conscious spirit be anything other than an absolute desire for God."[30] Instead of grace being an "extrinsic" addition to nature, grace brings natural abilities, natural

27. Abhishiktānanda, *Sagesse*, 47–48.
28. *Hindu*, 23.
29. Milbank, *The Suspended Middle*, 19.
30. De Lubac, letter to Maurice Blondel; see *The Natural Desire*, 628.

inclinations, and natural desires to their fulfillment. The implication of this Blondelian approach that regards grace as something that had an intrinsic connection with created human nature is well expressed in doctrinal documents such as the *Lumen Gentium*. In *Lumen Gentium*, divine grace unites itself to human spirit, elevating human beings in a way that human effort cannot equate, penetrating them in order to divinize them (*Lumen Gentium* 1 and 2). The *Magisterium* (teaching authority) will return with further doctrinal statements on the same point and elucidate it. For example, *Redemtor Hominis* informs that

> there is but a single goal to which is directed the deepest aspiration of the human spirit as expressed in its quest for God and also in its quest, through its tending towards God, for the full dimension of its humanity, or in other words, for the full meaning of human life. (*Redemptor Hominis*, 11)[31]

From the pioneering work of Blondel and de Lubac, the Council articulated the theological theme of the universal possibility of salvation by showing that *every human being* shares a natural desire for the supernatural end. However, the natural desire for the beatific vision is not grace itself. Grace meets the natural desire and fulfils it, but the natural desire is something imprinted in human nature (*imago dei*).

The natural movement of the human spirit toward God makes human beings open to unmerited grace. Through grace emanating from the Son, human nature receives from the inside the influx of the Holy Spirit and shares God's life. Grace penetrates the depth of human spirits, making human beings attuned to the Spirit of God. Simply put, grace is necessary for attaining communion with God. The supernatural in a mystical way unites the Spirit of God to the human spirit, transforming human nature for an intimate union with God that respects the distinction between God and human nature. By responding to grace in complete freedom, human beings come to a right relationship with God and are enabled to recognize God as their Abba (Romans 8:15, 26; Galatians 4:4–7). Decades earlier, Blondel had insisted that pure nature never existed: grace is actually operative interiorly in man and all men share in a supernatural vocation, a calling (the human spirit), that does not escape consciousness. Divine revelation is that which is experienced through the religious experiences of God's people in Scripture and in the church. The distinction between redemption and

---

31. Pope John Paul II, *Redemptor Homnis*. The Encyclical addresses the relationship between humankind and Christ.

revelation helps explain the point: the effects of redemption are universally available and are interiorly at work in mankind. Redemption is a supernatural order that is immanent and conscious, even though anonymously. The necessity of an external and objective contribution to faith represented by revelation guarantees the fulfillment. It is the relationship of the interior fact of soliciting grace and the external fact of revelation, or, incarnation and revelation, that together make up Christianity.

In the aftermath of the Council, Abhishiktānanda explored the theme of grace operating within in his book *Hindu-Christian Meeting Point*. Abhishiktānanda summarized his view in the first pages: he related real knowledge to notional knowledge by saying that the latter is reliant on the former; one needs to see in order to grasp. To put it differently, it is impossible to encounter Hinduism simultaneously at the level of real knowledge and at the level of notional knowledge.

> The Christians who desire to enter into contact with the Scriptures and the mystical tradition of India needs above all else an inward disposition [. . .] he needs the "knowledge" of those ultimate depths of the self, the "cave of the heart." [. . .] It is only when the contact has been established at this level that the true and spontaneous dialogue can begin at the level where concepts are formed and words are exchanged.[32]

Notional knowledge is a useful instrument for notion and formulation, but it is incapable of replacing the living experience of the Spirit. Notional knowledge, dignified by the tag of objectivity, can refer to a presence that is its origin and final end "only when" such a presence has been experienced. Is experience necessary for knowing? Abhishiktānanda conditioned the conceptual clarity of notional knowledge on the clarity of real knowledge; by doing so, he reframed the unity of intelligence of these two orders of knowledge within the heterogeneity of their functions. His apparent subordination of notional knowledge to real knowledge confirms the primacy of the experience in Abhishiktānanda's thought. In *Hindu-Christian Meeting Point*, he introduced a distinction between "Christian faith" and "the conceptual expression of that faith," in fact suggesting that revelation can be separated from its formal—its dogmatic and theological—expression.[33]

The more accomplished result of his efforts of reconciliation, however, was *Sagesse*, an Advaita-Trinitarian synthesis, written in 1962, published in

32. *Hindu*, 6–7.
33. *Hindu*, 15.

French in 1965, and posthumously in English in 1975. In *Sagesse*, Abhishiktānanda placed Hinduism among the cosmic religions outside the biblical revelation, and Advaita as "the acme of man's spiritual experience in the cosmic religions."[34] He felt compelled to reconcile Advaita and Christian theology via the theology of fulfillment: it is at the level of interiority, when the human search for God turns into a search within, that the human spirit discovers grace. At this point, the Christian mystic—that is, one who has real knowledge—realizes that Being is essentially co-esse, "being-with," and finds within his or her own relationship with God a mirror to the original, internal, non-dual relationship existing among the Members of the Trinity.[35] Christian revelation completes the action of human spirit and Holy Spirit, which when united lead human beings toward the Trinitarian God.

In *Sagesse*, Abhishiktānanda's prose was precise and his style, calm. A double movement was evidently at work: Christian revelation completes Hindu truths; Hindu experiences regenerate Christian faith. On the one hand, Abhishiktānanda framed the Indian-Christian relationship in terms of a compelling necessity—the necessity of a superimposition of Christian truth to Hindu truth:

> The integration of the advaitic experience into his own faith is for the Christian a necessary task. [. . .] If Christianity is unable to integrate it [Advaita] in the light of a higher truth, the inference must follow that *advaita* includes and surpasses the truth of Christianity and that it operates on a higher level than that of Christianity.[36]

On the other hand, he pointed out the need to recognize the spiritual component of the Christian faith. Too often Christianity selects one aspect of intelligence, usually the conceptual component, and accepts it as the full and final position. Abhishiktānanda responded to these unsatisfactory positions by proposing that the contemplative Christian come in contact with the Upanishad, and

> recognize something that he has known in his own depths, as he listens to the sages telling their experience. The summons presented to him by rishis and jnanis seems to arise from the depths of his own Christian heart.

---

34. *Saccidananda*, 67.
35. *Saccidananda*, 135.
36. *Saccidananda*, 47–48.

That is, to recognize that the Hindu Advaita is internal to the operations of the Spirit.[37] *Sagesse* represents an orthodox reminder that there is: (1) a dynamics of salvation at work that requires a movement from below upward (interior fact), and from on high downward (revelation); (2) a supernatural that is not only immanent but also conscious, even though anonymously; (3) an exigency for the revelation, that is, the necessity that the revelation be given in order for the interior fact to make sense; and (4) the internal operation and the external revelation are actively present one to the other, a relationship that reflexively confirms and intensifies while maintaining a critical distinction. Abhishiktānanda's effort to eclipse his previous idea to abandon conceptual knowledge without accepting the limits of conceptual knowledge is evident throughout the book.

Ultimately, the synthesis of *Sagesse* failed to satisfy Abhishiktānanda, and the subtitle "From Vedanta to the Trinity" was dropped in the English version, replaced with the more cautious "A Christian Approach to Advaitic Experience." A reading of the Introduction across two versions (French and English) and of some private letters is a good indication of the causes of this dissatisfaction. On the one hand, a dominant theme running through Abhishiktānanda's writings was the concern with a latent "extrinsicist" orientation of the Church of the West, as he called the Catholic Church, and the advocacy of a necessary integration of revelation with an interior spiritual gift from India that feeds the Christian life. In his early works, Abhishiktānanda claimed that only the option of a rich, interior, spiritually elevated Indian component could rectify Catholic moralism and give ultimate meaning and coherence to the Christian project. Is the spiritual gift as necessary for Christianity as revelation? This subject seems to remain the central concern in Abhishiktānanda's thought. After Vatican II, he continued to express objections to extrinsic accounts of authority, warning against ecclesiologies that assumed an intellectualist—"Greek," in his terms—conception of the church, or that were systematically confined to her exterior aspects without linking her structure to her underlying nature. The introduction of the English version of *Sagesse* can be read in this perspective.[38] On the other hand, Abhishiktānanda maintained that Advaita is irreducible to formulations. At the limit of its perfection, knowledge only becomes real on the condition that it ceases to be knowledge. Or, real knowledge is, in fact, no knowledge at all. Clearly, he was tempted to

---

37. *Saccidananda*, 13.
38. *Saccidananda*, xv.

totally abandon conceptual knowledge and embrace the pure experience when the limits of notional knowledge are exposed. In a letter to Panikkar, he complained that "whatever we do, is it not a qualified, *vivishta advaita?* And the *advaita* is lost as soon as there is qualification."[39] In sketching Advaita's irreducibility to formulations, Abhishiktānanda envisioned a form of union without formulation. His criticism of Christian intellectualism matches his principle of union without formulation, that is, the communion of Advaita and Christianity without the datum of the Christian revelation as delivered by the Magisterium.

He agonized over this contradiction for many years: Should he abandon his Christian faith? Should he turn his back on Advaita? There was no simple answer and he decided to leave the dilemma unresolved. "I think it is best to hold together, even though in extreme tension, these two forms of a unique faith until the dawn appears."[40] This unresolved dilemma brought him to the awakening.

Awakening

Since his early years in India, Abhishiktānanda faced the question of how to harmonize in human consciousness the overwhelming experience of Indian mysticism with the order of the external fact of the Christian revelation as delivered by the Magisterium for the supernatural destiny of the faithful. The question was the result of an intricate set of pre-assumptions on his side, namely (1) a lack of distinction between supernatural and natural mysticism; (2) an interpretation of the Church of the West in terms of a latent "extrinsicist" orientation, which in turn supports the advocacy of a necessary integration of revelation with an interior spiritual gift from India that feeds the Christian life; and (3) a communion of operations between the interior fact and the external fact through an interaction, which fails to maintain the distinction.

In the final years of his life, Abhishiktānanda returned to some of his initial intuitions, including that mysticism is, by its very nature, always supernatural in character. He benefited from the outcomes of the Council and reframed his assumption that mysticism tends by its very nature toward Christianity in terms of human spirit that naturally aligns to the Spirit. He also maintained the course initiated in his first period

---

39. Letter to Panikkar, June 11, 1964; see *Letters*, 163–64.
40. Letter to Odette Baumer-Despeigne, December 5, 1970; see *Letters*, 239.

in India, that is, that theological formulation that is extrinsicist to the interior experience. Moreover, he recovered his initial assumption on the commensurability of elements that unites the experience and the formulation, a commensurability that makes irrelevant a further investigation on the relationship between the experience and revelation. This specific point, however, deserves further consideration.

The "path to eternity," or salvation, is the attainment of the true status of the person. It is a transforming experience that is supposed to happen at the crossroads of the first afference—the spiritual experience—and the second afference: revelation. But in Abhishiktānanda's case, at least in the final period of his life, human consciousness is reframed in terms of silence. In a sentence that graciously unifies the movement of human spirit with the double-afference operation, he defines "the primary work of the Spirit" as "to impart to our spirits the interior silence of Jesus." In this same text, a letter to Sister Thérése de Jésus, he expanded the idea: "Silence cannot be institutionalized, nor even spoken of," to the point that "it [the silence] is a secret that only the Spirit tells to the spirit."[41] Abhishiktānanda reiterates the same principle in his correspondence, in which he links the experience of being in silence, so that "[the awakening] just *is*." De Lubac had already noted in his comment on *Guhantara* that for Abhishiktānanda, the experience—when pure and ultimate—surpasses the confusion of ideas necessarily present in formulation. Abhishiktānanda reiterates the same principle in a letter to Odette Baumer-Despeigne: "How can this silence be expressed for the theologians?"[42]

This is a convincing interpretation. Having said that, the evidence also sustains the possibility of another, more complex interpretation: in Abhishiktānanda's awakening, while human consciousness is reframed as silence, the external authoritative revelation is equated to cultural construction. It is the combination of these two steps, and not simply the former, that makes revelation better transmitted in silence from the inside out. I already stated that Abhishiktānanda's final step was to return to his original intuitions, that is, that mysticism is, by its very nature, always supernatural in character. However, he also maintained the belief that theological formulation is extrinsicist to the interior experience. "There is only the Awakening. All that is 'notional'—myths and concepts—is only its expression."[43] Should we read

41. Letter to Sister Thérése, March 18, 1970; see *Letters*, 230.
42. Letter to Odette Baumer-Despeigne, October 20, 1971; see *Letters*, 254.
43. *Diary*, 386 (September 11, 1973).

this sentence in the sense that Abhishiktānanda is setting up his awakening as a self-sufficient experience, one that neglected the external and objective signs of revelation, ultimately appropriate? One answer to this question asserts quite simply that this is the exact sense of Abhishiktānanda's comment. Another answer is that in Abhishiktānanda's opinion, the objective signs of revelation, that is, the external authoritative revelation, correspond merely to the level of articulation of faith. As a matter of fact, Monchanin wrote an essay on the existence of two distinct spiritual ways: *the way outside the sign* and the way of *the sign (of the mystery)*.[44]

The articulation of faith, or tradition, as Abhishiktānanda pointed out, operates at the level of "name (nāma) and form (rūpa)." As such, Christian tradition operates at the level of culture. More precisely, for Abhishiktānanda there were no non-cultural religious traditions. Every religion is rooted, encapsulated, and expressed in a culture, beginning with the most primordial and hidden archetypes that necessarily govern that religion's worldview. This suggests that there exists no pure primary experience or original consciousness.[45] Abhishiktānanda clearly expressed this idea in his diary, when he explained how the process from the primary experience to the dogma works.[46] Abhishiktānanda felt deeply the challenge he faced in experiencing and expressing the relativization of religious forms.

> The moment in history in which we are living calls us to a stern purification of all our means—institutional, intellectual, etc. To recognize the essential beyond all the forms in which it repeatedly embodies itself. [. . .] But then, in allowing the forms to yield their place, not to lose anything of the essential. The motives for abandoning forms are so mixed—just as mixed as those for keeping them intact. Who will be able to recognize the Spirit in all its purity? Who will be willing always to want nothing but the Spirit?[47]

We recognize the influence of Monchanin's essentialism here. Monchanin, Abhishiktānanda's co-founder, saw tradition as composed of two parts: an "infrangible core of the Revelation itself," the dogma in its pristine state, and several "constellations" formed around this nucleus, the subsequent development that began in the times of the apostolic fathers and carried on through the course of the European history of Christianity.

---

44. See Monchanin, *Esthétique*, 123.
45. Friesen, "Abhishiktānanda's Non-Monistic Advaitic Experience," 50.
46. *Diary*, 367–71 (February 2, 1973).
47. June 14, 1966; see *Letters*, 180.

He argued that "no medieval summa and no critical history of dogmas can surpass the theology of Paul and John."[48] In summary, the fundamental essence of tradition is pure and authentic and autonomous from its cultural clothes. For Abhishiktānanda, however, there was no pristine state; at the end of the day, the entire tradition is incidental. The line of demarcation between the essential and the incidental is reframed in terms of a change of status between the awakening and its articulation (the religious tradition). He said, "Hinduism is true. I know it," a claim grounded in his understanding of Christianity and Hinduism as religious traditions, which are true at level of faith articulation.[49]

Abhishiktānanda wrote that the two traditions, the Hindu and the Christian, are the "two forms of a single 'faith.'"[50] Which faith is that "single faith"? Here the notion of "I AM" comes to hand. Abhishiktānanda's identity as one who is "I Am"— (*aham asmi*, "I am Brahman" [Brhadaranyaka Upanishad 1.4.10 of the Yajur Veda] and *antequam Abraham fieret, ego sum*, "Before Abraham was, I am" [John 8:58])—trumps all his other nested identities. Abhishiktānanda would place his status as "I Am" above being French, Indian, or even being a monk, even if part of his Christianness. Abhishiktānanda summarizes his position on the matter: "The discovery of Christ's 'I AM' is the ruin of any Christic 'theology,' for all notions are burnt within the fire of experience." In what constitutes Abhishiktānanda's central argument against a worldly understanding of revelation, he concentrated on the relationship between grace and revelation. Revelation springs not from the outside (the external fact of doctrine), but rather from the inside (the internal fact of grace). This grace from the inside is—in the context of Abhishiktānanda's narrative—the awakening. "There is only the Awakening. All that is 'notional'—myths and concepts—is only its expression."[51] The tradition is an expression of the awakening. What about faith, then?

"Faith," Abhishiktānanda explained in a letter to his disciple Marc Chaduc, "is simply the acceptance that there is something beyond the rational." In the same letter, Abhishiktānanda pointed out that "the terrible contemporary crisis of faith" cannot be cured in "a new rationalization of the faith, but in the interior discovery of the level of experience."[52] The

48. Monchanin, *Théologie*, 86.
49. *Diary*, 348 (May 11, 1972).
50. Quoted in Dupuis, *Jesus Christ at the Encounter*, 90.
51. *Diary*, 386 (September 11, 1973).
52. Letter to Marc Chaduc, March 4, 1970; see *Letters*, 228–29.

value of faith lies not in its conceptualization, which is beyond the power of understanding, but in pointing toward the inward experience. His book *Hindu-Christian Meeting Point*, subtitled, "Within the Cave of the Heart," is a translation from the French by Sarah Grant. As she writes in the introduction, this book was written a few months before Abhishiktānanda's death, but after his experience of awakening, or "the reality of Upanishads and gospels." In this book, he carefully wrote and scrupulously edited the book, so that it might prove helpful to readers and drive them to "the awakening ... to awareness of the truth of their own being."[53]

The supernatural as a theological category not simply explains Abhishiktānanda's personal quest; it also connects such a quest to the all-embracing destiny of the church. He devoted much effort to redefining his idea of the awakening, especially in connection with the issue of the extension of the church and the historical phase in which she stood. The two issues—awakening and ecclesia—found a connection soon enough, even if a long period of gestation was needed before locating an acceptable degree of completion. The development of his thought can be followed in a few intermediate passages of his diaries. He says that "the Church is primarily all those men who are in the present state or in the potential state of their awakening."[54] Here Abhishiktānanda links the church with the state of awakening.

As a matter of fact, it is a Pauline move. Paul understood the coming of Christ not only for the twelve tribes of Israel, but also for the disinherited nations, nations that are the result of Yahweh's dispersal of the nations at Babel (Deuteronomy 32:8–9). Those disinherited should be appreciated with respect to Yahweh's inheritance, Israel, and the rectifying message of Jesus. Paul saw his ministry as instrumental in bringing back those people from the disinherited nations in Israel, and he interpreted himself as a conduit for their return to the true God: "And so all Israel will be saved" (Romans 11:26). The reality of the emerging church, the true Israel, including the disinherited nations, displaces the old identities and establishes a new one. In this context, Paul has multiple identities that he can adjust to accommodate gentiles, Romans, and Jews, because in the end, Paul's identity—like that of Israel's people—distils to one who is "in Christ." The unity of those who are in Christ (have faith in Christ) is far more important than adherence to any identity.

53. *Hindu*, 118.
54. *Diary*, 317 (August 25, 1970).

The same can be said of Abhishiktānanda's notion of Church of Awakening: the unity of those who are in Christ (those in the state of their awakening) is far more important than adherence to any religious tradition. Abhishiktānanda is self-identified as a Christian or a Hindu in many of his private writings, but his identity in "I Am" is his primary means of self-expression, specifically with himself. As a matter of fact, he identifies himself as "being in Christ," because "I Am" is Christ's name. He elaborates his view quite precisely. Abhishiktānanda clarifies that "Christ is not a *namarupa*. His true name is I AM."[55] So, Abhishiktānanda is Christian because he is in Christ. He follows Paul in his perspective to address the gentiles who are *in Christ*. When Abhishiktānanda writes of his Church of Awakening as "primarily all those men who are in the present state or in the potential state of their awakening," or, "all those who are already awakened to Christ," his readers are invited to superimpose another facet to their own eventually complex, multiple identities.[56] To put it differently, Abhishiktānanda's call to be part of the Church of Awakening necessitates some reprioritizing of the other facets of his readers' multiple identities. He urges his readers to put their "being" first, "their awakening," their "in Christ" first, as he has done, above all other components of their identity.

In Pauline terms, Abhishiktānanda frames the church as Israel, Yahweh's inheritance. For him,

> The Church is Israel extended to the Mediterranean world in the setting of the Roman Empire and its successors, but she is hardly extended beyond these limits even to our days. The Church is Israel, which does not recognize anymore the privilege of race and blood to enter the kingdom, but still recognizes members of the Kingdom those who have accepted integration into the human form of society in which she has developed.[57]

Abhishiktānanda reimagines, then, a world where the Church of the Awakening now functions as the true Israel. In his writings, he retells the story of the church to make a place for the awakened men (and women) as if they are the people of the disinherited nations. These writings capture him in the process of mythmaking, a process that incorporates the awakened people into the story of the church. Who are these awakened people? He is Christian, and his Church of Awakening falls under the umbrella of Christianity,

---

55. *Diary*, 357 (July 10, 1972).
56. *Saccidananda*, xiii.
57. *Diary*, 124 (September 6, 1955).

yet he does not imagine these people as members of the existing church; in fact, the church as a symbol is now exploding into symbols that are more powerful, more universal.[58] The church as Yahweh's inheritance is replaced by the church as Yahweh's all nations. Abhishiktānanda attempts to provide different ways of being Christian ("being in Christ"), specifically insisting on an apocalyptic rupture introduced by the meeting of Christianity with India, leading to a new church order without the doctrinal opposition so characteristic of his current church.

Once religious tradition is conceived as rhetorical rather than ritual or doctrinal, the religious barriers of the community are dismantled. The cultural dimension of tradition in Abhishiktānanda leads to the emergence of a new ecclesial reality, in which Christians are equated with Hindu. In the Church of Awakening, the Christian and Hindu identities are subordinated, superimposed by the status of "being in Christ." There is one more thing to note about Abhishiktānanda's handling of these two aspects, notably that the relationship between the awakening and church is not soteriological. That is, Abhishiktānanda does not use these terms to explain the presence of regenerate and unregenerate persons in the church, as others have used them. Rather, both aspects are far from being wholly ecclesiological in their usage; they are employed in understanding the constituency of the church, not the church as church.

In Abhishiktānanda's ecclesiology, the church is a universal symbol of salvation.

> The essential ministry in the Church is, consequently, the ministry of Presence. All the ministries are rooted in Christ, conformed to Him, and receive their value and their plenary efficacy from Him.[59]

Its ministry is not redemption but revelation. The Church of Awakening grants the recipients immission in the ecclesial community, the community that has the exclusive truth of the true God. Membership in the ecclesial community is important for specific reasons. Only this community has the truth, what Paul calls "the oracles of God" (Romans 3:2). Only this community has the truth in regard to the nature of the true God among all gods and how to be rightly related to him. Only this community knows truth. However, Abhishiktānanda never argued that membership per se either provides insured salvation or lessens any sinful impulse.

58. *Diary*, 373 (February 17, 1973).
59. *Eyes*, 61.

Conclusion

In this chapter, the spiritual search and Hindu-Christian synthesis of Abhishiktānanda are studied in light of his understanding of the supernatural. On the assumption that Abhishiktānanda interiorized the Blondelian framework of operation between internal and external afference, this chapter helps explain the consistency of Abhishiktānanda's work and identifies the supernatural as an element central to unlocking the guiding theological intuition that shaped his thought. Now it is time to address some of the implications of having the supernatural as a lens through which Abhishiktānanda's thought can be interpreted.

5

REINTRODUCING ABHISHIKTĀNANDA

"You were a poet."

—Panikkar, 1975[1]

Introduction

On the basis of the previous chapter's finding, that is, that the supernatural lies at the heart of Abhishiktānanda's thought, this chapter works as a correction to the traditional portrait of Abhishiktānanda as a theologian, or at least as somebody who deserves to be critically addressed in terms of strict theological categories. He was not a theologian and his writings resist an overly systematic or analytical theological scrutiny. Abhishiktānanda was primarily an artist—a poet—with a theological concern. He was not an acosmic, who was engaged in an individualistic yet heroic spiritual journey. He was a contemplative who maintained a "social" compass, where "social" can be understood in light of de Lubac's *Catholicism*, that is, in organic unity with the church and all humankind. I will address all these ramifications in this chapter.

In Search of an Identity

A *Jeopardy* answer might go something like this: "He was a founder of the most famous Roman Catholic ashram in India." The correct question in response is, "Who was Abhishiktānanda?" Another answer might be: "He

---

1. *Letter*, 438.

explored a pluralistic approach to the theology of religions before such an approach was even articulated." The question again is, "Who was Abhishiktānanda?" The life and work of Swami Abhishiktānanda have provided an inexhaustible source of wonder and whisper, acting as a continuous riddle to contemporary theologians and contemplatives who have been both appalled by Abhishiktānanda's thought and fascinated by his life. Part of the fascination is that his life is actually a puzzle: there is the silent, obedient, unpretentious Benedictine monk who entered St. Anne's Abbey in Kergonan, France, in 1929, known then as Dom Henri Le Saux. Then there is the contemplative missionary who joined Father Jules Monchanin in India to establish Shantivanam, a Benedictine ashram near Trichinopoly. Finally, there is the wandering *sannyasi* in orange, who spent the rest of his life in India *exploring* Advaita to an inexplicable degree of depth without compromising his Christian faith. So, who was Abhishiktānanda?

Between 1970 and the present, the numerous studies seeking a central key to unlock Abhishiktānanda's identity have yielded many insights into his life and work. The main tract of this identity can vary according to what the interpreter sees as the essence of Abhishiktānanda's life: the monk; the pioneer of Hindu-Christian dialogue; the theologian. An initial understanding of Abhishiktānanda emerged during his time in India thanks to a generation of friends and acquaintances who interpreted him as an ascetic monk. In a memorial letter addressed to Abhishiktānanda, Panikkar wrote,

> Central to you was your monastic commitment. You doubted whether, out of loyalty to yourself, you should quit the Church; you hesitated to give yourself fully to Advaita, but you never for a moment questioned your monastic consecration, your way of life.[2]

George Gispert-Sauch points out that "He came to India in 1948 as a Benedictine monk [and] at heart he remained Benedictine all his life."[3] His desire to be a monk—that monastic vocation—places contemplation and asceticism at the very center of Abhishiktānanda's life. He had a true contemplative vocation, and contemplation formed the deepest and most dominant part of his personality. One of Abhishiktānanda's first letters to Marc Chaduc, who would eventually become his one true and prominent disciple, states:

---

2. *Letter*, 446.

3. Later Gispert-Sauch elaborated that Abhishiktānanda came to India, first, to continue his search, and, second, to infuse a new life into the Benedictine tradition; see Gispert-Sauch, "In Search of Liberation," 40.

> The essential thing is to penetrate the interior mystery to which India bears witness so intensely. [. . .] Without a contemplative sense, to come to India is absolutely useless.[4]

Abhishiktānanda came to contemplation mostly because of a pure attraction to wordless union with the absolute. In most contemplatives, this motive remains in stark and painful contrast, or gradually coalesces with another, that is, an intense desire to flee a sinful self and world, but that was not the case for Abhishiktānanda. He instead encountered a profound spiritual experience in his early days in India; his advaitic experience deepened in the last months of his life, when he realized the truth of the Upanishads. Intimately interwoven with contemplation, Abhishiktānanda was committed to asceticism. He was able to push himself harder than almost anyone else while considering the severity of asceticism necessary.[5] He combined an inimitable spiritual journey with the intensity of his burning zeal to discover the truth. He felt a constant need to be a radical. When Abhishiktānanda lived in the monastery—a place for radical choices—this radicalism took the usual forms. He had aspirations of being a perfect monk, to go beyond, to see God Himself, not His gifts.[6] In India, he clearly embraced his experience with uncommon intensity along with the radicalism of his love for God. Should a Benedictine monk be interested in Hinduism or collect rice on the streets or sleep in caves? Father Monchanin used to say of him, "Le Saux went further than I did."[7] What is really distinct about Abhishiktānanda, though, is not only the magnitude of this commitment to stretch so far from his roots toward his encounter with India, but also his choice to go without hesitation straight to the core of the spiritual experience. Obviously, Abhishiktānanda was conscious of the scope of his spiritual journey:

> I have so much wanted holiness, without any qualification, for almost 30 years (9.1.28). And whatever particular follies there may have been, since that day this has been my only goal, the great goal (*mahat padam*), the Only One.[8]

---

4. Letter to Marc Chaduc, September 29, 1969; see *Letters*, 219.
5. Letter to Marc Chaduc, April 8, 1973; see *Letters*, 292.
6. Le Saux, "Amour et Sagesse," quoted in *Letters*, 5.
7. In 1957, on his deathbed in a Paris hospital, Monchanin opened his heart to Father Lemarié: "I was too Greek. Le Saux went further than me in the mystery of India."
8. *Diary*, 171 (November 24, 1956).

He was also aware that he belonged to an uncommon class of searchers:

> Some dive straight in from a rock into the deep water; others go gradually down the slope and advance only step by step into the water which beckons them. Blessed are they when a wave comes and swallows them up![9]

His long periods as a hermit in the caves of the holy mountain Arunachala and his courageous heart made him an emblematic and inspirational figure who left an indelible impression on his friends.

Further authoritative and engaging literature on Abhishiktānanda created the persona known to the world as Abhishiktānanda. This focus on Abhishiktānanda's private persona connects Abhishiktānanda the monk with Abhishiktānanda the man. James Stuart and Panikkar offered in great detail and with great care a portrait that much resembles the Abhishiktānanda scholars came to know from the work of Bettina Bäumer and Murray Rogers: extremely likable, guileless, exuberant, and wildly innocent. The ultimate impact of these portraits is that it sounds like everything that had happened to Abhishiktānanda had gone a little over his head. Indeed, part of the man's charm was his lack of pretension or self-importance. Out of these stories, Abhishiktānanda emerges as a real person, a "vivid" or "life-like" Man. He said and did things that seem convincingly like the kinds of things people say and do in so-called real life, even though Abhishiktānanda's "real life" was peculiar. He was a man of substance, of flesh and bone, fiber and liquids.

Abhishiktānanda was already known through his writings during his life, and through his writings comes the narrative of his life-journey—the evolution of his quest. Accordingly, in scholarship, Abhishiktānanda the Contemplative was soon partnered with Abhishiktānanda the Writer. In all the controversy about why he dealt with Hinduism, it is easy to forget how dedicated a writer he always continued to be. Panikkar noted that Abhishiktānanda's works were the product of years of intensive writing and rewriting.[10] If a person's identity, in the end, is a collection of habits, writing was the one habit Abhishiktānanda never lost. Even for a man not vowed to silence, Abhishiktānanda's several books would have been an extraordinary output, but considering the journal and letters—and these personal writings have spoken most powerfully—he must be recognized as a prolific writer.

---

9. *Arunachala*, 33.
10. *Letter*, 433.

For his readers, he was a spiritual writer. In the experience of the Catholic Church post-Vatican Council II (1962–65), Abhishiktānanda's account of his pilgrimage with Raimundo Panikkar to Gangotri, the sacred source of the Ganges, exemplifies a "new era" in the field of interfaith dialogue.[11]

Sometimes, Abhishiktānanda the Writer seems like an intruder on Abhishiktānanda the Ascetic. An ascetic monk is not in the best position to be well-informed about the outside world. Can a man committed to the wordless apophatic way be preoccupied with recording—and publishing—thoughts about his spiritual search? Apparently, he was not the only one who was redefining what it meant to be a monk. Gregory Zilboorg, a convert and a skilled psychoanalyst, warned Thomas Merton in the 1950s that his desire to leave the Trappist communal silence for the even more withdrawn life of a hermit—and still to write and publish—made him schizophrenic: "You want a hermitage in Times Square with a large sign over it saying *Hermit*."[12] Though not entirely fair to Merton, Zilboorg had a point. Surrounded as he was by books, papers, and even a typewriter, Abhishiktānanda would have conceded the point.

Like Merton, Abhishiktānanda entered the conversation without stepping outside the invisible monastery walls of his hut. Certainly, there was something paradoxical in silent monks who address the world in books and articles on topics such as peace and the Vietnam War (Merton) and the Hindu-Christian dialogue (Abhishiktānanda). The reclusive hermits who rejected the world with uncompromised fervor were at the same time coming to embrace the world with a deep compassion. As a matter of fact, the universal concern of the hermits is a well-established tradition in Christianity. Abhishiktānanda came to understand the fundamental unity of all humanity; he became concerned about the destiny of Christianity. His tendency to radicalism found its way into his ecclesiastic concerns, and the 1960s in turn provided him with a series of ecclesiastic questions to ponder: Vatican II, the Indian Church, Catholicism, and the materialism of the modern West.

An evolution in Abhishiktānanda's scholarship is the portrait of Abhishiktānanda as a theologian. Initially, his supposed attempt to elaborate a formal theological reconciliation of Advaita and Christian Trinitarianism was the object of intensive scrutiny. Abhishiktānanda made numerous attempts, across twelve books and several articles, to reach a theological synthesis

---

11. *Alle sorgenti del Gange*, 7.
12. Quoted in Mott, *The Seven Mountain*, 297.

between Advaita and Christianity, devoting a constant effort to nothing but theological synthesis. The depth of Abhishiktānanda's involvement with Hinduism made him a natural candidate for theological examination. When he became an advocate for Advaita, did he turn away from being a spiritual seeker toward being a thinker who would impact Christian theology? An argument could be made that he became wrapped up in a particular idea that he thought was correct, that is, the correct path for Christians in India, though not many people followed him down that road.

A Theologian?

In the first two decades after his death, Abhishiktānanda was considered by people who enjoyed direct contact with him and direct access to his original writings a spiritual author rather than a theologian. Most commonly, this generation of scholars produced studies of Abhishiktānanda's monastic experience and spiritual search. The new flux of theological analyses of Abhishiktānanda's work attempt to overcome the original distinction between theological work and spiritual narrative, in the meritorious attempt to reunify in a unique picture Abhishiktānanda the theologian and Abhishiktānanda the monk.

The whole idea of Abhishiktānanda as a theologian, however, is debatable. First, it means challenging previous comments from giants such as Monchanin and Panikkar (and later Dupois) on the theological value of Abhishiktānanda's thought, comments that have held an irresistible pull over scholars who until just recently claimed that, all in all, Abhishiktānanda never systematically and rigorously addressed theological issues. The theologian, as may be seen in painful detail in the *Diary*, never entirely settled down. His friends certified that Abhishiktānanda had no appetite for speculative investigation. Monchanin, Panikkar, Murray Rogers, James Stuart, Odette Baumer-Despeigne, George Gispert-Sauch, SJ, and Jacques Dupois were in close contact with Abhishiktānanda during the very period when his works were written, and these people had frequent opportunities to discuss his work. Monchanin first and then Panikkar considered him a spiritual searcher with no stamina for disciplined intellectual investigation. Already in the early 1950s, Father Monchanin made clear his discomfort in accompanying Abhishiktānanda into more uncharted spiritual adventures such as *Guhantara*, Abhishiktānanda's first intellectual exploration of Advaita.[13] Henri de Lubac welcomed the news of *Guhantara*, probably because of Abhishiktānanda's association with Monchanin and the high esteem that de Lubac maintained for Monchanin. When de Lubac received the manuscript, however, he did not conceal the extent of his reservation: "Firmer and more condensed, abbé Monchanin's thought is also more precise and more sure—right where it is more elliptic and bolder—than that of Le Saux."[14] Then Father J. Guennou, the ecclesiastic censor in Paris, found *Guhantara* full of heresies, and "redolent of relativism, modernism, quietism, modalism, and especially pantheism."[15] In his memorial *Letter to Abhishiktānanda on Eastern-Western Monasticism*, Panikkar comments in the foreword that Monchanin wrote to *Guhantara* that he, Monchanin, "tries to defend you," implying that Abhishiktānanda's work could not stand on its own and needed a pre-emptive defense from Monchanin.[16] Surely, Monchanin's hesitations and de Lubac's reservations with regard to the content of *Guhantara* and Panikkar's devaluation of the theological merit of Abhishiktānanda's work are difficult to discount.

As a matter of fact, Abhishiktānanda's theology suffered from some forms of monophorism. Abhishiktānanda maintained a conception of authority that suppresses "interiority," and came to privilege the initiative of the internal afference over the external one. Abhishiktānanda's monophorist system followed a three-stage logic: first, devaluation of external afference, marked by latent extrinsicism; second, focus on internal afference, generating spiritual life; and third, linking the inward supernatural to human consciousness (spirit) by means of silence. Abhishiktānanda turned Catholicism into a spontaneous movement of spirits—a movement from below upward—coupled with an understanding of tradition as a cultural construction: together, the two moves make notions and formulations irrelevant. He repeatedly and emphatically stressed the importance of recognizing the inner working of the divine gift, the doubly religious inclination of

13. Letter from Monchanin to Duperray, December 14, 1955; see *Letters*, 80.

14. Letter from de Lubac to Duperray, March 2, 1955. Unpublished correspondence communicated by Françoise Jacquin and quoted in Prévotat, "Henri de Lubac and Jules Monchanin," 70.

15. *Diary*, 86.

16. *Guhantara* (literally, "one who dwells in a cave") was never published. See *Life*, 70; *Diary*, 86 and, *Letter*, 446. Abhishiktānanda recognizes the value of the foreword but seems to link it more to the prestige of Monchanin and a greater possibility of publishing than he does his intellectual acume and theological prudence. See Stuart, 68. Monchanin's Preface is reproduced in *Mystique*, 269–73.

souls that are under the action of both grace and freedom. He ambiguously conveyed the necessity that the supernatural be given in order for the higher levels to make sense. Although Abhishiktānanda in his theological vision showed a propensity for a compartmentalization of the cavernous interior, he also maintained a notion of reality as a "continuum," in which no "walls of separation" divide one layer of reality from another.

The Abhishiktānanda's monophorist orientation is evident in comparison to de Lubac's Augustinian framework. In all fairness, Abhishiktānanda shared with de Lubac the aim to rebalance the equation to the side of the mystical; however, the affinity between Abhishiktānanda and de Lubac stops there. De Lubac's indisputable source was the Augustinian *"intelligentia fidei,"* the understanding of the mysteries of faith through "rational elaboration by theologians" after the illumination of a supernatural character has touched the holy soul.[17] To put it differently, de Lubac relied on the Augustinian dynamics of the eternal movement in which the act of faith always precedes the act of thinking, a certitude that our spirit already affirms God prior to all dialectic.[18] Nevertheless, de Lubac clarified in *Sur les Chemins de Dieu* that reflexive concepts are necessary; it is not theological positivism, but *via affirmationis* (cataphatic theology) that makes intelligible the primordial faith. Here is how von Balthasar explains the essential relationship between faith and thought in de Lubac:

> Each side of the thesis requires the other. Proofs for God are necessary. Genuine steps are taken [. . .] although in this process what was always already present is only brought into the light.[19]

De Lubac's thoughts on mysticism and theology were crystal clear: the necessity of the intellectual side as part of a system that unifies the mystical moment and the intellectual moment, although the latter follows and purifies the former; the recognition that the living mystery always transcends the historical forms and yet the historical forms are the way that the mystery expresses itself; and finally, the preference of the historical-eschatological orientation upon the mystical ascent.[20]

17. Quoted from *Corpus Mysticum*, 263.

18. The original quotation is: "prior to all dialectic [. . .] our spirit already affirms God." Quoted from de Lubac, *Chemins*, 134.

19. Balthasar, *The Theology of Henri de Lubac*, 95.

20. Another way to depict the framework is that the church has considered the influence of the Areopagite and the related upward orientation to the above (mysticism of ascent) as a dangerous alternative to the classic historical-eschatological orientation.

Abhishiktānanda himself does not seem to consider intellectual speculation as his primary interest. When Panikkar and Monchanin met for the very first time and—according to Panikkar—spent almost the entire night discussing the Trinity and forgetting all time and space, Abhishiktānanda was also present. But he quickly became tired of the loquacity of the two philosophers and quietly went off to sleep.[21] A few years earlier, de Lubac welcomed the news of *Guhantara*. When he received the manuscript, however, he offered Abhishiktānanda this straightforward evaluation:

> You take no account of the metaphysical synthesis that serves to underpin [the experience] [...] in many passages, the second term [i.e., conceptualization and formulation] is depreciated in relation of the first [i.e., mysticism]. Let scholars still discuss and theorize about it, he [i.e., the mystic, Abhishiktānanda] is satisfied just to be.[22]

Here de Lubac is certifying the notion that for Abhishiktānanda there was no value in an impeccably framed theological truth, in which only those termed "theologians" by virtue of some professional training would eventually show interest.

Today theologians see Abhishiktānanda as a heterodox thinker, who happened to exercise his talents and personality on a theological synthesis between Christianity and Hinduism with mixed results. The theologians' main criticism is that Abhishiktānanda's theological work is written "with a repellent look and [is] very abstract," is a subject of "concern and anxiety," and is "slightly romantic," that is, it is not theological enough, lacking intellectual rigor and discipline, and demonstrating a vague and inconsistent use of theological categories.[23] However, the crux of the matter is the distinction between a theological approach that is associated with a focus on the content of theological ideas rather than on their formal structure. The second approach is concerned primarily with the internal history of the discipline and doctrine. Abhishiktānanda can be properly investigated only through the former approach.

Abhishiktānanda introduces a third option, the downward orientation to the below (mysticism of descent).

21. Panikkar, *Tra Dio e il cosmo*, 13.

22. De Lubac to Henri Le Saux, January 23, 1955; see Monchanin, *Père Le Saux*, 253.

23. *Guhantara* "d'aspect rebutant et très abstrait": Monchanin to his mother, March 31, 1954; see Monchanin, *Mère*, 496. De Lubac to Henri Le Saux, January 23, 1955; see Monchanin, *Père Le Saux*, 253. "Slightly romantic" is a comment by Jacques Dupois, quoted as "somewhat romantic" by Gisbert-Sauch; see *Witness to the Fullness of Light*, 93.

Once placed in the context of the French pre-Vatican II spiritual and theological context in which he belongs, Abhishiktānanda recovers from the inconsistencies of the existing literature. Clearly there is an epistemological divergence, with the theologians treating his statements as epistemic—that is, based on beliefs that can be isolated and captured in assertions to be objectively assessed and directly compared to opposing claims, and Abhishiktānanda's deepest convictions embodied in his experience. In making his points, Abhishiktānanda was not trying to escape the traditional conceptual framework that assumes that at the foundation of well-founded beliefs lie beliefs that are founded too. He was not trying to build a new theory. In his writings, Abhishiktānanda was at the level of the primordial. He was just claiming that reality is abyssless and groundless at the same time. All attempts to justify—or deny—the statement on the truth of Hinduism would depend on a particular understanding of truth to justify the source of that statement. The right question is not which statement is true—that of the theologians or of Abhishiktānanda—but rather in which capacity Abhishiktānanda can be addressed theologically.

In the perspective of first-generation scholars' work, Abhishiktānanda was primarily an artist—a poet with a theological concern. Apart from all the circumstantial evidence that this study will be assembling in the next chapters, two immediate reasons remain for understanding Abhishiktānanda as an artist. By 1975, Panikkar had already established the primacy of the poetic nature of Abhishiktānanda's work as opposed to its purely theological elements. I already mentioned that Monchanin and Abhishiktānanda's friends considered Abhishiktānanda first and foremost a spiritual searcher. Murray Rogers thinks that Abhishiktānanda had a painful sense of inferiority since his *Guhântara* was rejected by the censor in Paris. Rogers describes the nature of Abhishiktānanda's writings in this way:

> More than once he used to say that all his writing was autobiographical, not intellectual thought or theology but personal experience. It is not therefore any new theology for which he will be remembered but the lived experience of a new life, a new way of being human, a new way of relationships between cultures, religions and peoples.[24]

Those close to Abhishiktānanda acknowledge that neither his gift nor his legacy was primarily theological. Among the most interesting things readers have learned from these scholars, some of whom were

24. Trapnell, "Abhishiktānanda's Contemplative Vocation," 170.

Abhishiktānanda's friends, are how well Abhishiktānanda expressed himself in prose, in French as well as English, how cogently he formulated his thoughts, and that he was an avid reader. He was a poet, an artist.[25] The opinion of these friends and scholars must be regarded as more authoritative than the subsequent inferences of those who have approached Abhishiktānanda with theological presuppositions and orientations. As a matter of fact, Abhishiktānanda identified himself as an artist.[26] In brief, an understanding of Abhishiktānanda as an artist recovers the integral portrait of Abhishiktānanda handed down from the first generation of friends and scholars and that has since been lost.

For those who investigate Abhishiktānanda as a theologian, his theology goes into great detail about a process that seems simple only when considered from a distance—figuring out what Abhishiktānanda was thinking, and then determining if this is acceptable according to the theological code and the doctrinal norm. This layered process of figuring out what someone else is thinking—of mind reading—on the basis of his writings is a common scholarly device. Theologians say they are convinced a dissecting analysis not only offers unexpected insights into individual texts, but that it may help answer fundamental questions about natural and supernatural orders of reality. Still, Murray Rogers warns that in the case of Abhishiktānanda, this type of exegesis risks not amounting to much more than dissecting a dead jellyfish.

> He was hurt when theologians and thinkers, better trained intellectually no doubt than he himself was, proceeded to dissect and analyze his words and experience in cerebral terms [...] and [...] failed to trust his Christian integrity and feared for his orthodoxy.[27]

Panikkar has a similar point: it was Abhishiktānanda who had the most heart and tried harder; he was not the better theologian. "You go and live the same kind of life and then we shall speak."[28] When theologians refuse to see the whole person, Abhishiktānanda becomes like the bodiless heads sometimes seen in circus sideshows. When Abhishiktānanda is removed

---

25. An unexpected recognition of Abhishiktānanda's poetic style comes from Sita Ram Goel, who suggests that Abhishiktānanda's poetry was so good to be mistaken for mystical experience. See Goel, *Catholic Ashrams*, 65.

26. *Letter*, 438. Talking about Panikkar, Abhishiktānanda explains that "He *also* happened to be an artist." See *Mountain*, 36 (emphasis is mine).

27. Rogers, "Swamiji—the Friend," 1.

28. *Letter*, 432.

from the context of his real life, like a fictional character that depends on his creator, he in turn becomes like a fictional character who belongs to the theologian who invented him.

Abhishiktānanda's theological concern is, indeed, *theological*, as Abhishiktānanda clearly shares with Mircea Eliade the opinion that a religious man can live only in a sacramentalized world. It is only in such a world that he participates in being, where he has real existence.[29] As a matter of fact, Abhishiktānanda's theological concern is a *Catholic* concern: in a Catholic universe, the natural sphere cannot run autonomously as if it disregards the supernatural end of redemption. The Catholic vision is that nothing is "purely natural." Since all is created, the supernatural order of things is already present within ordinary creation. The ordinary is extraordinary; therefore, the world can be recognized as filled with "mystery," that is, with the creative and redemptive presence of God, rather than a mere unfolding of material events.

Abhishiktānanda's theological preoccupation is that the Christian community—not simply Christian monasticism—no longer lives in a sacramentalized reality; therefore, symbols are no longer adequate and doctrines lose their meaning. This is the most decisive problem. The formulations are "secondhand."[30] Of course, the solution of this problem consists in new symbols that emerge from a world full of grace and spiritual enchantment: a sacramental imagination according to which created objects are sacraments that participate in the mystery of the heavenly reality of Jesus Christ.

An Acosmic?

Friends, acquaintances, and scholars often recognized Abhishiktānanda's profound commitment to solitude, contemplation, and asceticism. They have called his vocation as acosmic or asocial and placed him in a sort of "spiritual elitism."[31] The bottom line is that Abhishiktānanda has often been portrayed as a spiritual seeker pursuing an individual path of realization. Abhishiktānanda's search has been depicted mostly as an escape

---

29. For a comment on the identity between being and unity, see Kalliath, *The Word in the Cave*, 377. Eliade mentions a "sacred," not a "sacramental" world; see Eliade, *The Sacred and the Profane*, 64.

30. *Diary*, 345 (April 24, 1972).

31. Trapnell, "Abhishiktānanda's Contemplative Vocation," 165.

or refuge from the modern world, an ancient choice, a spiritual vocation that grew from the readings of the early church fathers and the encounter with the timeless sages of mystical India. By labeling Abhishiktānanda as a monk of acosmic inclination, scholars frame him as an acosmic engaged in an individualistic yet heroic journey to God and defuse the impact of his intellectual project and Catholic passion. Yet his predisposition for the supernatural and the sacramental character of reality is critical to our understanding of the social character of his search and his opposition to an individualist ecclesiology.

A predominant theme and discourse on Abhishiktānanda's life and thought revolves around his spiritual quest and a certain tension he experienced while resisting a form of total acosmism. As far as his spiritual quest is concerned, an individualistic yet heroic journey to spiritual enlightenment is only one among several options at hand. Is it possible that his mysticism, so to speak, was sacramental in character, that is, in organic unity with the church and the entirety of humankind? The term is supposed to denote a mysticism that is social in character, that is, becoming "one body" (1 Corinthians 10:17) in com-union with all and God.[32] In Abhishiktānanda's words, "simply feel the awakening to oneself in the universal community, in the Eucharist." As for a certain tension, scholars have seen Abhishiktānanda as an imperfect *sadhu*, interpreting his limitations as cultural or psychological where they were actually "social."[33]

At Gangotri, Abhishiktānanda praised the acosmic life of total solitude, and Panikkar provoked him, asking "Then why not you, here and now?" Panikkar remembers that Abhishiktānanda felt sad since he resisted the option to embrace such total solitude. Then Panikkar continued, saying that Abhishiktānanda did not remain at Gangotri.[34] So, from where did Abhishiktānanda's resistance originate? Scholarship has been shaped by Panikkar's mark on Abhishiktānanda: the "acosmic."[35] Yet the question needs now to be raised, in retrospect, whether, after all, scholars have correctly interpreted Panikkar's phrase, "You [i.e., Abhishiktānanda] are the acosmic."[36] The acosmic, for Panikkar, is surely the one who has left behind

---

32. Pope Benedict XVI, *Deus Caritas Est*, January 25, 2006. The Encyclical addresses the subject of God's love.

33. *Diary* (February 2, 1973), 370.

34. *Letter*, 442.

35. *Mountain*, 53.

36. *Mountain*, 53.

the world and already lives on the other shore of the river. Abhishiktānanda talked and wrote about the further shore, and for sure he envisioned himself leaving everything behind to reach the further shore.[37] But scholars have abundant evidence that he never actually left everything behind. For example, nine years after the episode at Gangotri, Abhishiktānanda received an invitation from Marc Chaduc to go to the mountains and to die near the Ganges.[38] Abhishiktānanda declined the invitation without further explanation and moved instead to Indore. We know the reasons he went there: "a homely atmosphere, medical attention, suitable food, and all that 'for the love of God.'"[39] Not your typical "acosmic," for sure. In the context of the dialogue between Panikkar and Abhishiktānanda at Gangotri—a dialogue focusing on cosmic priests and acosmic monks in which both the discussants, Panikkar and Abhishiktānanda, are priests—probably "acosmism" means something more specific than leaving the world behind. Panikkar claims to be the "cosmic" and more precisely the cosmic priest. The cosmic priest is, for Panikkar, the one who celebrates for the sake of maintaining and restoring the unity of the cosmos. For Panikkar, Abhishiktānanda is not a cosmic priest. He is the acosmic. The "acosmic" is the one who stops celebrating all rites (services, sacrament, liturgy). However, rites are essential to the well-being of the cosmos: stopping celebrating all rites is equal to letting the world collapse. If the priest does not celebrate, the entire universe collapses. Thus, what is at stake in the cosmic versus acosmic dialectic is the holding of the cosmos through the rites. This is Panikkar's position. Yet, Panikkar called Abhishiktānanda "the high priest of solitude" and called himself "the high priest of the crowd."[40] How to explain that? An answer will be provided in the next chapter. For now, it is important to note that Abhishiktānanda remained a priest and continued to celebrate the Eucharist until the end of his life. When reading his works, sometimes it is difficult to escape the sense that the contemplative and the priest in Abhishiktānanda switch roles according to the situation: when the monk deals with the abysses of acosmism, the priest operates as a reminder of the communal purpose of his quest; then the roles switch, and now it is the priest who benefits from the mystical insight of the contemplative to energize his theological and artistic vision for the sake of all.

37. It is the main topic of *Further*.
38. *Letters*, 316.
39. Letter to Odette Baumer-Despeigne, August 28, 1973; see *Letters*, 309.
40 *Mountain*, 47.

Abhishiktānanda's social inclination is an equally potential source of his visceral, immediate, and ultimately undefeatable resistance to individualism. Some scholars and commentators hold the misunderstanding that Abhishiktānanda was only concerned with his own quest, but this interpretation clouds the social character of Abhishiktānanda's enterprise. Abhishiktānanda was "social" not merely because he was not acosmic enough, or because he lacked courage; this was for him rooted primarily in the ecclesial character of his theological concern. Understandably, Abhishiktānanda saw the ecclesial character of his quest as intimately tied to his spiritual quest because the recovery of the supernatural implies the necessity of a close link— indeed, the identity—between personal search and ecclesial communion. Abhishiktānanda was "social" among other reasons because of the character of his ecclesial preoccupation underlying the reappropriation of the supernatural through Advaita. Several times he recognized the state of spiritual thirst of an entire institution effected by extrinsicism. Abhishiktānanda's personal search for God was not an individual enterprise, a form of escapism from the institution, but rather a mission with an ecclesiastical horizon, the recovery of the supernatural to Catholicism. His preoccupation likely had something to do with a personal problem he encountered in France, that is, his perceived impossibility to proceed, via a humble and serious experience, his search for God. In India, Monchanin provided Abhishiktānanda with the intellectual tools necessary to reframe his personal experience at the monastery into more general terms, that of a theological concern toward recovering a supernatural orientation within the church. Once we have established the ecclesial character of Abhishiktānanda's concern, the elusiveness of his social commitment conveniently disappears.

An Artist

In light of a reconstruction of the historical and theological context of French Catholicism in the first half of the twentieth century and of the suggestion to see Abhishiktānanda as integral to that context, readers can see Abhishiktānanda from a new perspective. Abhishiktānanda can be identified as an integral and authentically Catholic artist and a socially committed monk who exercised his talents and personality through literary work to recover a sacramental vision. This sacramental vision, in turn, is recovered for the sake of the renewal of the Church of the West, and it benefits from Hindu insights. The central weaknesses manifested in the sacramental imagination of the Western Church remained impressed into Abhishiktānanda's mind, framing and conditioning a main theological preoccupation of his life, while the engagement with Indian religion epitomized his remedy for such a preoccupation.

Reclaiming imagination is the work of an artist who can merge creativity, inspiration, and beauty and describe how the ultimate reality looks, evident and radiant in this very concrete world. Scholars, though, see Abhishiktānanda's work from a theological perspective, where they would do better to see him as an artist who engaged Advaita to re-empower sacramental imagination for the sake of Catholicism. They may even see him as a failed theologian, who lacked the intellectual stamina to grasp the complex reflections of Monchanin and his assessment of Indian thought. They would do better to see him as an artist who assimilated Monchanin's theological method to reach a generalized, imaginative solution to the problem of a desacramentalized vision of reality. It scarcely seems to have occurred to them that there might be more than a chance connection between the artist who described India as a sacramental place and the dissatisfied monk of the Abbey of Saint Anne de Kergonan. Theologians saw him as a contemplative who missed the final step, living in constant intellectual tension between two religions. He was instead an intergral and authentically artistically minded Catholic monk-priest who rather tried to change Christian consciousness for the sake of all, and for this purpose he had to be living in India and engaging with Hinduism.

By locating Abhishiktānanda within French Catholicism and recognizing him as an artist with a social compass, readers discover aspects of his life and thought previously hidden: the social character of his mysticism, the devotional life at the monastery, and the literary style of his writings. Moreover, this new narrative incorporates questions that require still deeper examination: why did Abhishiktānanda leave France for India? What did he learn from Monchanin? What was the true scope of his writings? And, in which sense was he an unreliable theologian versus a poet? In this portrait, Abhishiktānanda mends most of his troubles, recovers some consistency, and shows completeness.[41]

By reframing Abhishiktānanda as an artist, a more complete portrait can be painted. Certainly, Abhishiktānanda did not live to write, but his life and his literary work as a writer are intrinsically linked. His manuscripts

---

41. See the recent translation of Abhishiktānanda's French poems in Abhishiktānanda, *In the Bosom of the Father*.

are not speculative but autobiographical; they are born from experience and only later shaped by the writing. In Abhishiktānanda a circular motion exists between life and writing, writing and life, to the point that perhaps we can conclude that Abhishiktānanda the Artist makes himself available through his life and his writing—or that one complements the other.[42] To put it differently, the most remarkable achievement of Abhishiktānanda the Artist is the convergence of his life and his writing. But how we can claim that his life was an artistic life? Or, what can we claim made Abhishiktānanda an artist in the first place? When Abhishiktānanda calls Panikkar "an artist," he continues to explain that the latter was enchanted by the beauty of the landscape around him. "He never grew tired of marvelling at the sky, the snow, the changing colours in the sunlight."[43] These words suggest that for Abhishiktānanda, to be an artist meant to be artistically minded. Perhaps he adopted the same definition for himself. He called himself an artist because he saw the world from an aesthetic perspective. He turned his life, his quest, into a work of art in the sense that he was at the same time the artist and the artifact. A quest is a work of art and if that is true then surely it is the only art form in which the artist breaks himself down as he proceeds through his work—in which he breaks himself down to the point where the work is finished at the moment of the artist's collapse. Then the impact of the art, its capacity to move us, is determined solely by the artist's courage. Abhishiktānanda definitively took an artistic, emotive approach to his quest. He created a quest that inspired and provided emotions and helped people spend many hours in different places on the planet dreaming about a different form of Christianity, a different relation with Christ. Who else ever claimed that "Christianity is an explosion of the Spirit"?[44]

Abhishiktānanda did not write his life story; he did not share with his readers the struggle to answer a spiritual call. His life and artistic work are not à la Merton; he does not challenge his readers to give up their

---

42. Baumer-Despeigne made a similar, though not equivalent, comment when she said that Abhishiktānanda's spiritual journey could not be dissociated from his daily life. See Baumer-Despeigne, "Cheminement spirituel d'Henri Le Saux," 531. For a translation in English, see, "The Spiritual Way of Henri Le Saux," 20.

43. *Mountain*, 37.

44. Baumer-Despeigne, "The Spiritual Way of Henri Le Saux," 23. The meaning of the term *explosion* comes probably from the level of spiritual experience, as Abhishiktānanda will clarify a month later: "Everything explodes when you have reached the fourth mātra of the OM." Letter to Panikkar, June 25, 1973; see *Letters*, 301. A similar expression, "It is an explosion of the Spirit," is present in his *Diary*, 342 (April 8, 1972).

materialistic means for spiritual pursuits. Abhishiktānanda's theological concern focuses on the spiritual landscape. He writes about the spiritual experience that is reachable in India and let his French readers appreciate the difference. After spending weeks in a cave as a Christian hermit among Hindu solitaries in Arunachala, Abhishiktānanda describes his experience as, "The realization of the all-pervading Presence of God [. . .] in everything." The next year, in 1953, he added to his *Diary*:

> The Christian *sannyasi* discovers with astonishment that in reaching the peak of Arunachala, he has penetrated into the very heart of Hinduism. He, Christian as he is, has realized the fundamental experience of Hinduism.[45]

In India, the Christian monk has penetrated into the very heart of Hinduism and perceived the all-pervading Presence of God. He seems to ask: Why not in France? Why not into the very heart of Christianity? There is something paradoxical in a Christian monk who needs to go to India and act as a Hindu in order to reach the same God that he was unable to find in a Christian monastery in France. There is something paradoxical in Western Christianity. The artist who notes in 1966 that "Myth no longer carries any weight. Reason endlessly debates its conclusions" was not clearly thinking of the reality of Christianity in India.[46] He was more probably thinking of the rigid ecclesial atmosphere of his monastery, or the church's triumphalist mentality of the seminary. He was recalling the terrible insufficiency of life in a desacramentalized world that was entirely dedicated to celebrating the unquestioned and unquestioning certitude of the Catholic Church of the early twentieth century. As a matter of fact, it is in India, in the flowing waters of the Ganges, that the Christian signs recover all their value.[47]

An artist of Abhishiktānanda's profundity, independence, and originality did not engage in a theological enterprise simply on account of the personal influence of some meetings with extraordinary contemporaries. A priest of his eucharistic sensibility did not fail to see the "social" implication of the problem he encountered in France. The desacramentalized reality of the French Church and the related impossibility of pursuing a serious search for God is the problem with which Abhishiktānanda was *already* preoccupied when, at Monchanin's suggestion, he first made contact with

---

45. Baumer-Despeigne, "The Spiritual Way of Henri Le Saux," 21.
46. *Diary*, 288 (November 18, 1966).
47. *Diary*, 382 (June 30, 1973).

Sri Ramana Maharshi and was drawn into the fascinating path of Advaita. This influenced his life from then on. It is the problem of determining whose *practical* solution he saw in moving to India and the whole *intellectual* solution that engaged his mind *after* he got in touch with the saints of India in the first place that eventually became the foundation for the whole subsequent literary work of sacramental imagination with a Hindu stamp.

To put it differently, we must read Abhishiktānanda primarily as a Catholic artist with a theological concern that encompasses the church and eventually encompasses the entire human family. Of course, an artist is someone who creates art, but this definition is only partially useful in this case. In this book, Abhishiktānanda emerges as an artist with a mythopoetic sense, a mythmaker, and his life and literary work as an intellectual and experiential effort to create a new myth in which Christianity, or at least Abhishiktānanda, may find strength and meaning. However, a mythopoetic sense that embodies and empowers a eucharistic vision, a vision that rejects a narcissistic interpretation of spirituality, breaks barriers of space and time, and makes the entire church one body, whether her members are contemplative or not. Abhishiktānanda's contribution to Catholicism lies in the area of sacramental imagination, not of sacramental ontology. His is an explicitly literary contribution. He poured out an incarnational, sacramental worldview combined with his own personal passion and lucidity, a rare but fertile combination. Art and the poetic are the best filters through which to view Abhishiktānanda's work. We may get an authentic understanding of his theology by engaging with Abhishiktānanda as an artistic spirit that perceived himself as in the mission of recovering a pre-modern sacramental sensibility in India for the sake of Catholicism. He was not preoccupied with elaborating a theological synthesis that would lead to a theoretically impeccable notion of sacramental ontology.

Abhishiktānanda framed this world as non-dual and contended that Christians can recover the supernatural order within the original biblical ontology of Being through the encounter with Advaita. It is clear that Abhishiktānanda worked on the recovery of the supernatural, understood as the recovery of a sacramental character of reality—the unity of nature and the supernatural—through the representation in his literary work of a sacramental world that is infused with eucharistic meaning. I will deal with these two topics (the sacramental ontology of Being and the sacramental imagination) in the later chapters. Although Abhishiktānanda failed to articulate a relationship between the order of nature and the supernatural in proper theological terms, he developed a creative sacramental imagination that reflects a distinct understanding of the unity of nature and the supernatural. His contribution to Catholicism lies less in theological formulae than in his imaginative sensibility that restores a world replete with meaning at every level.

Conclusion

While the purpose of the previous chapter was to identify a central key to unlock the guiding theological intuition of Abhishiktānanda's intellectual project, this chapter explains why the search for such a focal point remains elusive: when placed in the context of pre-Vatican II French Catholicism, Abhishiktānanda's main intellectual preoccupation emerges clearly. He maintained a sacramental vision and wanted to reignite such a vision within Christianity. The portrait of Abhishiktānanda as a contemplative with a eucharistic sensibility helps frame his quest as spiritual and "social," a spiritual quest within a communal horizon. In the next chapter, I will provide a deeper study of Abhishiktānanda's priesthood and its relationship with the grand theme of the sacramental ontology.

6

ABHISHIKTĀNANDA'S PRIESTHOOD

> "[I am] consecrated to a ministry . . . that extends beyond . . . ecclesial manifestations."
>
> —Abhishiktānanda, 1971[1]

Introduction

IN THE PREVIOUS CHAPTER Abhishiktānanda was reintroduced as primarily an artist—a poet—with a theological concern, as well as a contemplative who maintained a "social" compass. A brief comment has been framed with regard to Abhishiktānanda's priesthood. Almost inevitably, Abhishiktānanda's priesthood brings to scholars' attention his difficult, at times polemical relationship with his church and his ambivalent relationship with liturgy: the acosmic is the one who stops celebrating all rites (services, sacrament, liturgy). Yet, there is probably no better theme than priesthood to correct the current interpretations of Abhishiktānanda as an "acosmic." Moreover, priesthood works to prove that the recovery of the supernatural is the theological intuition of Abhishiktānanda's intellectual project. Finally, priesthood operates as a privileged entry into Abhishiktānanda's idea of sacramental ontology. This chapter is dedicated to all of these subjects.

---

1. *Diary*, 335 (December 21, 1971).

Christian Unreadiness

In his private notes and published writings, Abhishiktānanda had often raised the problem of the "unreadiness of Christians." His main point was that Christians and Hindus can only meet in Christ. Abhishiktānanda wrote in *The Mountain of the Lord* that "it is only at the very source that the Meeting takes place we only meet each other when we meet God."[2] For Abhishiktānanda, Hindus and Christians can only meet in Christ. But, Abhishiktānanda observed, Christians are not ready to meet Hindus in Christ because they have not yet realized their total mystery in Christ. In a letter written a couple of months after his pilgrimage to Gangotri, Abhishiktānanda explained in plain terms that "the further I go, the more I believe that the essential task in India is not to bring the Gospel to the Hindus, but to convert the Christians to the *Gospel* [original emphasis] and to 'catholicism.'"[3] Thus, Christians still need to convert to the gospel. To put it differently, for Abhishiktānanda the church had yet to reach the hidden depths of her source. Christians needed to return to the source of their faith, which is the gospel, and ultimately Christ; only then will they be ready to enter in dialogue with Hinduism. In a letter to his sister, Abhishiktānanda described what seemed to be his vision of Christianity as totally converted to the gospel: "a life conformed to the Gospel . . . when the Church, or rather, Christians as a whole, radiate the pure light of the Gospel . . . then . . . the non-Christians will ask for baptism."[4] But what exactly is holding the church back? Why has she yet to discover her source?

What I called the church's unreadiness can be better defined as an ecclesiological problem: the church is sick. At a one level, Abhishiktānanda considered the church sick of rationalism.[5] In his opinion, Christianity was on the verge of a spiritual crisis, showing symptoms of a spiritual deficit that can only be cured through a return to the sources of Christianity. This crisis is not limited to the lay people; on the contrary, the crisis involved primarily the religious orders, including the monastic ones. "Monks *claim* (emphasis added) to belong to the Eschaton," he wrote in 1970. "But Benedictines think of the Beyond only under the form of an

---

2. *Mountain*, 42.
3. Letter to Sr Marie-Gilberte, August 11, 1964; see *Letters*, 165.
4. Letter to Mother Theophane, April 13, 1965; see *Letters*, 170.
5. For the remark on "rationalism," see, for example, Letter to Canon J. Lemarié, April 10, 1970, in *Letters*, 229.

abbey choir."[6] While he referred to rationalism, Abhishiktānanda had a much clearer diagnosis in mind, something that had to do with a theologically based sociological impossibility in the Christian reality of his days of reaching a true and total experience of Christ.[7] The solution, quite obviously, was to invite Christians to rediscovery the interior dimension of their faith: "Only an immersion in the real depth will save the Church. Launch out into the deep."[8]

However, there is a deeper level: in his personal journal, he mentioned the "Neolithic Church" three times. The first time was in 1956, eight years after his move to India and one year before Monchanin's death. Abhishiktānanda had already reached the point of considering the possibility of leaving Shantivanam to embrace the wandering life of the Indian sadhu. In his personal journal, he described the Neolithic Church as the church living in the Neolithic era, an era characterized by *nous* (mind, Greek) and *manas* (thought, Sanskrit)—an era "in which humanity 'builds' the earth for its own use and in its own style."[9] The Neolithic age is the time "of making plans, of rationalizing the world."[10] The Neolithic era is the era of the external world, of materialism, of the artificial. To put it differently, the Neolithic era is a non-atmic era, an era in which humanity has yet to reach undifferentiated awareness, a state of identification, not with individuality, not with groups of beings, "not through the medium of the intellect coupled with the external world," but with all pervading life itself.[11] Eleven years later, in 1967, Abhishiktānanda returned to the theme of the Neolithic era. "Church and religions," he claimed, "are tied to the Neolithic era which is coming to an end." They are provisional solutions in preparation of human beings taking control of themselves.[12] Finally in 1970, Abhishiktānanda wrote clarifying notes about the Neolithic Church. It is worthwhile to quote most of the passage:

---

6. Letter to Mother Theophane, March 18, 1970; see *Letters*, 231.
7. Beltramini, "Abhishiktananda and Roman Catholicism's Retrieval," 106–23.
8. Letter to Mother Francoise-Therese at Lisieux, November 30, 1972; see *Letters*, 279.
9. *Diary*, 140–41 (January 21, 1956).
10. *Diary*, 140–41 (January 21, 1956).
11. *Diary*, 140–41 (January 21, 1956).
12. *Diary*, 296 (October 22, 1967). It is well known that Abhishiktananda's original notebooks from 1966 to 1973 have been destroyed and what scholars can access is the manuscript written by Marc Chaduc out of the original notebooks.

> Pentecost inaugurates what is beyond religion. Christ lives in the Spirit, not in the Pope or in the formulas of the Creed. Realization after 2000 years of the Pentecostal era . . . . The Church, a transitory form between the descent of the Spirit and humanity's realization of the mystery of the Spirit – until such time as human evolution become capable of this purification (end of the Neolithic age). Christianity has been ossified into a religion.[13]

That passage contains much more than I want to disentangle here. For example, scholars of Abhishiktānanda recognize his critique of formulas, rites, names, and thoughts, and experts of Panikkar can detect a quote from *The Unknown Christ of Hinduism*.[14] In any case, the point is clear: the Neolithic era is the era of religion. It was supposed to end 2,000 years ago at the Pentecost, but it did not end there. In another note, written in the months before his death, Abhishiktānanda seemed to clarify his point about the path not taken:

> And then came the Councils! That means Hellenization with its transforming power, plus Roman legalism taking over from the Jewish Torah. And the Church feel into the intellectualism of the Middle Ages and the idolatry that went with it. What a shame that the Reformers were not able to discover the Spirit![15]

In brief, the church is still at the stage of formulas and rites; therefore, a purification is needed. Christians need to convert to the gospel before being ready to convert Hindus. It seems a brave statement, but it is worth remembering that on several occasions, his friend Panikkar also urged Christians to convert.[16]

Sometime in the decade between the second half of the 1950s and the first half of the 1960s, Abhishiktānanda and his friend Panikkar concluded that Christianity was not ready to convert India. The conversion of India can only happen at the source of both religions, with Christ being that source. Therefore, the conversion of India can only happen in Christ. And, the two friends concluded, neither Hinduism nor Christianity was ready to meet

---

13. *Diary*, 319 (September 9, 1970). The original French, however, reads, "Le christianisme a été scléroséen religion" (Christianity has been sclerosed (i.e., affected by sclerosis) into a religion). See Abhishiktananda, *La montée au fond du cœur*, 390.

14. "Christianity is 'foolishness,' because Christianity is provisional and not self-sufficient – being only for this temporal existence." See Panikkar, *The Unknown Christ of Hinduism*, 63.

15. *Diary*, 371 (February 2, 1973).

16. Beltramini, *The Unknown Christ of Christianity*, 67

in Christ. Abhishiktānanda and Panikkar argued that Christians "should seek God" (Acts 17: 27) but argued that they did not because they believed that they had already found Him. And because Christians believe as much, they transformed a wind of the Spirit into an edifice of laws and rituals, in which they worship God as He was *their* god. To follow is another way to put it: Christianity should be a nation of priests who introduce God to the nations (the non-Christians); here "introduce" stands for mediate. Christians should bridge the gap between God and non-Christians so that the latter are attracted by the former. This is true with regards to all non-Christians, including the habitants of India. Unfortunately, this is Abhishiktānanda's and Panikkar's position, that Christians are administrators of rituals before *their* God. How can Indians be attracted by God? How can Christians convert India? Abhishiktānanda and Panikkar articulated that position in distinct fashions and with different levels of profundity. Still, it is indisputable that they shared the same position.

Back to Abhishiktānanda. The difference between the level of the spiritual crisis of contemporary Christianity and that of the Neolithic Church is evident: the former requires a spiritual turn, a turn that cannot be led, in Abhishiktānanda's opinion, even by the contemplative religious orders within the Roman Catholic Church. The dialogue with Hinduism, in this perspective, is an opportunity to fill the spiritual gap that is troubling Christianity. The latter, however, is a different story: here the point is that at the Pentecost, Christians had the chance to enter into a post-Neolithic age, but they took another path. The relationship with Hinduism is framed in plain and firm terms: the institutionalization of Christianity into a religion in a very early stage of its history has consigned Christianity to a rank inferior to Hinduism. From here it follows that Christians need to convert (to the gospel): it is in and through living out the gospel that the Holy Spirit works and conversion takes place. If that is to happen, it takes time; in fact, in *The Mountain of the Lord* Abhishiktānanda suggested about generations. Therefore, Christians and Hindus live this time as a time in between, a time between the experiential, cognitive, and cultural levels, and a much deeper level. In summary, Abhishiktānanda believed that Christianity requires a return to the sources of its faith, to start over—that is, to start at the Pentecost a Pentecostal era. It is only at that point that Christians can meet Hinduism at the ultimate source—that is, Christ—and India will be Christian. Panikkar framed the same idea in 1964: "Hinduism and Christianity meet in the depths of death."[17] Both religions need conversion. "Christ is there in Hinduism, but Hinduism is not yet his spouse."[18] But, Panikkar argued, he has yet to complete another study, a volume called "The Unknown Christ of Christianity."[19] The unknown Christ of Christianity is the plastic representation of the gap that still exists in Christians' comprehension of Christ's Mystery that goes beyond Jesus Christ, a gap that precludes Christianity from receiving (i.e., meeting in Christ) Hinduism. The difference between the level of the spiritual crisis of contemporary Christianity and that of the Neolithic Church changes the meaning of Abhishiktānanda's invitation to Christians to return to the source. In the first case, it is an invitation to go inward, an invitation to experience God within and embrace spirituality. The second is instead an appeal to go back to the very sources of Christianity and start over.

Reflecting on the result of his spiritual clash with India, Abhishiktānanda perceived a deep spiritual crisis feeding the church of his day. Christians had strayed from its mysterious inner principle or power of spiritual life. His diagnosis: Christianity is in crisis because it had abandoned a collective sense of the faith supernaturally imparted by the Holy Spirit to the church. Thus, for Abhishiktānanda the problem of the church is essentially spiritual and the solution must be spiritual as well. His solution can be summarized as follows: the key to overcoming the spiritual crisis of Christianity is to reconsider the Christ-Holy Spirit relationship in a truly and deeply mystical perspective. For Abhishiktānanda, the divine sonship is thought radically, in terms of a spiritual dynamic that every Christian can potentially relive by opening up to the Spirit, that is, Christ as Spirit. Not surprisingly, Abhishiktānanda took up a famous passage from the Gospel of John (John 16:7) and stressed the need for Christ (visible Logos) to leave so that the Paraclete (unseen Logos) can come, thus highlighting how the physical humanity of the Son must be overcome in order for the Spirit to be generated.[20] The desire to focus on the visible rather than on the unseen, on the objective rather than on the subjective, in the final analysis, on Christ rather than on the Holy Spirit, was and still is, in Abhishiktānanda's opinion, the characteristic note of Catholicism, especially modern Catholicism. Modern Catholicism, for Abhishiktānanda, favors a certain primacy of

17. Panikkar, *Unknown*, 18.
18. Panikkar, *Unknown*, 1718.
19. Panikkar, *Unknown*, xiii.
20. *Diary*, 186 (November 30, 1956).

Christology over Pneumatology, with the consequent accentuation of the aspects of visibility, institutionalism, centralism, and rationality, in spite of those of mystery, communion, collegiality, and apophatic symbolism. To put it differently, in his private notes and published works, Abhishiktānanda confirmed the difference between a form of Christianity founded on a sacred book and that based on an ineffable experience. In fact, he spoke of a seemingly incurable contrast between the idea of a definitive and unchangeable revelation and, transitively, on a whole series of moral dictates and precepts, on one hand, and on the other an increasingly forgotten and marginalized notion of an experience founded on the inner awareness of an unspeakable mystery.[21]

A Priest

In their pilgrimage to Gangotri, Abhishiktānanda and Panikkar dissected the future of spirituality—understood in terms of where "the Spirit is drawing people"—in India and elsewhere. Panikkar was quite sure that the Spirit was at work "into the world itself," not in the contemplative orders of the "naked silent sadhus, sitting motionless at the back of their caves." Oh no, commented Abhishiktānanda, "there will always be some of these acosmics, naked and silent in their caves."[22] In his opinion, the more Christians accept involvement in the reality of world affairs, even if it means to bring peace and justice to the hungry and the thirsty, the more they need the comfort of spiritual people. The more Christianity is part of the historical movement of things and events, the more it requires these solitary hermits and wandering monks, the so-called "acosmics," to offer their stillness to keep the world still. The more the church embraces a reality based on an incessant becoming, the more she needs the presence of acosmics who reject rites and doctrinal formulations and remember to all *to be*. "They are," in Abhishiktānanda's words, "the pivots of this world."

As for himself, he considered himself a monk. He loved to spend weeks in silence, feeling at home in an abandoned Hindu temple or a cave in the hills. He used to visit Christians ashrams (he founded one of them) and Benedictine monasteries in India, but his heart was in sync with the

---

21. "One awakes everywhere and once for all, and the awakening cannot be confused with what one can see at the moment of the awakening, and therefore with that through which one becomes conscious that one is awake." See *Diary*, 385–86.

22. *Mountain*, 40–41.

naked and silent *sannyasins*, or Hindu ascetics, he met on the Indian roads or on the peaks of Himalaya. He engaged in long periods (weeks, months) of meditation, sometimes interrupted with the study of the Upanishads. He claimed that some passages were difficult and deserved more time than others, but then immediately corrected himself: "The Upanishads are not a science to be taught, but an experience which is communicated by spiritual generation."[23] He meant that the Upanishads are not a *gnosis*. Only those who have already experienced the spiritual generation, i.e., the generation of the Spirit within, are in the position to understand the difficult passages of the Upanishads. And it is from this vantage point of his interior experience of the generation of the Spirit, he believed—at least, so he wrote in his personal notes—that the Upanishads are true.[24] When comparing the literature of Christian mystics to the Upanishads, he could not hide his preference for the latter. "Just now I am rereading John of the Cross and Teresa of Avila. I can make out what they are saying, but how strange and complicated is their 'language.' By contrast, the language of the Upanishads shines of 'purity and directness.'"[25] Abhishiktānanda could access the ultimate meaning of the work of the Spanish giants of Christian early modern mysticism by way of correlation, that is, through the correspondences between his own spiritual experience and their experiences as described in their writings. But their descriptions looked "strange and complicated" to Abhishiktānanda in comparison with the descriptions included in the Upanishads. The latter, it seems to Abhishiktānanda, offer descriptions of their truths in a pure and direct way. To Joseph Lemarié, a French Benedictine monk with whom Abhishiktānanda corresponded for decades, he dared to complain: "I no longer know the language of the West; and so few of you are open to *our* language here" (emphasis added).[26] The French Benedictine monk had reached the point of interpreting Christianity along the Vedic lines of the Upanishads.

Abhishiktānanda considered himself a monk as well as a priest. Scholars are familiar with the dialogue between Abhishiktānanda and Panikkar during their pilgrimage to Gangotri, a dialogue that centers on the acosmic-cosmic polarities: Abhishiktānanda is the acosmic, i.e., the monk, and Panikkar is the cosmic, the priest. In the text, the acosmic-cosmic

23. Letter to Marc Chaduc, March 6, 1972; see *Letters*, 279.
24. Letter to Odette Baumer-Despeigne, May 28, 1972; see *Letters*, 279.
25. Letter to Marc Chaduc, June 13, 1972; see *Letters*, 272.
26. Letter to Joseph Lemarié, July 20, 1969; see *Letters*, 216.

counterpoint is repeated several times. The usual explanation suggested by scholars is that, in the dialogue, Panikkar's cosmism operates as an alternative to emphasize Abhishiktānanda's acosmism. According to this interpretation, Abhishiktānanda understood himself primarily as a monk, not as a priest. But an alternative interpretation is also possible: in the dialogue, Abhishiktānanda's acosmism serves as an alternative to emphasize Panikkar's cosmism. More than that, Abhishiktānanda's priesthood serves as an alternative to emphasize Panikkar's priesthood. In the dialogue, Panikkar's peculiar interpretation of priesthood is at stake. As a matter of fact, Abhishiktānanda recognized himself as an "acosmic," yet he refused to downplay his priesthood. He seemed confident that, as a monk, he could pass into the mystery and, as a priest, he could reveail that mystery. In the dialogue, Abhishiktānanda noted that he celebrated the Eucharist in "the Himalayan village of Gyansu" and in the caves of Arunachala.[27] His point is that Panikkar was not the only priest who had celebrated the Eucharist "often at various sacred places in India . . . where it has never been done before."[28] Yet, this important corrective did not seem to change the narrative: when it is Panikkar's turn to comment on Abhishiktānanda's words, Panikkar framed himself as the only priest: "we are both come [to Gangotri] as forerunners of the Church," Panikkar concluded, "I the priest, you the monk."[29] Panikkar's unwillingness to recognize Abhishiktānanda's priestly status seems more incomprehensible if it is remembered that Abhishiktānanda, like Panikkar, took his priesthood seriously and assigned a tremendous importance to his liturgy. Not only was Abhishiktānanda part of a monastic congregation in France that had been responsible for the liturgical renewal within the Roman Catholic Church since the second half of the nineteenth century, but he was also personally experimenting in India with the liturgy of the Eucharist by incorporating readings and chants from Hindu Scriptures into the regular Christian worship.[30] And Panikkar was well aware of all this, as Abhishiktānanda used to go to Varanasi to share his liturgical experiments with his friend.[31]

27. *Mountain*, 53 and 54.
28. *Mountain*, 53.
29. *Mountain*, 55.
30. Letter to Canon J. Lemarié, December 22, 1965; see *Letters*, 175.
31. For example, Abhishiktānanda went to Varanasi to discuss his liturgical improvements with Panikkar in December 1965.

What was Panikkar implying in his refusal to recognize Abhishiktānanda's priesthood? Was he implying that Panikkar and Abhishiktānanda were both priests according to the canon law, the corpus of ecclesiastical law that regulates the Roman Catholic Church, but in Panikkar's opinion, only Panikkar himself was primarily and ultimately a *true* priest, while Abhishiktānanda was primarily and ultimately a monk? Not at all. In the dialogue, in fact, Panikkar made the point that the monk "is the high priest of solitude and also the high priest of the crowd;" that is, he reframed monasticism in terms of priesthood. I can only speculate here.[32] In *The Mountain of the Lord*, two crucial distinctions are at stake in the dialogue between Panikkar and Abhishiktānanda. The first distinction runs between the priest of rites and the priest in spirit and truth (John 4:24). For both Panikkar and Abhishiktānanda, there is the level of rites, and there is the level of the Spirit. Accordingly, there is the priest at the level of rites, and there is the priest at the level of the Spirit. Panikkar refined the difference between the two levels of priesthood in terms of intermediation, that is, the administration of rites, the ministry at the service of a bureaucracy, and mediation between the Creator and His creation, the ministry at the service of the mystery. In Abhishiktānanda's words, the priest in spirit exercises the ministry of the "revelation to human beings of their own personally mystery and also of the total mystery in itself, what is called God or the Deity."[33] Both friends rejected the dominant interpretation of the priest within Catholicism as primarily "priest of rites" and envisioned an interpretation of priestly ministry that goes beyond its ecclesial expressions. In their celebre dialogue on their way to the sources of the Ganger, the crux of the matter is the priesthood in Spirit.[34]

Then there is the second distinction, one between the cosmic and the acosmic priesthood, or, in Panikkar's terms, between the priesthood of the crowd and the priesthood of solitude. A possible explanation of this distinction is that Panikkar was the cosmic priest and Abhishiktānanda was the monk-priest, the priest who reveals the mystery precisely because as a monk, as an acosmic, he disappears into the mystery. Panikkar was assuming several strands of high priesthood: "the high priest of solitude and also the high priest of the crowd," and of course the high priest of peace, i.e., of

---

32. *Mountain*, 47.
33. *Diary*, 335 (December 21, 1971).
34. *Mountain*, 36–60.

unity.[35] Eventually for Panikkar, each of these stands took on its own specific nature, although the plurality of stands is the expression of the one and same high priesthood that is constantly at work. In the end, these stands all maintain, renew, and cement the relationship between creation and Creator. In this way, all the high priestly essence flows together in the ensemble of strands and are fused into unity. Or, it can be said that the high priest of solitude, the high priest of the crowd, and the high priest of peace are like the rays of the sun, the sun being "the high priesthood."

The distinction between the priest of rites and the priest in Spirit is explained in a note from Abhishiktānanda's notebook: "There is the priest at the level of rites and there is the priest at the level of the Spirit."[36] Abhishiktānanda struggled to be a priest of rites. His private notes are a testimony of the ambivalent relationship he maintained with rites during his time in India. He celebrated Mass and performed the Eucharist until the end of his life, yet he believed that to go beyond rites was part of his vocation. He never doubted, however, to be a priest in Spirit. Like Ramana, he wrote, "every guru, is a priest in spirit and truth" (John 4:24). Of course, true priesthood can only be the mutual interpenetration of the priesthood of rites and the priesthood in spirit. This is the explanation of one of Panikkar's most straightforward remarks on his own priesthood:

> I have always considered myself a priest, although I entered [priesthood] through a very narrow door, the Roman Catholic door . . . you have to open the door wide; and then, once you enter this realm of mediation, you must get rid of any mentality or ideology that can make you a bureaucrat, or the representative of a particular clan. . . . In any case, I am a Catholic priest.[37]

One enters priesthood through the priesthood of rites, then one reaches the priesthood in spirit and never goes back. One must, so to speak, throw away the ladder after he/she has climbed up it. Yet, once one reaches the level of the Spirit, his/her priesthood of rites is not replaced, abolished, or terminated, but instead elevated, that is, fulfilled and brought to fullness. In summary, true priesthood is a sacramental communion of the priesthoods of rites and in Spirit.

Abhishiktānanda's priesthood was probably the same. If so, the distinction between the priest of rites and the priest in Spirit helps to clarify

35. *Mountain*, 47.
36. *Diary*, 335 (December 21, 1971).
37. Panikkar, *Entre Dieu et le Cosmos*, 60. Translation is my own.

Abhishiktānanda's complex relationship with priesthood: he was ambivalent about rites, and for this reason was called "acosmic." But he was a priest, and he was rightly recognized as such. He recognized himself in such a profile. Twenty months before his death, he wrote a note on the occasion of the thirty-sixth anniversary of his sacerdotal ordination. He considered himself "consecrated for a ministry," but a ministry that extended "beyond the so-called ecclesial manifestation."[38] He was a priest, a Roman Catholic priest, a priest in spirit and truth.

Cosmic Christ

In the next chapters I will study the way in which Abhishiktānanda attempted to frame the sacramental ontology theologically, and why he failed. I will also address his more successful effort to empower sacramental imagination. In this last section of this chapter, however, I focus on Abhishiktānanda's idea of Cosmic Christ as a form of sacramental ontology.

By clashing with the reality of India, Abhishiktānanda discovered cultural galaxies which had reached spiritual peaks without any connection with the biblical revelation and whose mental frameworks do not integrate the Judeo-Hellenistic Christ of the Christian tradition. In turn, the Christ of the Christian tradition, forged into Judeo-Hellenistic mental frameworks, was unable to integrate and supersede the truths generated into, and manifested by, Indian cultural galaxies. By clashing with the reality of India, that is, Indian gurus and *sanniasis*, Hindu sacred mountains and holy temples, Vedic scripture and nonduality (or Advaita Vedanta), Abhishiktānanda discovered a cosmic conception of the divine, an a-historical as well as non-anthropocentric view of the divine. In his words:

> India, free from history and especially free from . . . that impossible "people of God"! and also free from the *logos* and the concept [*eidos*], immediately grasped the universal mystery, the Purusha who, outside all history and every *eidos* . . . appears at the origin of everything, at the origin of the cosmic whole.[39]

Thus, in Indian religiosity he found the traits of a cosmic vision of the mystery.

---

38. *Diary*, 335 (December 21, 1971).
39. *Diary*, 363 (December 25, 1972).

In India Abhishiktānanda reached the conclusion that the twenty-centuries long history of Christianity was the result of an enormous, unfortunate misjudgment: Christ has been located at the level of rites, not at the level of spirit. One of the consequences of this is that Christianity has been developed as a religion. "Christianity has been ossified into a religion." This is, pure and simple, Abhishiktānanda's dramatic and conclusive opinion on the church. "By becoming a religion," he wrote, "Christianity has lost its mystery" and its redemptive power.[40] Christianity also lost its most precious gift, that is, total openness to the total human community.[41] In his personal journal Abhishiktānanda described the spiritual deficit of the modern church, and he declared the twenty-centuries old church as the Neolithic Church, that is, the church living in the Neolithic era, an era characterized by *nous* (mind, Greek) and *manas* (thought, Sanskrit)—an era "in which humanity 'builds' the earth for its own use and in its own style."[42] The Neolithic age is the time "of making plans, of rationalizing the world."[43] The Neolithic era is the era of the external world, of materialism, of the artificial. The Neolithic era is the era of religion. It was supposed to end 2,000 years ago at the Pentecost, but it did not end there.

Christ is addressed on the level of rites, not at the level of the spirit. It is through the incarnation that the Spirit has penetrated the universe and now everything shines with the brightness of the Spirit. Christ is Spirit that blows freely, but he is worshiped by Christians as a tribal god, as *their* god (the impossible people of God, as Abhishiktānanda noticed). Once Christ is worshiped at the level of rites, he is transformed into a national god. Abhishiktānanda framed the situation through "terrible" statements: "The Jew burdens God with his own personality. Everything is centered on himself (sic!) for the Jew. God must fight for his people, exterminate his enemies. . . . Yahweh is a national God. The Christian Israel has inherited Jewish chauvinism."[44] Later in life, Abhishiktānanda synthetically returned on the same subject: "The Church [is] committed to the unification of the world in God. It is for God alone that the Church draws the world together, for God in himself, not for the God it adores."[45] The church should serve God

40. *Diary*, 367 (January 2, 1973).
41. *Diary*, 343 (April 24, 1972).
42. *Diary*, 140–41 (January 21, 1956).
43. *Diary*, 140–41 (January 21, 1956).
44. *Diary*, 151 (July 19, 1956).
45. *Diary*, 305 (January 15, 1969).

for God in Himself, not because He is *her* god. Unfortunately, the church today does not recognize the privilege of race and blood for entry into the kingdom, but still recognizes as members of the kingdom those who accept certain laws, forms of worship, and doctrines.

But Christianity is not and cannot be a religion like any other religion (and by "religion" I mean a system of believes, practices, and doctrines). Christianity is purely and simply the spiritual kingdom of God. Christianity, if one still wants to use this term, is humankind in the post-Pentecostal era, after the effusion of the Spirit. "Christ lives in the Spirit," according to Abhishiktānanda, "not in the Pope or in the formulas of the Creed."[46] Thus, Christians are not the members of a religion among the others with its rites and doctrines, rather those who carry the Spirit. "We must bring people today to recognize the Spirit, much more than the story of Jesus."[47] Christians carry the Spirit as well as ferment creation. As Panikkar put it, Christians' task is to be salt, to give more flavor to all things so that everything is more beautiful and better (Mark 4:11–12).[48] Their task is to act as cooperators between the divine and all creation, to be synergic to the coming of the kingdom (1 Peter 2:8).[49] Previously, Abhishiktānanda had used the same words: "The primordial role of Christian, to be leaven in the dough; by his (sic!) own humility, sincerity, etc., to make whoever approaches him more humble, more sincere."[50] When he applied to Christ this distinction between the level of rites and the level of spirit, he recovered from the Pauline letters and patristics the notion of "Cosmic Christ." In Abhishiktānanda's words, "Christ is the cosmic Man, the *Parusha*.[51] Christ is God manifested in the totality."[52] A distinct Christopneumatic interpretation of the nature of the fundamental Christian fact, that is, the coming of Christ in this world, was at stake in Abhishiktānanda's reflection: Christ is Spirit and the ones who

---

46. *Diary*, 319 (September 9, 1970).

47. *Diary*, 319 (September 9, 1970).

48. Panikkar, *La Nuova Innocenza*, 115; see Panikkar, *Christianity: Opera Omnia*, 29.

49. Quoted in Panikkar, La nuova innocenza, 50' Puntata 3 di *Una serie a cura di Werner Weick e Andrea Andriotto*, Lugano, Televisione Svizzera Italiana, 2000. The series was composed of three episodes: (1) the art of living; (2) the smile of the wise man; and (3) the new innocence, from which the quote above is taken. Translation is my own.

50. *Diary*, 273 (May 11, 1964).

51. Nonduality (or Advaita Vedanta) is a sub school of the Hindu philosophy of Vedanta. Its core principles and teachings are referred to as a monastic system of thought. The canonical texts include the Upanishads, the Bhagavad Gita and the Brahman Sutras.

52. *Diary*, 283 (October 19, 1966).

worship Him must worship in spirit and truth (John 4:24). Or, in Abhishiktānanda's words: "Jesus said to his disciples: It is good for you that I go away. And in effect he disappeared, . . . the one who dies, rose, ascended to heaven is therefore no longer 'known' except in the *pneuma*, the Spirit, in a spiritual, *pneumatikē* form."[53] Christ is no longer known except in Spirit.

Conclusion

In a previous chapter, I reframed Abhishiktānanda as an artist with a theological concern. In this chapter I reintroduce him as a priest, not only because his priesthood was an essential element of his identity, but also because his priestly consecration helped him to anchor his spiritual search into a proper ecclesial, social context.

In the next chapter, I will provide a brief summary of Abhishiktānanda's comments on the recovery of the supernatural in Western Catholicism and a sketch of his sacramental ontology. In the following chapter, I will investigate Abhishiktānanda's sacramental imagination. Then to follow is a brief conclusion to end the study.

---

53. *Diary*, 149 (April 15, 1956).

7

SACRAMENTAL ONTOLOGY

"You remained [...] a disciple of Parmenides."

—Pannikar, 2005[1]

Introduction

IN A PREVIOUS CHAPTER, I placed Abhishiktānanda's spiritual search and interreligious dialogue within the framework of the Christian supernatural. The intention was to prove that the supernatural can be seen as Abhishiktānanda's guiding theological intuition, the idea that centers his thought and provides coherence to his work. Here I continue to explore the role of the supernatural in Abhishiktānanda's thought. Certainly, he understood Roman Catholicism as a supernatural religion, although not exactly in line with the thinking of Maurice Blondel, Henri de Lubac, and his own close friend, Jules Monchanin. In the encounter with Hinduism, I argue that Abhishiktānanda found a supernatural perspective to apply to Catholicism. He showed an understanding of reality in terms of sacramental Being, a particular ontology, one that is sacramental in character. His work on the recovery of the supernatural, or sacramental ontology, is interesting, although not of the same quality and originality as his efforts to reignite a sacramental imagination within Catholicism. While this chapter is focused on sacramental ontology, in the next one I will examine Abhishiktānanda's literary efforts to deliver this notion of sacramental Being.

---

1. *Letter 2*, xiv.

A Preliminary Remark

While the risk that the voices of scholarship alter the original in the process of interpretation is a common concern, it is particularly relevant in the case of Abhishiktānanda. Some of his writings have been heavily edited and his portrait so specifically characterized that some would claim that Abhishiktānanda's original thought has been diluted. The last part of the *Diary* (from November 1966 to 1973) was copied by Marc Chaduc, so scholars have only Chaduc's transcription of what was in that part of the *Diary*. No one knows what might have been left out, and Panikkar suspects that these existing extracts only partially cover the notes from those years.[2] That said, hundreds of pages have since been dedicated to drafting a possible theological synthesis between Advaita and Christianity, and readers have only a few concluding pages of Abhishiktānanda's diary to consult; the result is that theologians are now faced with a string of dogmatic statements about the Holy Grail, collapsing synthesis, and the declaration that "there is only the awakening."[3] If theologians see these final statements of Abhishiktānanda about "the myth of the Church [that] is left behind, as is the myth of Christ" exclusively as an episode in the story of his engagement with theology, one significant feature of the statements remains totally mysterious. In these final pages, he used his writing skills to reveal a critical attitude toward the contemporary Christian world and its structures. He does not reject them—he criticizes them from within. More importantly, he contends that Christians can recover the supernatural order within the original biblical ontology of Being through the encounter with Advaita. For Abhishiktānanda, the engagement with Hinduism is not an escape from Christianity, but rather a spiritual vocation that grows from the depths of extrinsicism toward the heights of the supernatural in order to return to the original sacramental ontology. Abhishiktānanda delves and interprets the experience of the "Being" (Nirvana, Brahman, or Atman).

---

2. "Sono ancora profondamente commosso dalla lettura di gran parte dei tuoi diari. Mi spiace che quelli scritti dopo il 1965 siano stati distrutti e che, quindi, tranne pochi estratti conservati, tutti i riferimenti a quegli anni siano di seconda mano." I am greatly moved by most of your personal journals. I regret that those written after 1965 have been destroyed and, therefore, with the exception of a few preserved extracts, all the references to those years are secondhand. See *Letter*, original version (not the 1982 canonical version, in which this passage is omitted). See also: *Diary*, xxx.

3. *Diary*, 386 (September 11, 1973).

Abhishiktānanda's general thesis is that the error of the Catholic Church consists in her distancing from the "I am" of the Gospel of John. The abandonment of this original ontology, that is, the Being of the gospel and the choice of "formulation" instead, is the problem of the church. "Formulation" is the path of the insufficiency, the contingent space where the forms of Western Christianity, with its religious and social institutions, have moved away from the original biblical ontology. In choosing not to respect the teachings of the Gospels and in embracing the reality of the "formulation," the Western Church has found herself in a situation without an obvious exit, and that has brought about the present condition of inauthenticity and inconsistency. In view of all this, the church must return to the Being. Abhishiktānanda brings to light the radical sense of the contraposition of the Being to the "formulation" and investigates the absolute sense of these two notions, understanding in an experiential manner what had not been clarified by the great Christian myths.

Being

At the end of his life, Abhishiktānanda realized that the Being is.

> I have found the Grail. [. . .] It is yourself that you are seeking through everything. And in this quest you run about everywhere, whereas the Grail is here, close at hand, you only have to open your eyes. And that is the finding of the Grail in its ultimate truth, Galahad's direct sight of the inside of the vessel, and no longer just being fed by the Grail which mysteriously passes through the hall, nor even drinking from the Grail [. . .].[4]

According to Abhishiktānanda, Being is not something emerging out from the shadows of obscurity: the truth cannot be hidden. Being is always "existing," the truth always shines. Being means that every moment of reality "is," that it does not come to existence and does not return to nothingness. Being is the "existing" that exists before one even recognizes its existence. There is no need to get out of the cave of non-truth to finally see the truth, no need for a search. One does not have to seek the sun at night; the sun is high on the sky. It is a light that rises from the darkness and illuminates things. But your eyes are closed and you think it is night time. "You only have to open your eyes," Abhishiktānanda argues, to recognize that the

---

4. *Diary*, 386 (September 11, 1973).

Being is and to drop the veil that hides the truth of the Being.[5] The unveiling is not a human act.

Moreover, Abhishiktānanda discovers that he is. The Grail is the discovery that the very "I" is the un-veiling of the eternal. The discover of the Grail "is in the depth of yourself, it is that very 'I' that you are saying in every moment of your conscious life, even in the depth of your consciousness when you dream or sleep."[6]

The essence of the human is the eternal appearance of the eternal. You are in a quest because you think you are not eternal, because you believe that the eternal is outside of you; however, you are pure sight uncorrupted by the finitude, in the same way that a mirror is not contaminated from the image reflected in it. The unveiling of Being constitutes the human. It lights in the depths of every human being as a hidden diamond. It lights even in those who do not know to be its manifestation.

What is Being for Abhishiktānanda? Being is simply Being. This is not, however, a perfect tautology. He affirms that "Being is" because the Being is immediately known. At the order of Being, the thought is the immediate, that is, the immediately known. The term "thought" means here the actuality or the immediate presence of Being. It is the immediacy of Being that makes the phrase "Being is" self-evident. "It simply is, *etad vai tad*! That, just that!"[7] In this context, "thought" is also the name of "experience." The experience is immediately present in the thought. The immediacy of Being is the awakening, the experience "of simply BEING."[8]

Being is the ontological original structure of the world. When one awakes to the Being, because even the simplest of beings is related to the original structure of the world, he or she awakes to all. A person awakes to the Totality, the already existing—an unchanging, ungenerated, indestructible whole. "As soon as you awake, on account of the essential connectedness of all human beings, you awake with, on behalf of, all."[9] For Abhishiktānanda, the Being is not just the opposite of "not being." The being is beyond the same contraposition of Being versus "non-being." The essential property of the Being is that its denial is unable to act as such without presupposing the Being itself; as such it cannot deny the Being.

---

5. *Diary*, 386 (September 11, 1973).
6. *Diary*, 386 (September 11, 1973).
7. *Diary*, 388 (September 12, 1973).
8. Letter to Murray Rogers, September 10, 1973; see *Letters*, 311.
9. *Diary*, 369 (February 2, 1973).

SACRAMENTAL ONTOLOGY

In other words, the Being is such precisely because it has in itself every possible negation, which means that the totality of its past, present, and future possible negations do not exist outside the Being. Abhishiktānanda makes the same point in terms of non-duality: "There is [. . .] the source and the non-source, and that is not two."[10]

The situation of life/death actually occurs within the order of Being. If death is part of the order of "not being," it is nothingness and it cannot affect the Being. If Being is the eternal, it cannot become "not being." The Being has significance beyond what one typically intends when using this term. "[The not-born] seizes one and takes one beyond everything."[11] Not only that:

> I felt all the ensuing days as if *Mrityu* wanted me, was claiming me . . . and yet, without my feeling it, there was that, the angel of life, the urge to life that was fighting against the death-urge. [. . .] Something within was struggling so that I should survive, in opposition to that which was struggling within me to carry off.[12]

Abhishiktānanda does not seem to assume that the Being can change nature and become "not being" in the sensible world. The very notion of becoming is banned in the kingdom of Being. Death belongs to the order of what is eternal; it is an event internal to this order.

> No one is either born or dies! / nor he born from anywhere, nor does he become anybody [. . .]. [Being is to be free] from every *loka*-situation, even from the *loka*-situation of life/death.[13]

Abhishiktānanda maintains that in the order of Being, all is eternal, referring not only to every human and thing, but also to every life moment, every feeling, every aspect of reality. Nothing disappears, nothing dies. Every feeling and thought, every form and nuance of the world, every gesture of every human is eternal, and that includes all that appears every day and in every instant: the first fire lit by man, the weeping of Jesus at his birth, the oscillations of the lamp in the ashram. Eternal are every hope and every instant of the world; with all the contents of the instant, eternal is the

---

10. *Diary*, 388 (September 12, 1973).

11. *Diary*, 388 (September 12, 1973).

12. Letter to Christian Belle; see Baumer-Despeigne, "The Spiritual Journey of Henri Le Saux," 328.

13. *Diary*, 387 (September 11, 1973).

conscience that sees things with their eternity. "At every moment of life, in fact in every circumstance, *I wake up*."[14]

According to Abhishiktānanda, the awakening "comes about in any circumstances."[15] Every act operates not in terms of functionality or aim, but has its own value, independent from any will. This value is unrelated to the situation. "There is only the Awakening. All that is 'notional' [. . .] is only its expression." Accordingly, there is a distinction between experience and testimony: experience is beyond the meaning as expressed in the word. The relationship between the experience and the testimony can be of representation, where the testimony represents the experience, or it can be of symbol, where the testimony is a sign. Perhaps Abhishiktānanda is saying here that the awakening can happen at every moment of life in a unique, revelatory moment. Awakening happens in *that* moment, in that moment only "the moment of the awakening [. . .] through which one becomes conscious that one is awake," and that moment is no different in character than any other ordinary moment.[16] Awakening happens *hic et nunc*, although its effects are permanent. Or perhaps Abhishiktānanda is saying, more precisely, that the awakening happens permanently, as there is an infinite number of awakening moments, and the flow of time is the sequence of these awakening moments. In this case, time is not the becoming, but the gradual appearance of the eternal.

What does it mean? It means that everything is eternal, not only the past and the present but also the future. The future is what is not yet, but not because it is not yet, but because it does not appear yet. There is no time that can come out of no time, therefore the future time already is. The time is the gradual appearance of the immutable Being: every moment is therefore the appearance of the eternal in the world of perception, like the frames of a film. The frames of course already exist in the film, but the facts appear one after another in sequence, creating the perception of movement (similarly to the Zenonian conception of motion). Via this analogy, the film is the Being—the film that is already shot and eternally saved—while the individual frames are the moments that flow over time, illuminated by the light of Being.[17] Therefore, each moment appears as finite in the

---

14. *Diary*, 386 (September 11, 1973).
15. *Diary*, 386 (September 11, 1973).
16. *Diary*, 385–87 (September 11, 1973).
17. The flow of time is like the flow of objects on the surface of a mirror, in which things are (exist) before they enter into the mirror and are seen and continue to exist

common perception, since it appears and disappears from the phenomenal. In reality, though, there is a eternal moment for every single moment that constitutes the chain of time. The moments, one after the other, give origin to time and to movement. There is thus an eternal moment in which we experience the Being; there is an eternal moment in which we become conscious that we are awake, and so on.

What spectacles are shown, if they are shown, in Being? "The non-born is manifested by a—what?—a brilliance, a light, a glory that envelops everything."[18] The Being is identical to itself, or rather, the Being that is manifested is no different from the permanent Being.

> The word "illusion"; maya, is misleading [. . .]. "Appearance" would be better, provided you realize that it is the Real [. . .] which thus makes its appearance. An appearance which is *not* other than the Real.[19]

Thus, there is the immutable Being that leaves the door open to manifestations, which do not contain any part of Being but show parties of it that are always different.[20] Being, for Abhishiktānanda, is what is manifested in the unveiling. He argues that "when once you have reached the heart of the sign, you realize that everything is essentially an epiphany, a manifestation of the Lord."[21] In ancient Greek the word *alétheia* is usually translated as "truth," but an appropriate and even more literal translation is more precisely "disclosure" (where the prefix *dis* corresponds to the alpha privative *a-létheia*). For the Greeks, "truth" is an unveiling.[22] What one sees is not a

---

even when they are out of the mirror and disappear and seem no more (Plotinus). Augustine of Hippo, with a similar image, defined the time as the moving image of the Eternal, although here—in the case of Abhishiktānanda—the becoming is not only the eternal God, but also extends to all beings that manifest the Eternal.

18. *Diary*, 388 (September 12, 1973).

19. Letter to Marc Chaduc, April 12, 1973; see *Letters*, 330.

20. When Chaduc was ecstatic, Abhishiktānanda said that this ecstasy was "a quasi-eternal sign" of something deeper that they both experienced. Can the expression "quasi-eternal sign" work as a tentative description of the manifestation of Being? See Letter to Marc Chaduc, June 3, 1972, *Letters*, 270.

21. *Guru*, 42.

22. Is this a good translation of the meaning of Abhishiktānanda's words? Had Abhishiktānanda in mind the Greek identification of the unveiling with truth, when he wrote about the discovery of the Holy Grail? A good translation should be accurate—that is, it must reliably replicate the meaning of the text. These words are part of the last part of Abhishiktānanda's *Diary*, which Marc Chaduc copied as extracts from the originals. Thus, our translation should be taken cautiously.

creation of Being, but only its appearance in the horizon of the phenomena, the way in which the Being enters the realm of its appearance. The Being exposes the fundamental illusion of the phenomenological level of reality ("the Grail which mysteriously passes through the hall", etc.), as the Being shines through the "non being."[23] One cannot accept the fact that the Being moves, because to move it should pass from one place to another and proceed in an element, that is, an empty space. This should allow for movement, which is contradictory. The becoming of the Being is therefore an untrue opinion, an illusory appearance of which mortals who follow the course of appearance become convinced. All is eternal means that every moment of reality "is." It also means that the triumph that we usually reserve for Christ should also be given to the most humble and impalpable notion of Purusha. "Jesus reveals to the human being what he [sic] is, what everyone is" and "Above all, [. . .] the I AM that Jesus is."[24]

Finally, to speak of Being kills the Being, because the deep vein of gold cannot be seen and what comes out is only a specter, a myth at best—a strange discourse of an unbalanced writer or mystic. Being is not something that can be known or something about which one can talk. Being can only be experienced as such. "Neither Jesus nor Buddha described their Awakening."[25] Abhishiktānanda applies the category of "Being" to God and offers the investigation of a non-Greek Being that in some way differs from the "Supreme Being," as Western theologians sometimes name God, and from God as "Beyond Being," the theology preferred in the East. In Abhishiktānanda there is a sense of the Being that is open and dynamic, although at the phenomenological order.

At the very end of his life, Abhishiktānanda identifies the Being with the Trinity. The Trinity is the original structure: "The 'being' of the Trinity—this is my absolute experience of being, there is no being except there, Sat = atman = Brahman."[26] And also: "The eternal basis of the Church is [. . .] the Trinity itself."[27]

In a nutshell, Abhishiktānanda's criticism toward the church is simply that she accepts the world of the formulation as an extreme approximation to the world of the Being. In his view, the church maintains a conviction

23. *Diary*, 386 (September 11, 1973).
24. *Diary*, 388 (September 12, 1973).
25. *Diary*, 378 (April 21, 1973).
26. *Diary*, 379 (April 28, 1973).
27. *Diary*, 372 (February 17, 1973).

that there are immutable truths of Being that can be formulated. The church assumes that Christianity can be framed by a formulation that pretends to organize the world. Already from these observations, one can argue that the church is destined to take a central position in Abhishiktānanda's thought on Being: in fact, the church attempts to exclude, in the name of the evidence of the formulation, the immediate reality of the immutable Being that, with its existence, would controvert and reduce to simple appearance such evidence.

Abhishiktānanda states that the order of "formulation" is not the truth and that institutions are only "names and forms," their determinations. As a matter of fact, he is ready to concede that those who live at the level of "names and forms" experience Being in terms of manifestation, and "that is all correct."

> Those who live at the level of *namarupas* will have the experience of Jesus in the manifestations, *namarupas* of the Spirit [. . .]. That is all correct.[28]

Abhishiktānanda provides a hierarchically structured world in which the order of manifestations has its unique and indispensable place, so that no one is degraded to belonging to a lower rather than a higher order. He has words of respect and appreciation for the order of symbols. Here is an example:

> All these symbols [i.e., family, tribe, homeland, religion, Christ, etc.] are inadequate because of their essential limitation but they allow the human being to live in some fashion the mystery of this unity [togetherness, ekatvam].[29]

Most of Abhishiktānanda's personal writings are dedicated to the "mental," "formulation," and "thought." In his view, both the phenomenon (the historical and natural reality) and the "immutable" (the reality of the thought: dogmas, theologies, doctrines) belong to the order of the impermanent. Christianity also belongs to the order of the manifestation.

> The whole formulation of Christianity . . . valid in its own order, the order of manifestation [vyavaharika] (and so provisional), and not of the Absolute [paramarthika].[30]

---

28. *Diary*, 384–85 (July 8, 1973).
29. *Diary*, 372 (February 17, 1973).
30. *Diary*, 322 (October 23, 1970).

In his writings, Abhishiktānanda puts limits on the sphere of the manifestation from the outside. He sets a limit to thought from the other side of the thought; that is, he seems able to go beyond thought.

> The "being" of the Trinity—this is my absolute experience of being, there is no being except there, Sat = atman = Brahman. All the rest is a world filled with ideas and myths.[31]

In an attempt to capture the domain of thought, he summarizes the development of the patristic doctrines as a matter of abstractions and modalism:

> Greek speculation made this [the divine-human] into abstractions; these abstractions, when brought to the concrete level of average intelligence, became modalism or tritheism.[32]

By placing the formulations of Christianity at the level of the manifestations, Abhishiktānanda concludes that our understanding of the eternal God exists only at the order of the phenomenological. Therefore, such an understanding is an abstract opinion, an illusory appearance of which mortals who follow the course of manifestations, that is, of appearance, become convinced. In itself, it is ineffective to reach the order of the Being.

> The more thought seeks to find, to penetrate this deva, this purusha, the more it feels itself ineffective, abstract.[33]

It is not easy to comprehend Abhishiktānanda's message thanks to his unusual language and because his works are the result of a long process lasting more than two decades, during which the concept of truth was deconstructed in its link to the divine. Christ, the church, the Eucharist, and God are nothing more than symbols because they belong to the order of the appearance.

> And then came the Councils! That meant Hellenization with its transforming power, plus Roman legalism taking from the Jewish Torah. And the Church fell into the intellectualism of the Middle Ages and the idolatry that went with it.[34]

---

31. *Diary*, 379 (April 28, 1973).
32. *Diary*, 388 (September 12, 1973).
33. *Diary*, 380–81 (April 30, 1973).
34. *Diary* (February 2, 1973), 371.

Abhishiktānanda argues that the formulation is in an attempt to grasp the essence of "Being." He saw that modern theology tended to sink into inauthenticity and inconsistency precisely because it assumes the truth of the formulation. Reflecting on Christianity and on the history of the Western Church, which stands at the center of the formulation, Abhishiktānanda arrived at the affirmation that the confusion between Being and the formulation is the primary mistake, the eclipse of Being. The original sin of Christianity occurred after Jesus, when Greek thought, instead of considering only the "existing," also evoked the formulation intended as a visible dimension where things originate from Being.

But what is "the transforming power" of the church? Following Abhishiktānanda, we could describe it as the essence of the principle of instrumentality, according to which it is possible to transform Being into formulation: "what exactly is meant by Jesus' formulation [. . .] Certainly not what the Councils imagined a few centuries later."[35] In comparison with the Greek sense of Being (Hellenization), which is the basis of Christianity, Abhishiktānanda opposed the original manifestation of Being. Because he believed that the church is mistakenly confusing the formulations with the eternal Being, he undertook the task to bring Being back to the very center of the church. In his view, the church should be committed to the lived experience of sacramental Being, to the Absolute Reality of God in the communal daily life. He overturned tradition: it is not necessary to refer to a temporal and immanent formulation; the Being itself, which is eternal, is before us.

Supernatural

Although it is reasonable to assume that both Monchanin and Abhishiktānanda were addressing the same topic (the recovery of the supernatural in unity with nature for the sake of a healthy sacramental ontology), it is equally reasonable that they were adopting frameworks that were only partially based on common ground (both were the progeny of Gregory of Nyssa, but both were not the progeny of de Lubac). Monchanin was more orthodox on the doctrine of tradition, believing that many properties and relations are contingent and can be morphed without fundamentally altering the core entity. These in turn are conceived as truths or meanings, which remain constant regardless of changes in context. Abhishiktānanda located

---

35. *Diary* (February 2, 1973), 371.

the fundamental problem in the way theologizing suspends our ongoing engaged search for God, with its tacit as well as explicit recommendation of how to use words and interact appropriately with different types of entities, including sacred entities, to take up a disengaged theoretical posture. In other words, Monchanin assumed a Platonic view of truths or meanings as contained within a doctrine that remained constant in an atemporal ground while contingently applied to different context; Abhishiktānanda claimed the displacing effect of theological notions on our ordinary, humble mastery of words and things, that is, in our *finitude*. He emphasized the spontaneous immediacy that bypasses theoretical considerations and high-level abstract reflections. From his perspective, restoring the pre-reflective, intuitive reasoning not only undermines the theological certainties that foundation theologies have long defended, but also functions as the groundwork for quests that fit finite creatures like us.

What is distinctive about Abhishiktānanda's work—and I think so puzzling to many theologians—is the way in which he constructs through alternatives. These alternatives, in turn, do not so much refute the traditional theory as prevent it from arising in the first place. Theologians are used to exploring the ramifications of a thesis and offering arguments for or against it. Abhishiktānanda, on the other hand, tried to show that the underlying ideas, far from being self-evident and foundational, actually rest on and perpetuate a whole host of historicized presuppositions. While in his early works he surveyed the positions that were on the board at the time, the way he carried out his project and the ideas he "discovered" in the process proved profoundly original. Abhishiktānanda's insistence that "we have to go to the other side" shows that it is not so much a matter of clearing up the distinction between Trinity and Advaita or determining one or the other as the solution, but of seeing that the former is a concept that exists only on the basis of premises so basic and self-evident that they have escaped notice until then.

This was highly problematic for Monchanin, who claimed that "I experience a growing horror at the forms of muddled thinking in this 'beyond thought' which most often proves to be only a 'falling short of thought,' in which everything gets drowned."[36] This sentence, included in a letter to Duperray in 1955, has been reported innumerable times and employed as an example of simple disagreement or implicit evidence about Abhishiktānanda's lack of intellectual rigor. While these interpretations are surely valid,

---

36. Quoted in *Letters*, 87.

the alternative is that Monchanin was echoing the dictum of his friend de Lubac: true Christian thought requires that the mystical and the intellectual, or the mystical and the theological, are inseparable. It is the interaction of the two poles, the Augustinian dynamics of the eternal movement in which the act of faith always precedes the act of thinking. It is the certitude that our spirit already affirms God prior to all dialectic.[37] In all fairness, de Lubac's concern was rather to rebalance the equation on the side of the mystical. In *Paradoxes* and then *Nouveaux Paradoxes* de Lubac moves the dialectic between the act of faith mystical and the intellectual even further, to the point that Christianity in its fullness should recover the relationship between sacred and unsacred.

> Two things are demanded of us: that we "rediscover the sense of the sacred" and that we "integrate the sacred into all our daily life." There are certainly two opposed aspirations—although, of course, all reality can (and should) be sacralized, the universe has as a whole a sacred goal, and the Resurrection of Jesus has become the promise of its resurrection. But not everything is, so to speak, sacred by nature.[38]

Not everything is sacred by nature, and yet we have to rediscover the sense of the sacred and integrate it in our life. Here the sense of the sacred seems to coincide with the sense of an incipient historical-eschatological orientation.

Although only *Paradoxes* was published (in 1945) before Monchanin expressed his remark on the "*muddled* modes of thinking," a previous version of *Sur les Chemins de Dieu* was published in 1941 (with an imprimatur from 1941) as *De la Connaissance de Dieu*. In general it can be assumed that Monchanin was aware of de Lubac's thoughts on mysticism and theology: the necessity of the intellectual side as part of a system that unifies the mystical moment and the intellectual moment, although the latter follows and purifies the former; the recognition that the living mystery always transcends the historical forms and yet the historical forms are the way the mystery expresses itself; and finally, the preference of the historical-eschatological orientation upon the mystical ascent.

Abhishiktānanda seemed to proceed in the opposite direction from de Lubac and Monchanin, suggesting the heterodox option that any rational

---

37. The original quotation is "prior to all dialectic [. . .] our spirit already affirms God." See de Lubac, *Chemins*, 134.

38. Henri de Lubac, *Nouveaux Paradoxes*, 162.

elaboration on the mystical moment is irrelevant. Beyond that, according to Abhishiktānanda, the intellectual moment—theology—sediments in our psyche and ultimately halts the flow that naturally guides our engaged spiritual activity, transporting us to grounds in which spiritual phenomena are rare or hard to find, when in reality they are ubiquitous, although invisible. They do not need to be examined or "purified" in the same way and for the same reason that ordinary phenomena in familiar situations do not necessitate further reflections: because of their constant presence. The ever-presence of Being—the awakening—renders unnecessary any conscious rumination on proper or improper mystical moments.

Borrowing the comment of Lee Braver on a philosopher, there is something inexhaustible about Abhishiktānanda's work, so that it can never be neatly dissected and definitively classified. This is why he remains so puzzling and so provocative, and that is why his work maintains its vitality. The unconventionality of his position also explains his unusual writing style, since he had to battle the connotations of a vocabulary suited to inherited notions. His poetic prose and sparse argumentation have given rise to a promising industry of exegetical work and scholarly contention that focuses on evaluating his ideas rather than elucidating or applying them to contemporary topics. He was compared to a poet and complimented as a religious prophet of the interreligious dialogue or a searcher for God.

Although he did not articulate an orthodox version of sacramental ontology, this is only part of the story, albeit the part that has dominated most interpretations of his early work until fairly recently. In his attempt to restore an original sacramental ontology, to retrieve a primordial sense of the supernatural, Abhishiktānanda was struggling with the same problem with which Monchanin and de Lubac and Blondel dealt. The problem was the solidification of a notion of nature in rationalistic form that had for centuries contaminated French cultural life, at least since the birth of Jansenism. The whole question was not a form of intellectual distraction, but rather the unintended source of the modern secularism within the church, a deviation from the patristic-scholastic line of thought that unfitted theologians who aimed to protect the order of grace against the natural desire to extend "beyond what lies in the natural capacities" regrettably delivered.[39] Rather than reaching the sources of the juridical-naturalist framework that ultimately affected the clarity and authenticity of the fundamental conception of Aquinas—that

---

39. Quote from de Lubac, *Augustinisme et Théologie Moderne*, 202

is, that the desire for the vision of God constituted the essence of the created spirit—Abhishiktānanda turned to Indian wisdom.

Conclusion

In the last part of his *Diary*, which was summarized and revised by his disciple Marc Chaduc, Abhishiktānanda described Christianity as he saw it from the vantage point of the end of his life: the expression of a myth that can no longer be recovered. Born in 1910 into a solid Catholic family and spending thirty-eight years of his life within the boundaries of the institutional church, Abhishiktānanda experienced the ossification that had befallen Christianity from a standpoint of self-confessed privilege. The extrinsicism of the old order is widely visible in the picture he conjured up, thousands of miles away from anywhere he could call home. The encounter with Hinduism ended his career as a European missionary, destroyed most of his extrinsicism, and left him in a state of permanent flight. Abhishiktānanda has been dismissed by many as a second-rate thinker whose work hardly counts as theology and attacked for his lack of orthodoxy in confronting the Hindu spirituality. He has also been a target of admiration on account of his courageous spiritual search for God. In his writings, however, Abhishiktānanda envisioned the recovery of the sacramental ontology of Being. In this chapter I tried to demonstrate how Abhishiktānanda articulated his sacramental ontology. It was, however, the goal of the renewal of sacramental imagination in Catholicism that attracted his main efforts. The next chapter will offer a view of his sacramental imagination.

8

SACRAMENTAL IMAGINATION

"I found the Grail."

—Abhishiktānanda, 1973[1]

Introduction

In this chapter, I recast the discussion on Abhishiktānanda in terms of sacramental imagination, since most scholars' and readers' fascination with Abhishiktānanda has more to do with imagination than theology. Many of the stories that he narrates reside in the theological margins of Catholicism, largely left out of Western theological texts and thus unfamiliar to most readers. When considered in the context of sacramental imagination, Abhishiktānanda aimed to reawaken the divine within the church, a goal that was a reaction to his perception of a diseased Catholic Church's imagination. In order to recover a healthy Catholic imagination, Abhishiktānanda suggested de-categorizing the Catholic narrative of creeds, liturgies, and practices, and then connecting them to places and people to restore full humanity. The chapter also examines the context of Abhishiktānanda's sacramental imagination, specifically the role of place in a spiritual quest and the particular importance of India. A literary-theological evaluation of Abhishiktānanda's sacramental imagination is proposed at the end of the chapter: he thought he could reimagine the world in a way that reshapes Catholic "social" performance of identity as people living in a sacramental universe.

1. *Diary*, 386 (September 11, 1973).

SACRAMENTAL IMAGINATION

A Form of Remythologization

The term *cosmic mountain* has been used in the study of ancient Near Eastern religion, especially Mesopotamian mythology. However, the term has also been applied to other ancient religions, including in Canaan and the Old Testament. In Canaan and in the Hebrew Bible, some mountains are given religious veneration. In the Hebrew Bible, the cosmic mountain is Mount Zion, a low and undistinguished mound that is nonetheless described in the Bible as the tallest mountain in the world. Mount Zion, as well as the other cosmic mountains, is the meeting place of the gods, the meeting place of heaven and earth, the place where gods meet humans, a place of theophany.[2] Basic to the interpretation of the cosmic mountain is an understanding of the reality where a relationship was established between the natural and supernatural worlds. As a matter of fact, Abhishiktānanda saw a mountain as a unity of worlds, the symbol of human-divine co-habitation, fusing the dualism of the natural and the supernatural. The mountain is, of course, Arunachala, a sacred peak in the Tamil regions of southern India where Abhishiktānanda, living in a cave between 1949 and 1955, spent long periods of silence.[3] Here, in the caves of the Holy Mountain, in the deepest recesses of the "cave of the heart," he awakened to the mystery of non-duality.

Abhishiktānanda not only recognized the myth of Arunachala, the sacred mountain, but he acknowledged the cosmic mountain *status* of Arunachala and linked it to another cosmic mountain of the Hebrew Bible, Mount Horeb.

> *Arunachala is a symbol*
> *and Arunachala is a Reality,*
> *a high-place of the Dravidian land,*
> *all ruddy, aruna, in the rays of the rising sun,*
> *where is worshipped the linga of fire,*
> *the elemental sign of the Living God,*
> *he who appeared to Moses in the burning bush*
> *and on the summit of Mount Horeb,*
> *Fire that burns and Fire that gives light,*

2. Clifford, *The Cosmic Mountain*, 3–5.

3. Abhishiktānanda was not the first Western seeker to discover the holy mountain. Paul Brunton (1898–1981) visited Arunachala in 1931. He also wrote two books about his experience: Brunton, *A Message from Arunachala* and *Search in Secret India*.

Deus Ignis consumens
Lux mundi
Paramjyoti
Phos hilaron
the joyful light of the immortal glory
of the Blessed One,
Bhagavan![4]

Abhishiktānanda did not simply embrace this supernatural worldview of the Bible; he both assumed and articulated a supernatural worldview. In his writing—and in his own life—Abhishiktānanda recovered this premodern sense of reality, this sacramental sense of reality. In his universe, humble solitaries prostrate before a mountain, and mountains hide secrets. In his universe, a deserted temple is the place of the highest spiritual experience.[5] In his universe, the supernatural erupts into the natural to the point that landscapes both symbolize and contribute to a larger world of grace.

> The scenery [...] arouses aesthetic delight in those who appreciate natural beauty, but even more, to those who can discern everywhere the traces of God's handiwork and his smile, it gives a call to spiritual joy and thanksgiving.[6]

Here he deliberately describes a world that contains different levels of reality and that has not yet been desacramentalized.

> When Arunachala was shrouded in cloud and impregnably solitary, its secret was more mysteriously revealed that it could ever be on days of bright sunshine.[7]

In his writings, Abhishiktānanda conducts us from a dream of separateness to a special world, the world of landscapes that mirror spiritual conditions and ignite mystical experiences. The whole illusion of a separate supernatural order is a dream. Abhishiktānanda showed how he entered other worlds and ultimately revealed that entering other worlds today, including Heaven in Earth, is possible:

---

4. *Arunachala*, 53.

5. For example, the week of spiritual retreat at the little temple at Ranagal, besides the Ganges, July 10–14, 1973.

6. *Mountain*, 14.

7. *Arunachala*, 123.

Really a door opened in heaven while I was lying on the pavement. But a heaven which was not the opposite of earth, something which was neither life nor death, but simply "being," "awakening" [. . .] beyond all myths and symbols. [. . .] That coronary attack was only a part, but an essential one, of a whole process of grace.[8]

He did not accept the historic, demythologized interpretation of Christianity. He clarified that there is no need for a kind of Christianity that expels ("like Bultmann, by demythologizing") supernatural events such as the incarnation, to cite just one example on which he relies in his writings.[9] He did accept myth as a sign of the way Christians may understand what it means to experience an authentic life (awakening). According to Abhishiktānanda, the myth is important, but in order for Christians to grasp its truth, such modern thought-forms must be abandoned or dismissed.

Demythologization is the process of reinterpreting portions of Scripture that are considered by some as *mythical*—that is, taking the true stories of Scripture and deeming them implausible because, well, they're *supernatural*. In order to make the Bible more palatable (and believable) we reinterpret those portions to find the moral, the "deeper"—the more spiritual meaning. Abhishiktānanda reacted against the demythologization of the original Christian revelation. The term remythologization in Abhishiktānanda's case means the recoding of natural patterns into the original Christian mythical patterns of thought in the Scriptures. Abhishiktānanda believed that contemporary Christian thought demands a spiritual view of the universe that interprets reality in terms of the supernatural. Such a view recovers the possibility of the supernatural defined as supernaturally caused events. Not every event has a natural cause; rather, every event has a supernatural cause. As he said, "the cosmic order is simply the outward sign and substructure" of the spiritual order.[10]

To put it another way, Abhishiktānanda believed that the old myths of the Bible and of Hinduism are alive. He maintained a pre-modern sense of reality that receives its source of meaning not from the self, but from the hidden powers of angels and gods. Despite the humility of tone and simplicity of style, there are traces of an epic register in his writings, a sense of a reality that is both mysterious and meaningful. Abhishiktānanda described landscapes neither as a context for his characters nor as the fixed

8. Letter to Murray Rogers, September 10, 1973; see *Letters*, 311.
9. *Diary*, 370 (February 2, 1973).
10. Abhishiktananda, *Hindu-Christian Meeting Point*, 82.

reality of a story, but as a mythopoetic source from which his readers can drink. Abhishiktānanda's writings are not secularized literature that presents a rectified view of the world, a grace-full reality, the irruption of the supernatural in the natural: "the mystery of the Presence in the depth of himself and of its potent manifestation under the enchanting form of the Mountain."[11] He created a pre-modern sense of the world, a mythopoetic sense, in which created reality is a sacrament, that is, a revelation of the presence of God: "Every earthly peak [of mountains] is a sign" of Christ.[12] In his literary works, Abhishiktānanda presented reality both as a symbol and a participation of the supernatural. The stories he tells are made to provide a world for the supernatural rather than the opposite. With regard to his writings, Abhishiktānanda needs to be considered a Catholic author, or an author who sees the world from a Catholic perspective. As an artist, he poured out a sacramental worldview combined with his own personal spiritual search and lucidity, a rare but fertile combination. He was mostly interested in the real, in being, rather than in the illusion of immutable religious structures. In his writings he addressed the topic of the sacramental with an eye to the Church of the West and to her renewal.

If we take Abhishiktānanda seriously as an author, we may conclude that the subject of his writings is the action of the supernatural in a territory that is already meaningful. To put it differently, the subject of his work is discerning the action of grace in territory held largely by "the gods."[13] The sacramentality is everywhere in Abhishiktānanda's portraits of (human) nature. His sacramental orientation can be discerned in a passage that may be considered out of place. In this passage, he connected the need for revelation with the universal manifestation of Christ:

> Jesus was amazed that people needed him to appear to them. He never appeared to John or to his Mother. [. . .] The manifestation of God in every being, in every person, is so much important than all those 'quasi-revelations.'[14]

What is Abhishiktānanda's point? Simply that by our senses we may see only creatures, but the Creator is manifesting Himself in the entire creation, in all creatures.

---

11. *Arunachala*, 118.
12. *Mountain*, 21.
13. *Mountain*, 9.
14. Letter to Marie-Therese Le Saux, April 14, 1969; see *Letters*, 211–12.

SACRAMENTAL IMAGINATION

Abhishiktānanda rejected the idea that we have grown beyond myth and instead implied that we can recover something of the original innocence; he believed we were able to rescue our original sacramental vision through myth and mythmaking. It is through imagination that human beings can reconnect the supernatural with nature. A restored vision, Abhishiktānanda asserted, does not take us in the direction of heaven, but provides us the way to see the palpable signs of God's grace. He argued that

> The entire universe must be consecrated to the Lord, all must be "sanctified" (John 17:17–19). The Eucharist is its sign, annunciation, call and eschatological realization of all together under the veil of the sacrament.[15]

Life, including a life of solitude, is mainly the discovery of meaning, a mythopoetic operation, and these discoveries are offered to those open to the gift. These discoveries are offered not to confirm, but to defamiliarize our vision of the world; by doing so, we recover the true vision of the world. To understand silence is to see, once again, what reality is. Imagination takes us out of this disenchanted world in the direction of the supernatural.

Recovery brings back the original vision, to see things as we were meant to see them. However, the mythopoetic purpose of Abhishiktānanda's works is also consolation. In discussing this, he always offered a happy ending and suggested the re-enacting presence of God.

> If one accepts, totally, if one embraces, if one hugs this solitude, this silence of the books, this very silence of inward speculation, with all one's heart, with no mental reservation, without trying to create a substitute, it seems to me that the "lotus" is bound to open itself in an already interiorized soul. The more the days go by, the more all seems far, far away and the essential alone remains.[16]

This is a fairy tale in which the end brings joy, not only hope. The point here is that the modern mind can be skeptical about the happy ending and cynical about the possibility of a fairy tale, but not the pre-modern mind that links experience with gospel. For such a mind, the miraculous ending echoes the redemptive resurrection of Christ. The more everything seems far and lost, the more that defeat seems at hand, and the more the essential remains, the more the victory becomes imminent and inevitable.

---

15. *Eyes*, 65.
16. Letter to Mother Francoise-Therese, February 3, 1960; see *Eyes*, 141.

By tracking Abhishiktānanda's writings from beginning to end, we can conclude that his goal was to inspire the reader with the passion he had for his subject, to provoke the imaginative response that Abhishiktānanda himself sought to ignite. His writings are an invitation to understanding and enjoyment and an invitation to appreciate the Catholic imaginative world and to open the doors of our own perception. Abhishiktānanda's works are mythopoetic theology, the return not to a pre-scientific and imaginary world of superstition and fiction, but to a sacramental vision able to discern the shadow of the Trinity. This shadow is what he called the "Night" of India, a reinterpretation of the dark night in an Indian context.[17]

The Present Crisis

It is clear that Abhishiktānanda worked on the recovery of the supernatural, that is, the recovery of a sacramental character of reality—the unity of nature and the supernatural. His literary work reveals as much in the representation of a sacramental world that is infused with eucharistic meaning. In which sense is the sacramental "sacramental" in Abhishiktānanda? In the sense that Monchanin explains in his Preface to *Guhantara*, where he summarizes the Western Christian mystical tradition in three distinct moments (*moments*): the affirmative, the negative, and the eminence (*suréminente*) moment. The moment of eminence, he adds, seems to contain the same anthropomorphic statements of the affirmative moment, although it is not subject to the same limitations. But "the way of eminence is not a return backwards" from the second moment to the first moment; rather, it is "a surmounting" of the second moment "without even denying it. What is negated is irrevocably negated."[18] In other words, the third moment does not signal a return to a *via affirmativa* after the *via negativa* of detachment and disenchantment, but instead signals a sacramental movement from mystical experience back to the life of service to others in the ordinary universe. It is the "there is only the awakening" of Abhishiktānanda, the consecration of the mundane existence. In this third moment, however, nothing is denied, except denial. After the first moment and the second moment, regarding questions of belief and disbelief, the third moment allows for a specific appreciation of "the thing itself." The two preparatory moments operate as positive and negative capabilities for the moment, which paves the

---

17. Letter to Mother Francoise-Therese, February 3, 1960; see *Eyes*, 142.
18. Monchanin, *Mystique*, 271–72.

way for the deepest wisdom of reality. This moment of pure attention is the sacramental vision of the everyday, the eucharistic character of the sensible world, or Abhishiktānanda's notion of the Holy Grail.

The third moment is the sacramental entry to the holiness of the everyday. The term "sacramental" is used here in a wider sense than that of ecclesial "sacraments," although it includes these, to cover the reawakening of the divine within the singular events of quotidian existence. The term *sacramental* refers to the embodiment of the transcendent in the immanent, the extraordinary in the ordinary, the not-yet in the now. Monchanin said that this moment is "not an infinitization of the finitude" (*une infinitisation des finitudes*).[19] In fact, it is the finitization of the infinite, or the infinite embodying itself in daily acts of eucharistic love. It is sacramental incarnation, that is, the quotidian sacramentalization of life/world, the constant daily coming into flesh/nature of the divine. In this movement of transcendent immanence, it is important that the "sacramental nature" infiltrates into a fragment of space, and that the flesh-smitten divine is treated in all its ontological depth. The flesh/nature is not matter, but rather an element of Being. A desacramentalized world, in which the divine is removed, threatens to plunge such a world into a state of non-Being or nothingness. To put it differently, Abhishiktānanda's sacramentality is the sacramentality of the sensible world, the eucharistic character of the sensible. The divine does not infiltrate the flesh/nature from above, but instead from below and from within.

Abhishiktānanda's main concern was the ultimate inability of the Catholic theology to encourage genuine intimacy with God and fraternal communion with people and cosmos. According to Abhishiktānanda, Catholic narrative has faltered in its imagination to maintain human intimacy with God. Why has Catholicism, a religion premised upon intimacy with God and neighborly love, failed in its attempts to connect with the divine and to heal social divisions? The answer is as follows: Catholic theology has ended up forging Christian doctrines rather than encouraging the encounter with the Presence. Over the centuries, Western Christianity has greatly impoverished our sense of deep belonging to each other as the body of Christ. We truly cannot imagine authentic intimacy with God and Christian connection across cultural and religious differences. Abhishiktānanda made his position clear in a communication to Mother Marie-Gilbert:

19. Monchanin, *Mystique*, 272.

> The further I go, the more I believe that the essential task in India is not to bring the *Gospel* to the Hindus, but to convert the Christians to the Gospel and to "catholicism" . . . then only the proclamation of the Gospel will be able to make a serious impact on religious India.[20]

According to Abhishiktānanda, this poverty of belonging continues to live inside Christian theology, and acknowledging this reality is the first step toward a new ecclesial future. These convictions helped him propose a way in which Catholics can better understand and tell the story of the life of Jesus as "I am," a story that stands in contrast to the general thrust of society's corrupted imagination.

In his courageous and imaginative experimentation, Abhishiktānanda does not "speak of" or "speak for," but rather he dares to "speak *from*" the ancient tradition of Hinduism. In this way, he generated a counter-discourse that challenged rather than extended existing constellation of habits. The crux of the matter is that Abhishiktānanda's account offers the ancient tradition as the resources that could bring those outside Catholic practices and beliefs into the conversation; his work attempts to so do in a way that avoids imposing another version of the tolerant liberal caricature. He brings those resources because he believes that they can be worthwhile in the spiritual growth of Catholics toward the healing of their diseased sacramental imaginations.

Abhishiktānanda's basic intuition was that the inner world of the modern Christian spiritual searcher is not so easily ordered as were Dante's levels of the *Divina Commedia*, and that the church must take some responsibility in that. He did not think of spirituality and Catholicism as contradictory, but instead recognized that in spirituality—deep spirituality—there is certainly more of the orthodox lineage than the Catholic Church assumes in our age. Our age, according to Abhishiktānanda, shows "so much evidence of worldliness that its [church's] spiritual and contemplative character has often almost disappeared from sight."[21] His attention was not on the spirit, but rather on the absence of it. He believed that it is impossible for a spiritual searcher to be without God, yet what makes this world of the "Church of the West" a despiritualized world was that the church herself inhibited the search. Abhishiktānanda questioned not the identity of the searcher or how the search was conducted, but instead

---

20. Letter to Mother Marie-Gilbert, August 11, 1964; see *Letters*, 165.
21. *Life*, 201.

what inhibited the search and who or what was guilty of doing so. And as there are countless forms of guilt, he attempted to describe some of them, beginning with the rationalization of transcendence and the corruption of the Christian sacramental imagination.

In India, Abhishiktānanda wrote manuscripts concerning his increasing recognition of the concreteness of spiritual reality and, accordingly, of the materialism of the Church in the West. He identified the "present crisis in the Church" as spiritual in character, a contemplative deficit that makes Christianity groundless.[22] He investigated at length the consequences of the separation of the church from the Source. At the same time, he explained why no theology is adequate to define spiritual reality. For the majority of his writing career, then, Abhishiktānanda quietly introduced fissures of ambiguity into the Catholic community's pronouncements on dogma, theology, and even on spirituality to establish enlightening connections between theological abstractions and inner experience, all with the warmth and poetic melancholy that is characteristic of his work.

Abhishiktānanda's effort to reignite a proper sacramental imagination with Christianity is based on the premise that the greatest literary works are almost inevitably a response to the perplexities and conundrums their authors faced. In this specific case, these disarrays were twofold, as the initial disappointment for the poverty of the spiritual landscape in the West was rapidly coupled with the further discovery of an abundance of spiritual gifts in the East. There, he plunged into the depths, going beyond the institutional boundaries of Catholicism, and to his surprise, he found the whole. In his mind, the fact that Catholics aspire for immortality was one of the profound contradictions of human existence, and he indeed fervently believed that there is a special access to the divine within the church, when all the evidence in his spiritual life in India argued against that. He himself certainly had such a longing. Either he was delusional, or Catholicism is incomplete. He realized that sacramental imagination opens the door to experiences larger than ourselves, an appreciation of nature, a sensitivity to the world, a feeling of shared connection with other living realities, and a desire to encounter God in a way people less fortunate than him can only dream. All these things can occur within and outside Catholicism. He recognized, outside the boundaries of his religion, something that we may call "spiritual sensibility"—the rooted, sensible intuition that God is the only reality that ultimately matters, even if we cannot

---

22. *Life*, 200.

explain how. One thing he was admired for, but actually was a source of tremendous anguish to him, was his treatment of Hinduism, which he did not equate to atheism or pantheism, or as an adversary to all things metaphysical. He even expressed a surprising sympathy, surprising at that time, for the revealed and scriptural truths of the Hindu books—and that sympathy proved more than traditional decency.

Abhishiktānanda's work, in other words, is essentially not a work of theology, but rather a work of art. It does not presume to discover specific knowledge but rather to express mirabilia and desperation in a drama that goes beyond the finitude of the author to reach the universality of the church. How has the church assumed control on the spiritual quest, leaving a solitary individual unable to assert freedom? With prudence, Abhishiktānanda wrote with a passion and urgency rather uncommon in a monk, purporting that a spiritual quest had something to do with self-making and with personal choice, and suggesting that it was not enough to know all the truths that Catholic tradition could tell us. He did not deny the validity of the basic categories of Christian theology but claimed that spiritual life cannot be reached and then fully understood in terms of them. As a writer, Abhishiktānanda was particularly drawn to the limits of Catholic thought on contemplation. He claimed that thinking about spiritual existence required new categories not found in the conceptual repertoire of current Western monasticism, which was still rooted in the principle that spiritual search requires diligent acceptance of uniformed paths and devoted human beings who interacted within a world of rules. His powerful literary depictions of the human condition of a spiritual searcher wrestling with the very core of his faith exerted a profound influence on readers, placing Abhishiktānanda among the great spiritual writers of the past century who managed to give Catholics true archetypes (the archetype of the self-restraint spiritual searcher, or, the spiritual searcher who is chosen by the Spirit and not trained by the church).

"Mythopoiesis" (or "mythopoei") refers to the creation of myth. Usually it refers to the natural process of myth-making throughout centuries of oral tradition; eventually it can refer to a myth that does not evolve naturally but as an act of literary making. In fact, *myth* in ancient Greek (*muthos*) means "word," and *poesis* in the same language means "to make." So, mythopoiesis (or mythopoei) means "myth making," and the myth creator is "a maker." However, this definition needs clarification: we live in a present context of conceptual thinking, in which "ideal" means "abstract," or "non-real." A myth maker looks like an inventor of a fictional world. An "inventor," from the Latin *invenire*, is somebody who discovers something that has never been found in nature; a "fiction" is from Latin *fingere*, that is, to give form, not in the realm of nature but of concept. So, a myth maker can easily be associated with the notion of somebody who gives form to something that has never been found in nature, eventually a myth or a mythical reality that never existed other than in the mind of its author. Moreover, "creation" is a term that has been saturated by biblical associations, primarily the significance of out of nothing. This is not what mythopoiesis means.

Abhishiktānanda does not engage in a creation, but rather in a re-creation of an ancient world, in which nature is more than biology, and human nature is more than a historical construction. As a matter of fact, creation in the human world is always creation of the second order, a rearrangement of matters already created. Coleridge would say in this regard that creation is imagination, that is, "a repetition in the finite mind of the eternal act of creation in the infinite I AM."[23] Accordingly, the myth maker is a creator in the sense that he/she penetrates the reality of language and reaches the origin of it, recreating the primordial unity between the literal and the metaphorical. Myth operates at the very origin of language, before the unity between the literal and the metaphorical and between the natural and the ideal broke down. Myth is about words, but words that are embodied of an original unified perception, and therefore bring us into a level of consciousness that is primordial. Thus, mythopoiesis is not synonymous with "invention," a liberal act of an individual, but rather the reconciliation of the literal and the metaphorical, an act of recomposing the unity of consciousness.

Conclusion

The mythopoetic gift of an artist is "artistic genius" or creative imagination, an imagination that brings together the notion of the defamiliarization of our current demythized vision: an imagination that inspires the generation of a new myth, which transforms the mythmaker, who in turn uses the myth to bring visions to others. In this chapter I brought to a conclusion some arguments introduced in previous chapters. The first is that the core of Abhishiktānanda's work is sacramental imagination. The second is that his work is a work of art. With a few final remarks in the next chapter, I will conclude this work.

23. Coleridge, *Biographia Literaria*, 302.

CONCLUSION

"Perhaps I am a little too Cartesian."

—Abhishiktānanda, 1973[1]

Introduction

THE OBJECTIVE OF THIS study was to answer two questions: what constitutes the guiding theological intuition of Abhishiktānanda's intellectual project, and why has the quest for such a focal point remained elusive? The answers lie in a reinterpretation of Abhishiktānanda and his writings. More specifically, this research reintroduces Abhishiktānanda and repositions his legacy in light of one specific argument: the supernatural. Once placed in the context of the French theological attempts to recover the supernatural for the sake of Catholicism, we acknowledge that the supernatural stands as Abhishiktānanda's main preoccupation and we gain a better appreciation of the character of his life and work.

Chapters 1 to 4 identify the central point of Abhishiktānanda's thought in a recovery of the supernatural within Catholicism. Chapters 5 and 6 suggest that while numerous scholars have considered Abhishiktānanda both as a monk and/or a theologian, few have extensively studied him as a priest and an artist. Chapters 7 and 8 focus on Abhishiktānanda's sacramental ontology and sacramental imagination and argue that the former is an unorthodox accomplishment while the latter provides the critical link between Abhishiktānanda's artistic inclination and his theological concern.

---

1. Letter to Murray Rogers, September 2, 1973; see *Letters*, 311.

CONCLUSION

The present chapter will summarize the conclusions reached thus far and offer suggestions about the potential for further study.

Brief Summary

The Introduction considers previous research by scholars and friends on Abhishiktānanda and his work. I concluded that despite intense scrutiny, it remains difficult to identify the guiding theological intuition of his thought. To that end, I regrouped the body of scholarly output on Abhishiktānanda under a "spiritual" interpretation, based on this singular premise: to deal with Abhishiktānanda is to deal with an individual spiritual search. The implications of this search can vary according to what the interpreter sees as the essence of Abhishiktānanda's thought—contemplation, interreligious dialogue, or theology.

Chapter 1, "The Recovery of the Supernatural," introduces the notion of Catholicism as a supernatural religion. It describes how the work of Blondel and de Lubac established the recovery of the supernatural as a key theological category in French Catholicism during the years Abhishiktānanda spent at the seminary and then at the monastery in Brittany. Chapter 2, "Escaping Extrinsicism," points out that in order to identify the theological concern behind Abhishiktānanda's work, we have to survey his years at the Abbey of Saint Anne de Kergonan, the years well before his move to India and his encounters with Father Monchanin, Sri Ramana Maharshi, and Sri Gnānānanda. The chapter elaborates on the deep "dissatisfaction" he experienced at Kergonan, a dissatisfaction that Panikkar frames as a "sociological impossibility" to reach the spiritual highest. In the chapter, I identify this potent dissatisfaction as an effect of extrinsicism and discuss it as a practical cause behind Abhishiktānanda's move to India. Chapter 3, "Meeting Monchanin," offers refinements to the general conclusions of the previous chapter and explains how the clash with India and meeting with Monchanin helped Abhishiktānanda reframe his practical problem in theological terms. He realized that extrinsicism operated on one hand as a practical cause for him to move to India, and on the other, as a theological disease that affected the church as a whole.

Chapters 4 to 8 investigate the ramifications of Abhishiktānanda's intellectual commitment to the supernatural. Chapter 4, "A Theologian?" addresses the interpretative issue, the elusiveness of the central point of Abhishiktānanda's thought. The chapter argues that the supernatural is the axis of Abhishiktānanda's thought, a topic that occupied his thought since the early days spent in India. The chapter examines how the spiritual search and interreligious dialogue can be seen in Abhishiktānanda's writings in light of his understanding of the supernatural.

Chapter 5, "Reintroducing Abhishiktānanda," shows Abhishiktānanda primarily as an artist—a poet with a theological concern. Scholars have pointed out that Abhishiktānanda went to India as a spiritual seeker but embraced Hindu forms of renunciation to the point that he was labelled an acosmic. In this chapter I confront that supposed acosmism and I claim that, as a matter of fact, he was a monk with social, ecclesial concerns. He was also a priest, a contemplative who maintained "social" concerns, where "social" can be understood in light of de Lubac's *Catholicism*, that is, in organic unity with the church and all humankind. In Chapter 6, "Abhishiktānanda's Priesthood," I investigate further the meaning of Abhishiktānanda's priesthood and how priesthood works as a privileged entry into Abhishiktānanda's recovery project of the sacramental. The chapter also states that Abhishiktānanda's priesthood operates as an additional rejection of the Abhishiktānanda's supposed acosmism. Chapter 7, "Sacramental Ontology," explains the difference between sacramental ontology and sacramental imagination and argues that Abhishiktānanda struggled practically with the former (in search of an ontological middle that composes the dualities such as cosmic-acosmic, immanence-transcendence, ahistorical-historical). The chapter also claims that Abhishiktānanda's sacramental ontology provides the link between Advaitic ontology and an eucharistically based ecclesiology. Abhishiktānanda connects Hindu ontology and the Christian Eucharist and represents in his literary work the image of a sacramental world that is infused with eucharistic meaning. Chapter 8, "Sacramental Imagination," provides a proper study of Abhishiktānanda's sacramental imagination. The chapter also explains that Abhishiktānanda deliberately empowers this image, this myth, as the artist that he is and through a mythopoietic component that operates as a creative force in his effort to recover a sacramental sensibility.

Abhishiktānanda Revised

Abhishiktānanda remains a puzzling figure for interpreters of twentieth-century Catholicism. In the forty years since his death, interest in Abhishiktānanda has not faded, although his influence on the shape of

CONCLUSION

Catholicism at large, especially in the fields of spirituality, theology, and inter-religious dialogue, is still open to interpretation. Abhishiktānanda is one of the most visible Western expatriates in India, and beginning in the 1950s he drew controversy for his radical approach to monastic spirituality and appreciation of Hinduism. His first manuscript—an attempt to record his new understanding of Advaita—made him suspect to the theological establishment in Rome and left a mark on his orthodoxy. While it is generally agreed that Abhishiktānanda remained faithful to Christianity with certain theological inconsistencies, identifying which idea is positioned at the center of his thought and deciphering the inner coherence of his work remain open to interpretation.

It is how he wrote as well as what he wrote that makes Abhishiktānanda difficult to interpret. Panikkar declared that Abhishiktānanda was a poet and Abhishiktānanda called himself "an artist." Four specific factors stand as impediments to decoding Abhishiktānanda's body of writings: the originality of the topics addressed; his lyrical tone, including the use of fictional characters; the evolution of his thought; and the incompleteness of his writings. First, the engagement with Hinduism brought Abhishiktānanda into an unknown territory. As a result, he was forced to improvise, drawing resources from the previous readings of patristic and medieval authors and from the vast Hindu tradition. His writings lack the clarity that a foundation within the more classic spiritual tradition would have provided, and in turn layered his insights with some semblance of familiarity. Second, in comparison with other spiritual writers, Abhishiktānanda exhibits a particular lyrical tone, a poetic framework that demonstrates divergence from theological systematization and methodological rigor. Abhishiktānanda often avoids speaking in his own voice, instead expressing his opinions through fictional characters. Whatever the underlying cause may be for avoiding the first person, his style hinders easy discovery of the theological considerations guiding his work. Third, Abhishiktānanda's writings are responses to the evolution of his thought. Establishing theological coherence among his various writings remains a problem because these works are notoriously difficult to reduce to clear and consistent positions. Abhishiktānanda was notoriously dissatisfied with his own writings, even his more structured and logically constructed output. He assumed that only one among his many writings would survive, and most of his works were released posthumously. A final obstacle to discerning the coherence of Abhishiktānanda's theological reflection is the incompleteness of his writings and the editorial work that they received. To sum up, unifying features and foundational insights are not easy to pin down.

In general, Abhishiktānanda's writings are biographical stories with theological intent; they are never a disengaged narration of the facts. Not surprisingly, interpreters are divided between those who focus on the biography and those who study instead the theological underpinnings. Early interpreters have suggested that Abhishiktānanda's primary *personal* problem was his spiritual quest, while more recent scholars argue that his main *intellectual* concern was theological in character. Two main lines of thought come out of this second option: Abhishiktānanda was primarily interested in building a bridge between Christianity and Hinduism or focused on elaborating a synthesis between Advaita and Christian theology, namely a non-monistic understanding of Advaita. While the first suggestion is well received, the second one confirms the deepest suspicions of contemporary professional theologians about the quality and rigor of Abhishiktānanda's theological insights.

In this book, I reorganized the entire output of scholarly interpretation according to one premise: most scholars have studied Abhishiktānanda under the presumption that he was concerned mostly with an individual quest for spiritual realization. Accordingly, scholarly interpretation of his writings reflects an assumption, that is, that there exists a unity between the nature of his spiritual quest and the intellectual concerns that the quest raised, although the definition and outlines of those concerns vary according to the interpreter. Moving beyond spiritualist and individualist accounts, I proposed a correction to this established interpretation, suggesting an interpretation that centers instead on sacramentality. In other words, I emphasized the sacramental character of Abhishiktānanda's vision as the basic unifying feature of his thought. According to this interpretation, the principal problem that Abhishiktānanda addressed was that of the desacralization of the Catholic imagination, a problem that he encountered during his time in Kergonan. While the *practical* problem of a diseased Catholic imagination for Abhishiktānanda was solved by moving to India, the *intellectual* dimension of the problem became the focus of Abhishiktānanda's thought for the rest of his life.

I contended that the path to a recovery of sacramentalization is the basic structure that informs Abhishiktānanda's writings and intellectual concerns. After he moved to India, he began to rethink a Christian view of reality, one that takes seriously God's ongoing presence in the world, in light of the philosophies of Shankara and other Hindu sources. While Abhishiktānanda outlined the sketch of a possible ontological synthesis between Advaitá and Christology, I suggest readers consider sacramental imagination as his most lasting legacy. In other words, if sacramental *ontology* became a motive of tension for Abhishiktānanda, in his writings he addressed his overarching concern for sacramental *imagination* and outlined the remedy for an unhealthy Christian imagination. The central question that emerged concerned the relationship between the non-dual ontology communicated in Hindu Scripture and the unifying power punctuated by the Eucharist. In Abhishiktānanda's thought, sacramentality provides the link between Advaita and a eucharistically based ecclesiology. Without a eucharistic vision, non-dual reality fails to appear; without advaitic ontology, a eucharistic sensibility ceases to be sacramental. Panikkar argues that the cosmic character of the Eucharist acts as a counterbalance to Abhishiktānanda's aspiration to become an acosmic.[2] In this study, I suggest that the Eucharist also plays a role in Abhishiktānanda's imagination.

In claiming the Eucharist as one of my entry points into a fuller understanding of Abhishiktānanda and his legacy, I suggest that we survey other aspects of his life, *in primis* his priesthood, in a new light. We have been under the effect of the Panikkar-esque refrain of "You, the monk—I, the priest" since the publication of *Une Messe aux Sources du Gange*. Of course, Abhishiktānanda wrote the piece, but the speaking voice here belongs to Panikkar, who defines the roles and establishes the polarization. Abhishiktānanda listens and walks beside his friend and simply reports his words, with no additional comment. Panikkar's account of the exclusivity of Abhishiktānanda's vocation has prompted scholars toward a monastic interpretation of his life; however, the exclusivity of Abhishiktānanda's vocation does not imply its uniqueness. Panikkar's polarization of Abhishiktānanda does not help us see that Abhishiktānanda was, in effect, a priest. Indeed, he remained a priest until the end of his life, when he was still ready to blame himself for not having given Marc the Eucharist.[3]

Once we pay attention to his priesthood, his love to the Eucharist, and his concern for sacramentality, we can see Abhishiktānanda firmly settled within Catholicism. When I speak of Abhishiktānanda as Catholic, I don't mean to imply that an appreciation of Abhishiktānanda is limited by the Christian tradition—quite the contrary. Abhishiktānanda's

2. *Diary*, xx.
3. Letter to Marc Chaduc, May 30, 1972; see *Letters*, 269.

work in the area of Hinduism allows religions in the diversity of mythic horizons to come into dialogue and mutual fecundation. I mean that he envisioned his quest as a "social" project, in the service of the church, on behalf of the entire human family—"social" in the sense of de Lubac's communion ecclesiology. For Abhishiktānanda, God's salvation is social and what is received is received to be given away to others; so much for the *individualized* spiritual quest.[4]

Sacramental imagination—whether in regard to a Christian-Platonic horizon or a Christian-Advaitic perspective—suggests that the principal categories of Abhishiktānanda's theology are literary rather than philosophical. This work is a reinterpretation of Abhishiktānanda as an artist toward securing a strong case that Abhishiktānanda should not be interpreted in an overly systematic or theological manner. He never elaborated in a systematic fashion or coordinated the various aspects of his thinking. Yet his various literary interventions evince a common structure organized around a theological concern, that is, the relationship between Advaita and (ecclesial, social, cosmic) communion. Abhishiktānanda's sacramental imagination, which arose against the backdrop of a secularized reality in France and an inspiring, spiritual landscape in India, constitutes for this book the organizing principle and stands as the guiding theological intuition of his diverse literary projects.

All in all, I think that a serious appreciation of Abhishiktānanda's artistic mindset and his apostolic consecration can beneficially correct an interpretation of Abhishiktānanda as exclusively a theologian and a contemplative. First, his friends regarded him as "an acosmic" who just happened to be a priest, but he saw himself as both a contemplative and a priest. The definition of "an acosmic in the cosmos" is not mine; it is his own.[5] Second, he was an artist with a theological concern, which means that we should see his writings as literary and evaluate them as such, even as we recognize their theological intent.

Abhishiktānanda was a monk spiritually gifted, with a contemplative sense that helped him identify the geographical place in which his quest could be better pursued. Abhishiktānanda entered monastic spirituality without intellectual or practical preoccupation, but then he faced a sociological obstacle and decided to move to India. In India he found his place. Abhishiktānanda moved to India because he recognized as a "sociological

---

4. *Way*, 24.
5. Letter to Marc Chaduc, April 8, 1973; see *Letters*, 293.

impossibility" the pursuit of his spiritual quest in France. But for him, India was more than instrumental; he was *the* place, and with that I mean an indispensable ingredient of his spiritual quest. At the end of his life, he suggested to Marc to find *his* place, "because we are flesh" and the encounter with the Mystery implies a space (and a time). So, "we have great need [. . .] of places."[6] As for Abhishiktānanda, India was his place. But not only that: he easily conceded that India was not only the place in which he found God. It was the place that gave him joy: "the flowers and the hills [. . .] the caress of the Ganges [. . .] the sound of the jungle."[7] India was the place that gave birth to him.[8]

Gispert-Sauch argues that Abhishiktānanda's call was to bring the contemplative tradition to the Church of India.[9] This study capitalizes on Gispert-Sauch's insight: Abhishiktānanda's call was to draw from the source of the spiritual treasures of India and offer them to the whole church in order to recover the ancient unity of both natural and supernatural by way of a sacramental imagination. Contemporary Roman Catholic theology insists that Catholics need to appropriate the sacramental ontology of the early church as generated by the encounter of Platonism and Christianity and formulated by the *ressourcement* theologians. Abhishiktānanda shared with the *ressourcement* theologians the belief that the revitalization of the sacramental participation of nature in the spiritual, eternal reality of Christ is the only viable answer to the modern separation between the natural and the supernatural. Abhishiktānanda's basic intuition was "from becoming to being" as he summarized in his *Une Messe aux Sources du Gange*, a particularly inspired book across whose pages flows the strength of an intense spirituality.[10] The expression—from "becoming" to Being—stands for a shift from the relativity of religious formulation to the absoluteness of Being, as Being is a central theological category serving an overall sacramental ontology. However, this intuition ultimately served to inspire his writings and revitalize the sacramental imagination.

Did he make it right, that is, theologically sound, orthodoxically irreproachable? Can we recognize signs of a consistent theological orthodoxy that permeates Abhishiktānanda's sacramental imagination? In my

6. Letter to Marc Chaduc, October 9, 1973; see *Letters*, 315.
7. Letter to Marc Chaduc, October 4, 1973; see *Letters*, 315.
8. Letter to Odette Baumer-Despeigne, November 13, 1973; see *Letters*, 316.
9. Gispert-Sauch, "In Search of Liberation," 41.
10. "Du devenir à l'Etre." See Abhishiktānanda, *Une Messe aux Sources du Gange*, 71.

opinion, sacramental imagination suggests that the principal categories of Abhishiktānanda's thought are literary. Accordingly, his work deserves to be evaluated from a literary standpoint. The lasting contribution of his writings does not reside in a rigorous conceptual solution that is immune to speculative attack, but rather in the effect that they make on others. How can we examine the imagination? We can't. The stock-in-trade questions of academic theology are not appropriate here. Abhishiktānanda simply presented us with the image of a sacramental universe infused with eternity and joy, and in doing so, he is of course at his most profoundly theological. Nobody reading his writings can be left with any doubt as to Abhishiktānanda's emotional engagement with his subject matter. The questions Abhishiktānanda's poetry and prose raises are eternally contemporary. His writings don't ask us "Is this true?" but, "Can you see it?" In fact, Abhishiktānanda's task is to help us see that which we do not readily see with our own eyes. The dual role of art and artist has a particular vocation in this regard. Abhishiktānanda's contribution lies in an ability, through his writings, to inspire generations, as well as to nurture artists, poets, writers, musicians, singers, and architects who can both enact and contribute to bringing twenty-first-century men and women to encounter and experience the church's sacramental imagination. It is for *this* contribution that he should be scrutinized.

The Importance of This Study

Abhishiktānanda (also known as Henri Le Saux, OSB), is among the most studied Roman Catholic expatriates in India, yet the idea at the center of his thought and the inner coherence of his work still need a definitive interpretation. This work suggests that Abhishiktānanda's fundamental vision was guided by the supernatural, by the recovery of a unified vision of the supernatural and nature, and that the supernatural operates as a basic unifying feature of his thought. In light of a reconstruction of the historical and theological context of French Catholicism in the first half of the twentieth century, this study invites the reader to see Abhishiktānanda from a new perspective—namely as an integral and authentically Catholic artist and a socially concerned monk who exercised his talents and personality through literary work to recover a sacramental vision. This vision, in turn, is recovered for the sake of the renewal of the Church of the West, and the vision benefits from Hindu insights.

CONCLUSION

In light of those insights, this book maintains that Abhishiktānanda worked on the recovery of the sacramental Christian reality—the unity of nature and the supernatural, according to which created objects are sacraments that participate in the mystery of the heavenly reality of Jesus Christ. More precisely, he worked on the recovery of the sacramental Christian reality through his "sacramental imagination," that is, the representation in his literary work of a sacramental world infused with eucharistic meaning. Abhishiktānanda framed this sacramental world as non-dual and contended that Christians can recover the sacramentality of an original biblical worldview of Being through the encounter with Advaita.

This study takes up the argument that sacramentality needs to be considered as Abhishiktānanda's organizing principle and guiding intuition. It frames Abhishiktānanda's sacramental sensibility, first in terms of reaction to a personal problem he encountered in France, and then as the focus of his intellectual projects—the restoring of the sacramental imagination within the church through the mythopoetic power of his writings. In India, Abhishiktānanda produced literary works that embedded the insights of Hinduism and the theological method of Monchanin in order to replace an old myth with a new one, where Christians, or at least Abhishiktānanda's spirituality, can flourish. The arguments that Abhishiktānanda can be viewed as a Roman Catholic artist with a theological concern, and that his literary work can be analyzed in light of his priestly vocation and artistic mindset, are also addressed.

This work places Abhishiktānanda's theological concern in a broad context, along a trajectory of thought that includes Blondel, de Lubac, and Monchanin. As an artist, and not as a theologian, Abhishiktānanda's relevancy for Roman Catholicism lies in his attempt to recover a sacramental sense not in the West but in India, and not through the Platonist-Christian myth but through an Advaitic-Christian myth.

This text contributes to the scholarship that re-Catholicizes Abhishiktānanda. From this perspective, he attempted to draw from the source of India's spiritual treasures and offer them to the whole church to restore sacramentality by way of a restored sacramental imagination. Abhishiktānanda invites us to change the lenses through which we are looking at our worlds and the languages by which we are presently limiting it.

This book is a work of reinterpretation. Abhishiktānanda has been subject to certain individualist, spiritualist representations that ignore the "social" character of his thought and work. Due to this, the prevailing interpretation of Abhishiktānanda and his work is in need of correction. This study offers ways to advance the interpretation toward grasping the complexity and sophistication of his thought, as well as uncovering the richness and beauty of his sacramental vision. This scope is significant because it has proved to be difficult to delineate the one element within Abhishiktānanda's writings that gives insight into his thought. By targeting sacramentality as uniquely central to Abhishiktānanda's writings, I provide details about one of the deepest motivations permeating his life and work: in other words, to identify sacramentality as the organizing principle of his thought represents a significant correction of the whole of Abhishiktānanda's interpretation.

Limits of This Study

A main limitation of this study is methodological and is concentrated in chapter 2. The chapter is focused on making the supernatural the main intellectual concern of Abhishiktānanda before his move to India. This point cannot be made by appealing only to direct evidence taken from within the text of his writings or memories of those who met him in that stage of his life. Inevitably, much of the argument to confirm my present account of Abhishiktānanda's pre-Indian preoccupation depends on circumstantial evidence. Given the social, cultural, and theological situation I depict here, and given also Abhishiktānanda's own family background and education, we can see that he was uniquely placed (1) to feel the full force of that problem; (2) to engage the problem; and (3) to elaborate a satisfactory general and literary solution. However, to suggest that I do this out of spite or from some illicit purpose is to ignore the experimental nature of this enterprise, which I admit in the Introduction. Just because an inquiry is recognized does not mean that it is settled. Important in this regard is a brief sketch of Abhishiktānanda's theological concern on the supernatural against the background of his appropriation of Monchanin's interpretation of de Lubac and in light of Blondel's insights on that subject.

Another limitation of this study is that it involuntary yet inevitably downplays the influence of Hinduism on Abhishiktānanda's thought. My project, in fact, rarely involves the use of Western hermeneutics in dialogue with indigenous interpretations. This can and does often lead to a minimization of the impact of Hinduism and Indian philosophy on his works. True, without the encounter with Monchanin and Sri Ramana Maharshi

CONCLUSION

and Sri Gnānānanda after him, Abhishiktānanda could never have written the works as we know them. While some may not agree with the conclusion of this work, it would be useful to argue on the level of method, or to present contrary evidence, so that a more balanced reinterpretation emerges. At the end of his life, Abhishiktānanda confessed to his friend Murray Rogers that "perhaps I am a little too Cartesian, as a good Frenchman, and perhaps others might find a way out of the atomic mushroom."[11] The same can be said about this book: perhaps this research sides a little too closely with Abhishiktānanda's French background, and perhaps other scholars will find the way out to a more balanced interpretation.

Possible Objections

The main objection to my work, of course, is that the "spiritual" interpretation has survived for forty years. How do I respond to that? First, I made clear that the inspiration for most of the ideas in this study come from the portraits and memories of the first generation of friends and scholars who met Abhishiktānanda. Examples of these ideas that I borrowed from these interpreters are (1) the integration of the intellectual with the human; (2) the artistic dimension; (3) the sociological concern; and (4) the Eucharist. In other words, the "sacramental" interpretation is not rootless, but comes out of an unexplored research avenue that was opened up by Baumer-Despeigne, Panikkar, Rogers, and Stuart. Second, the "sacramental" interpretation is not a replacement but rather a (significant) corrective to the "spiritual" interpretation. There are merits to speaking of Abhishiktānanda's spiritual quest. Yet there are also limitations. Probably the main limitation lies in this: the "spiritual" interpretation assumes that the predominant themes and discourses within Abhishiktānanda's work revolve around the monastic call rather than the priesthood and, more precisely, the Eucharist. It is a significant limitation: the priesthood is crucial to decoding Abhishiktānanda's trajectory in India. Most of his inconsistencies in a sense come out of the fact that he never acted as an acosmic although he indeed felt the impulse to be one; when these perceived oddities are put in relation to his priesthood, however, they become intelligible. It is because he was a priest that he perceived "so many things which hold" him back and prevent him from staying hidden in some mountain cave.[12]

11. Letter to Murray Rogers, September 2, 1973; see *Letters*, 311.
12. *Mountain*, 46.

The Eucharist is an indispensable element to understanding Abhishiktānanda. Panikkar points out in the introduction to the *Diary* that Abhishiktānanda's "rootedness in the earth," that is, his cosmic motif, was related to the Eucharist.[13] Atop a mountain, or at the sources of Ganges, all of reality—the sun, the earth, the water, the breath, the human hands, and human eyes and that dimension of divine mystery intersecting the human and the cosmic—became present to Abhishiktānanda as a sign of the Christian sacrament. Priesthood and the Eucharist also testify to the "social" character of Abhishiktānanda's quest. Gispert-Sauch acknowledges that we would be better to see Abhishiktānanda not as "an individual seeker" because he always interpreted "that search in a communitarian perspective."[14] The communitarian perspective mentioned by Gispert-Sauch was a Catholic perspective, an affair of universal solidarity.

While the priesthood operates as a corrective to the interpretation of Abhishiktānanda as acosmic, his artistic mindset and the literary character of his writings suggest that he should not be interpreted in an overly systematic or theological manner. The "spiritual" interpretation delivers us a portrait of Abhishiktānanda as an acosmic who just happened to be underequipped for theological reflection. The "sacramental" interpretation helps us see him as an integral and authentically Catholic artist who rather tried to change Christian consciousness, and for this purpose he had to be living in India and engaging with Hinduism. When it comes to his writings, their literary style rather than their theological rigor requires assessment. I wonder if an interpretation of Abhishiktānanda as an artist can bring to rest the discussion on Abhishiktānanda's theological claims, including the *vexata questio* of how much one can deem his theology as canonical (a topic I discussed in the Introduction).

Further Directions

This research maintains that the current interpretation needs correction if we hope to find the inner coherence of Abhishiktānanda's corpus. In this regard, a "social," sacramental interpretation can work better than an individualist, spiritualist interpretation. However, not all the theological implications of the former are investigated in this research. In light of paying closer attention to Abhishiktānanda's concern for sacramentality, an

---

13. *Diary*, xix.
14. Gispert-Sauch, "In Search of Liberation," 41.

interesting area of research is a reframing of other aspects of his writings, thought, and life in light of his sacramental sensibility.

A more promising area of research lies at the intersection of theology and cultural studies. In short, I want to bring attention to the optic dimensions of our interpretations. If I am correct to say that any interpretation is imagination-dependent, the status of our imagination is an important factor to consider before assessing the plausibility of the "sacramental" interpretation, or any interpretation, for what it matters.

My point is articulated on different levels. A first one investigates the individualistic character that resides in the imagination from which the "spiritual" interpretation depends. In other words, did we interpret Abhishiktānanda's spiritual search as individualist in character because we are affected by an imagination that tends to focus on internal character traits over environmental factors when explaining human behavior—an imagination that assumes the Western idea of the individual who is separated from the context? If yes, we inherited the way of the individualistic habits of mind; how can we pretend to understand Abhishiktānanda and his sacramental imagination? Perhaps we interpreters see Abhishiktānanda's imagination through the lens of our individualistic understanding of spiritual search, which in and of itself is a product of a secularized imagination.

A second level can be articulated around the notion of "not seeing," and "not imagining." In short, can we see what Abhishiktānanda saw? Can we imagine what Abhishiktānanda imagined? If I understand Abhishiktānanda correctly, he left France and moved to India because of a kind of blindness that attends modern Christian existence and especially modern Christian theology when it comes to addressing sacramentality. Are we—the interpreters—entrapped in such a blindness? Eventually, such blindness affects interpreters' theology to the point that they cannot imagine a kind of imagination such as Abhishiktānanda's. If Abhishiktānanda is correct on the status of our imagination, we cannot see and imagine what he saw and imagined.

A third level addresses the status of theology as an authentic site of creative imagination. The plague of individualism is *entailed* in Christianity and its dominant forms of theology and it blinds us and corrupts our imaginative capability. Most Christians tend to ignore the notion that salvation is a communal horizon that promotes universal solidarity. And they clearly see salvation as individual, that is, they ignore the ongoing doctrine and eventually the monastic spirituality of Abhishiktānanda by reducing salvation to an individual intentional act. This individualizing of Christianity is quite complex, attending to converging forces that are rarely named in full, especially in the work of a theologian. More important, this individualizing happens to operate *unacknowledged*. Consequently, the dominant role of an individualistic imagination in theology passes unquestioned.

Finally, I want to bring attention to Abhishiktānanda's claim that he could not do in France what he was later able to accomplish in India. He did not consider it as the individual problem of one monk, but rather as a "sociological impossibility," a collective problem for most, if not all. Abhishiktānanda left France for a more congenial spiritual landscape, one in which he could benefit from more sociological support for his search. He developed an "Indian self" because he was very much influenced by the place where he lived. If he was correct, places count, and some places are better than others for a spiritual quest. Or, some places are affected by a social landscape that affects negatively the origination of spiritual seekers.

Conclusion

This study concludes with an invitation to recover place and geography in theology and spirituality and to bring together typically isolated disciplines such as geography, postcolonial theory, and comparative theology toward framing a new "social" imagination to replace an "individualist" one. It is an invitation to traditional Western theologians who have rightly been concerned with questions of orthodoxy and intellectual edification to recognize how crucial are land, language, bodies, and "literary space" in informing theological construction and evaluation.

BIBLIOGRAPHY

Abhishiktānanda. *Ascent to the Depth of the Heart: The Spiritual Diary (1948–1973) of Swami Abhishiktananda*. Edited by Raimon Panikkar; translated by David Fleming and James Stuart. Delhi: ISPCK, 1998. French edition: *La montée au fond du cœur. Le journal intime du moinechrétien—sannyasihindou (1948–1973)*. Introduction and notes de Raimon Panikkar. Paris: OEIL, 1986.

———. *In the Bosom of the Father*. Translated by Jacob Riyeff. Eugene, OR: Resource, 2018.

———. *The Further Shore*. Delhi: ISPCK, 1975. Reprint with addition of *The Upanishads and the Advaitic Experience* and poems, 1984. Reprint 1997.

———. *Guhåntara: Au sein du fond* (written 1952–53; only extracts published so far. Part of chapter 3 published in *Initiation* (I.A.14). Parts of chapters 4–7 published in *Intériorité* (I.A.19).

———. *Guru and Disciple*. Containing *A Sage from the East—Sri Gnånånanda* and *The Mountain of the Lord*. London, ISPCK, 1974. A new translation of *A Sage from the East—Sri Gnånånanda* was published as *Guru and Disciple*, London, ISPCK, 1990. *Guru and Disciple: An Encounter with Sri Gnanananda, a Contemporary Spiritual Master*. New and enlarged edition by Swami Atmananda Udasin. Chennai: Samata, 2012.

———. *Hindu-Christian Meeting Point—Within the Cave of the Heart*. Bombay: CISRS, 1969. Reprint, Delhi: ISPCK, 1976.

———. *Lettres d'un sannyasi chrétien à Joseph Lemarié*. Introduction, presentation, and comment by Joseph Lemarié et Françoise Jacquin; preface by Jacques Dupuis. Paris: Le Cerf, 1999.

———. *Mountain of the Lord: Pilgrimage to Gangotri*. Bangalore: CISRS, 1966. Reprint in *Guru and Disciple*. London: ISPCK, 1974. Revised by the author as *Une messe aux sources du Gange*. Paris: Le Seuil, 1967.

———. *Prayer*. Delhi: ISPCK, 1967. Rev. ed., 1972. Reprint, London: ISPCK, 1972. Reprint, Philadelphia: Westminster, 1973. Revised by the author as *Éveil à Dieu, essai sur la prière*. Paris: Le Seuil, 1984. This revision includes an additional essay, "Le chrétien en verité." Translated separately as *In Spirit and Truth*. Delhi: ISPCK, 1989. Revised and newly translated as *Prayer*. Delhi: ISPCK, 1999. *Prayer: Exploring Contemplative Prayer through Eastern and Western Spirituality*. New and enlarged edition by Swami Atmananda Udasin. Foreword by Rev. Dr. James Stuart. Delhi: ISPCK, 2015.

———. *Sagesse hindoue mystique chrétienne: Du Védanta à la Trinité*. Paris: Centurion, 1965. Revised as *Saccidânanda: A Christian Approach to Advaitic Experience*. Delhi: ISPCK, 1974; rev. ed., 1984.

———. *Alle sorgenti del Gange: Pellegrinaggio spirituale*. Quaderni di Ricerca, 46. New edition by Milena Carrara and Espedito D'Agostini. Troina: Servitium, 2005.

———. *Souvenirs d'Arunâchala: Récit d'un ermite chrétien en terre hindoue*. Paris: Epi SA, 1978. Translated as *The Secret of Arunâchala*. Delhi: ISPCK, 1979. Rev. ed., 1987.

———. *Swami Abhishiktānanda: His Life Told through His Letters*. 2nd ed. Edited by James Stuart. Delhi: ISPCK, 1995.

———. *Swami Parama Arubi Anandam: Fr. J. Monchanin 1895-1957*. Shantivanam, Tannirpalli: Saccidananda Ashram, 1959.

———. *Les yeux de lumière: Écrits spirituels*. Introduction of André Gozier et Joseph Lemarié. Paris: Centurion, 1979. Rev. ed., Paris: OEIL, 1989. Translated as *The Eyes of Light*. Denville, NJ: Dimension, 1983.

Acharya, Francis. "Saccidananda Ashram Reminiscences and Swami Abhishiktananda: A Memorial Tribute." *Kurisumala: A Symposium on Ashram Life* (1974) 61-62; 71-74.

Ad Gentes. Second Vatican Council's Decree on the Missionary Activity of the Church. Promulgated by Pope Paul VI. December 7, 1965.

Aleaz, Kalarikkal Poulose. "Dialogical Theologies: A Search for an Indian Perspective." *Asia Journal of Theology* 6 (1992) 274-91.

———. "The Experiential Theology of Swami Abhishiktananda." In *Christian Thought through Advaita Vedanta*, 128-47. Delhi: ISPCK, 1996.

Augustine. *Confessions*. Translated by Maria Boulding. Hyde Park, NY: New City, 1997.

Bailey, Raymond Hamby. *Thomas Merton on Mysticism*. New York: Image, 1974; originally "The Evolution of the Mystical Thought of Thomas Merton." PhD diss., Southern Baptist Theological Seminary, 1973.

Balthasar, Hans Urs von. *Bernanos: An Ecclesial Existence*. Translated by E. Leiva-Merikakis. San Francisco: Ignatius, 1996.

———. *Dare We Hope "That All Men Be Saved"? With a Short Discourse on Hell*. San Francisco: Ignatius, 1988.

———. *The Theology of Henri de Lubac*. San Francisco: Communio, 1976.

———. *The Theology of Karl Barth*. Translated by Edward T. Oakes. San Francisco: Ignatius, 1992.

Bäumer, Bettina. "Abhishiktananda and the Challenge of Hindu-Christian Experience." *Bulletin of Monastic Interreligious Dialogue* 64 (May 2000) 34-41.

———. "Abhishiktananda and the Upanishads." *Vidyajyoti* 50 (1986) 469-77.

———. "Henri Le Saux—Abhishiktananda." In *Grosse Mystiker*, edited by Gerhard Ruhbach and Josef Sudbrack, 338-54. Munich: Beck, 1984.

———. "An Introduction to the Diary of Swami Abhishiktananda." *Setu (Bulletin of the Abhishiktananda Society)* 20 (November 1999) 16-22.

———. "Swami Abhishiktananda—Henri Le Saux OSB, Pilgrim and Hermit: A Bridge between Hinduism and Christianity." *Bulletin of Monastic Interreligious Dialogue* 72 (May 2004) 18-20.

———. "Swami Abhishiktananda: Il mistico del dialogo interiore." In *I mistici nelle grandi religioni: Omaggio a Raimon Panikkar*, edited by Milena Carrara Pavan, 165-76. Milan: Jaca, 2009

BIBLIOGRAPHY

Baumer-Despeigne, Odette. "Cheminement spirituel d'Henri Le Saux: Textes inédits." *La Vie Spirituelle* 144 (1990) 531–43. For an English translation, see "The Spiritual Way of Henri Le Saux—Swami Abhishiktananda." *Bulletin of Monastic Interreligious Dialogue* 48 (October 1993) 20–25.

———. "The Spiritual Journey of Henri Le Saux- Abhishiktananda." *Cistercian Studies* 18, no. 4 (1983) 310–29.

———. "The Spiritual Way of Henri Le Saux—Swami Abhishiktananda." *Bulletin of Monastic Interreligious Dialogue* 48 (October 1993) 20–25.

Baumgartner, Jacob. "Der Aufstieg ins Innere: 'Henri Le Saux—Swami Abhishiktananda.' Neue Zeitschrift für Missionswissenschaft" *Immensee*, 45, no. 1 (1989) 37–43.

Beltramini, Enrico. "Abhishiktānanda: A Reception History." *Journal of Hindu-Christian Studies* 31, no. 10 (2018) https://doi.org/10.7825/2164-6279.1702

———. "Abhishiktānanda and Roman Catholicism's Retrieval of the Sacramental Order of Reality." *Vidyajyoti Journal of Theological Reflection* 83, no. 1 (2019) 106–23.

———. "Can One Person Belong to Two Faiths? The Experience of Three Catholic Monks in India." *Studies in World Christianity* 20, no. 2 (2014) 103–23.

———. "Roman Catholic Streams of Hindu-Christian Dialogue." *Exchange: Journal of Contemporary Christianities in Context* 47, no. 4 (2018) 313–34.

———. *The Unknown Christ of Christianity: Scripture and Theology in Panikkar's Early Writings*. New York: Lang, 2020.

Blake, William. *The Marriage of Heaven and Hell*. Oxford: Oxford Paperbacks, 1975.

Blanchette, Oliva. "Why We Need Maurice Blondel." *Communio* 38.1 (2011) 138–67.

Blée, Fabrice. "L'Occident chrétien et l'Inde hindoue: un rendez-vous à ne pas manquer: Rencontre entre Robert Vachon et Henri Le Saux." *Theoforum* 39, no. 1 (2008) 5–38.

Blée, Francis. "Exil et errance chez Henri Le Saux: Une source d'inspiration pour le Dialogue Interreligieux Monastique." *Bulletin francophone du D.I.M.* 43 (January 2011). hhttps://www.aimintl.org/fr/2015-05-29-13-29-48/presentation.

Blondel, Maurice. *L'Action: Essai d'une critique de la vie et d'une science de la pratique*. Paris, 1893. A commercial version of the early *L'Action* was reprinted in 1950 with identical pagination by Presses Universitaires de France as *Les premiers écrits de Maurice Blondel* 1. English translation, *Action (1893): Essay on a Critique of Life and a Science of Practice*. Translated by Oliva Blanchette. Notre Dame, IN: University of Notre Dame Press, 1984.

———. *Carnets intimes*. 2 vols. Paris: Cerf, 1961–66.

——— (under the pseudonym La rédaction). "L'*Encyclique Pascendi* Dominici Gregis." *Annales de philosophie chrétienne* 155 (October 1907) 5–9.

———. "Histoire et dogme: Les lacunes philosophiques de l'exégèse moderne." A series of three articles in *La quinzaine* 56 (January–February, 1904) entitled "Histoire et dogme, les lacunes philosophiques de l'exégèse moderne," and one article in *Bulletin de littérature ecclésiastique de Toulouse* (February-March, 1905) entitled "De la valeur historique de dogme." Facsimile reproduction in *Histoire et dogme: Extrait de la "Quinzaine" des 16 janvier, 1er et 16 février 1904*. La Chapelle-Montligeon: Librarie de Montligeon, 1904, 224. All four articles have been reprinted in *Les premiers écrits de Maurice Blondel* 2, 149–245. Paris: Presses Universitaires de France, 1956. Its English translation is found in *The Letter on Apologetics and History and Dogma*, translated by Alexander Dru and Illtyd Trethowan, 220–87. New York: Holt, Rinehart & Winston, 1965.

BIBLIOGRAPHY

———. "Lettre sur les exigences de la pensée contemporaine en matière d'apologétique et sur la méthode philosophique dans l'étude du problème religieux." *Annales de Philosophie Chrétienne*, January-July, 1896.

———. "La Semaine Sociale de Bordeaux et le Monophorisme." Originally appeared in his journal *Annales de philosophie chrétienne* between October 1909 and May 1910. Reprint, *Catholicisme Social et Monophorisme: Controverses sur les Méthodes et les Doctrines*. Paris: Bloud, 1910. Facsimile reproduction, *Une alliance contre nature: catholicisme et intégrisme: La Semaine sociale de Bordeaux 1910*. Preface by Peter Henrici. Introduction by Michael Sutton. Bruxelles: Editions Lessius, 2000.

Blondel, Maurice, and Auguste Valensin. *Correspondence (1899-1912)*. Paris: Aubier, 1957.

Blondel, Maurice, and Joannes Wehrlé. *Correspondance 1*. Edited by Henri de Lubac. Paris: Aubier, 1969.

Boersma, Hans. *Heavenly Participation: The Weaving of a Sacramental Tapestry*. Grand Rapids: Eerdmans, 2011.

———. *Nouvelle Theologie and Sacramental Ontology: A Return to Mystery*. New York: Oxford University Press, 2009.

———. "Sacramental Ontology: Nature and the Supernatural in the Ecclesiology of Henri de Lubac." *New Blackfriars* 88, no. 1015 (2007) 242-73.

Bonino, OP, Serge-Thomas, ed. *Surnaturel: A Controversy at the Heart of Twentieth-Century Thomistic Thought*. Translated by Robert Williams; revised by Matthew Levering. Ave Maria, FL: Sapientia Press of Ave Maria University, 2009.

Boyd, Robin H. S. "Swami Abhishiktananda (1910–1973)." In *An Introduction to Indian Christian Theology*, 287–97. Madras: Christian Literary Society, 1975.

Braine, David. "The Debate between Henri de Lubac and His Critics." *Nova et Vetera* 6 (2008) 543–90.

Brunton, Paul. *A Message from Arunachala*. London: Rider and Company, 1936.

———. *Search in Secret India*. London: Rider, 1934.

Bruteau, Beatrice. "In the Cave of the Heart: Silence and Realization." *New Blackfriars* (July-August 1984) 301–19.

Buzaré, Jimmy. "Il y a trente ans mourait le Père Henri Le Saux (1910–1973)." *Lettre aux Amis de l'Abbaye Sainte-Anne de Kergonan* 2 (2003) 9–16.

Calasanz, Eduardo Jose E. "Echoes of the Centennial of Maurice Blondel's Action." *Budhi* 1, no. 1 (1997) 147–56.

Calloc'h, Jean-Pierre. *Ar en deulin* (à genoux). Brest: Kendalc'h, 1963.

Calza, Sonia. *La contemplazione: via privilegiata al dialogo cristiano-induista: Sulle orme di J. Monchanin, H. Le Saux, R. Panikkar e B. Griffith*. Milan: Paoline Editoriale Libri, 2001.

Caron, Francois. *An Economic History of Modern France*. New York: Columbia University Press, 1979.

Carré, Nicole. "Expérience et connaissance de Dieu: Henri Le Saux à la rencontre de indouisme." *Nouvelle Revue Théologique* 136, no. 2 (2014) 247–70.

Chardronnet, Joseph. *Histoire de Bretagne: Naissance et vie d'une nation*. Paris: Nouvelles Editions Latines, 1965.

Cheruvally, Santosh Sebastian. *Jesus Christ: Quest and Context of Abhishiktananda*. Delhi: ISPCK, 2011.

Cicero, Marcus Tullius. *Cato Maior—De senectute*. Cambridge: Cambridge University Press, 1988.

BIBLIOGRAPHY

Clifford, Richard J. *The Cosmic Mountain in Canaan and the Old Testament.* Cambridge: Harvard University Press, 1972.
Coff, Sr. Pascaline. "Abhishiktananda: An Interview with Odette Baumer-Despeigne." *Bulletin of Monastic Interreligious Dialogue* 51 (October 1994) 17–24.
Coleridge, Samuel Taylor. *Biographia Literaria.* Princeton: Princeton University Press, 1985.
Coles, Laura. "Hindu-Christian Dialogue and the Blurred Boundaries of Religious Identity." PhD diss., Canterbury Christ Church University, 2013.
Comans, Michael. "Swami Abhishiktananda (Henri Le Saux) and Advaita: The Account of a Spiritual Journey." *Indo-British Review: A Journal of History* 19, no. 1 (1993) 99–116.
Concernat, Jean-Paul. "Calloc'h." *Sked* 1 (1947) 9–23.
Conio, Caterina. *Abhishiktananda sulle frontiere dell'incontro cristiano-hindu.* Assisi: Citadella, 1994.
———. "Dolore e salvezza nell'esperienza di Henri Le Saux (Svami Abhishiktananda)." *Quaderni del Centro Interreligioso Henri Le Saux* 6 (1988) 143–53.
Couture, André. "Altérité et religions dans l'expérience de Dom Henri Le Saux." *Chemins de Dialogue* 2 (1993) 27–53.
Daley, Brian. "The Nouvelle Theologie and the Patristic Revival: Sources, Symbols and the Science of Theology." *International Journal of Systematic Theology* 7, no. 4 (2005) 362–82.
Daniélou, Jean. "Les orientations présentes de la pensée religieuse." *Études* 79, no. 249 (1946) 5–21.
Davy, Marie-Madeleine. *Ecrits.* Selected and introduced by Marie-Madeleine Davy. Spiritualités vivantes 91. Paris: Albin Michel, 1991.
———. *Henri Le Saux—Swami Abhishiktananda: Le passeur entre deux rives.* Paris: Le Cerf, 1981; rev. ed., Paris: Albin Michel, 1997.
De Chardin, Pierre Teilhard. *Lettres intimes à Auguste Valensin, Bruno de Solages, Henri de Lubac, André Ravier, 1919–1955.* Edited by Henri de Lubac. Paris: Aubier-Montaigne, 1972.
De Chateaubriand, François-René. *Le Génie du Christianisme.* London: Ulan, 2012.
———. *Mémoires d'outre-tombe, tome 1: Livres I à XII.* Paris: Le Livre de Poche, 2001.
Delatte, Paul. *Commentaire sur la Règle de st Benoît.* Paris: Mame, 1922.
De Lubac, Henri. *At the Service of the Church: Henri de Lubac Reflects on the Circumstances That Occasioned His Writings.* Translated by Anne Elizabeth Englund. San Francisco: Ignatius, 1993.
———. *A Brief Catechesis on Nature and Grace.* Translated by Richard Arnandez. San Francisco: Ignatius, 1984.
———. *Catholicisme.* Paris: Cerf, 1938. Translated into English by Lancelot C. Sheppard. London: Burns and Oates, 1950.
———. *Corpus Mysticum: The Eucharist and the Church in the Middle Ages.* Translated by Gemma Simmonds et al.; edited by Laurence Paul Hemming and Susan Frank Parsons. London: SCM, 2006.
———. *The Mystery of the Supernatural.* Translated by Rosemary Sheed. New York: Crossroad, 1998.
———. *The Splendor of the Church.* Translated by Michael Mason. 1956. Reprint, San Francisco: Ignatius, 1999.
———. *Sur les Chemins de Dieu.* Paris : Cerf, 2006.

———. "A Witness of Christ in the Church: Hans Urs von Balthasar: Eulogy." June 30, 1988. https://www.crossroadsinitiative.com/media/articles/hans-urs-von-balthasar-eulogy-de-lubac/.
De Smedt, Marc, ed. *Christ et Védanta, L'expérience d'Henri Le Saux en Inde*. Gordes: Albin Michel, 1991.
Doyle, Dennis M. "Henri de Lubac and the Roots of Communion Ecclesiology." *Theological Studies* 60, no. 2 (1999) 209–27.
Du Boulay, Shirley. *Abhishiktananda Centenary*. Conference presentations, Gaunt's House, July 15–18, 2010.
———. *The Cave of the Heart: The Life of Swami Abhishiktananda*. Maryknoll, NY: Orbis, 2005.
Dupré, Louis, and James A. Wiseman. "Henri Le Saux (Abhishiktananda)." In *Light from Light: An Anthology of Christian Mysticism*, edited by Louis Dupré and James A. Wiseman, 415–31. New York: Paulist, 1988; rev. ed., 2001.
Dupuis, Jacques. "Eveil à soi—éveil à Dieu dans l'expérience spirituelle d'Henri Le Saux." *Nouvelle Revue Théologique* 111, no. 6 (1989) 866–78.
———. *Jesus Christ at the Encounter of World Religions*. Translated by Robert R. Barr. Maryknoll, NY: Orbis, 1991.
———. "Swami Abhishiktananda ou l'expérience spirituelle d'un moine hindou-chrétien." In *Jésus-Christ à la rencontre des religions*, 98–115. Paris: Desclée, 1989.
———. "Swami Abhishiktananda, or the Spiritual Experience of a Hindu-Christian Monk." In *Jesus Christ at the Encounter of World Religions*, 67–90. New York: Orbis, 1991.
Edwards, Felicity. "Spiritual Experience in Three Contemporaries: Dom Henri Le Saux, Vandana Mataji RSCJ and Fr. D. S. Amalorpavadass, and Its Significance for Interreligious Dialogue and Social Responsibility." In *Religion and the Reconstruction of Civil Society*, edited by John De Gruchy, 75–89. Pretoria: University of South Africa, 1995.
Eliade, Mircea. *The Sacred and the Profane*. Translated by Willard Trask. New York: Harcourt Brace Jovanovich, 1959.
Euverte, Marie-Françoise, et al. *Henri Le Saux, moine de Kergonan*. Saint-Maur: Parole et Silence, 2012.
Feingold, Lawrence. *The Natural Desire to See God According to Saint Thomas and His Interpreters*. Roma: Apollinare Studi, 2001.
Flipper, Joseph S. *Between Apocalypse and Eschaton: History and Eternity in Henri de Lubac*. Minneapolis: Fortress, 2015.
Flynn, Gabriel, and Paul D. Murray, eds. *Ressourcement: A Movement for Renewal in Twentieth-Century Catholic Theology*. New York: Oxford University Press, 2012.
Fouilloux, Étienne. *Une Église en quête de liberté, La pensée française entre modernité et Vatican II, 1914–1962*. Paris: Desclée de Brouwer, 1998.
Friedrich, Thomas. "Henri Le Saux' Gott der Saccidananda-Trinität. Eine Hindu-Christliche Integration." *Zeitschrift für Missionswissenschaft und Religionswissenschaft* 87, no. 3 (2003) 181–99.
Friesen, John Glenn. "Abhishiktananda: Hindu Advaitic Experience and Christian Belief." *Hindu-Christian Studies Bulletin* 11 (1998) 31–38.
———. "Abhishiktānanda's Non-Monistic Advaitic Experience." PhD diss., University of South Africa, 2001.
Gadille, Jacques. "Jules Monchanin, a Prophet in the Culture and in the Church of his Day." In *Jules Monchanin (1895-1957) as Seen from East and West: Acts of the Colloquium*

Held in Lyon-Fleurie, France and in Shantivanam-Tannirpalli—India, vol. 1, 18–30. Delhi: ISPCK, 2001.

Gelineau, Fr. Jean-Gabriel. "Dom Henri Le Saux—La présence dans l'absence." *Bulletin francophone du D.I.M.* 43 (January 2011). https://www.aimintl.org/fr/2015-05-29-13-29-48/presentation.

Gianfreda, Fasto. "Abhishiktananda's Theology of Awakening." *Religion East and West* 8 (October 2008) 55–73.

Gillespie, George. "The Language of Mysticism." *Indian Journal of Theology* 32, nos. 3–4 (1983) 45–62.

Giri, Swami Nityananda. "Abhishiktananda's Christ Expérience." In *Bulletin of Monastic Interreligious Dialogue*, edited by Swami Nityananda Giri and Sadguru Sri Gnanananda 64 (May 2000). https://www.aimintl.org/en/2015-05-29-13-29-49/presentation.

Gispert-Sauch, George. "Abhishiktananda's Influence on the Theology of Jacques Dupois." In *Witness to the Fullness of Light: The Vision and Relevance of the Benedictine Monk Swami Abhishiktananda*, edited by William Skudlarek et al., 85–102. Brooklyn: Lantern, 2011.

———. "Exploring the Further Shore." *Vidyajyoti* 40 (1976) 502–6.

———. "Jacques Dupuis and Swami Abhishiktananda." In *In Many and Diverse Ways: In Honor of Jacques Dupuis*, edited by Daniel Kendall and Gerald O'Collins, 146–57. Maryknoll, NY: Orbis, 2003.

———. "In Search of Liberation." In *God's Harp String: The Life and Legacy of the Benedictine Monk Swami Abhishiktananda*, edited by William Skudlarek, 39–44. Brooklyn, NY: Lantern, 2010.

———. "The Spirituality of Swami Abhishiktananda." *Ignis Studies* 10 (1985) 41–47.

Goel, Sita Ram. *Catholic Ashrams: Sannyasins or Swindlers?* New Delhi: Voice of India, 1988; rev. ed., 1994.

Gozier, OSB, André. *Un éveilleur spirituel, Henri Le Saux*. Magny-les-Hameaux: Soceval, 2004.

———. *Henri Le Saux, un moine chrétien à l'écoute des Upanishads*. Paris-Orbey: Arfuyen, 2008.

———. *Le père Henri Le Saux à la rencontre de l'hindouisme*. Paris: Centurion, 1989.

Grant, Sara. "Swamiji—the Man." *Clergy Monthly* 38, no. 11 (1974) 487–95.

———. "Time-Bomb or Tomb-Stone? Reflections on the Private Journal of Swami Abhishiktananda." *Vidyajyoti* 52 (1988) 83–97.

Grumett, David. "Eucharist, Matter and the Supernatural: Why de Lubac Needs Teilhard." *International Journal of Systematic Theology* 10, no. 2 (2008) 165–78.

Hackbarth-Johnson, Christian. "Interreligiöse Existenz. Spirituelle Erfahrung und Identität bei Henri Le Saux (OSB) / Swami Abhishiktananda (1910–1973)." PhD diss., University of Munich, 2001; published by Frankfurt am Main: Lang, 2003.

Hélias, Pierre-Jakez. *Le Cheval d'orgueil: Mémoires d'un Breton du pays bigouden*. Paris: Plon, 1975.

Irudayaraj, X. "Sannyasa—Swami Abhishiktananda." *Clergy Monthly* 38, no. 11 (1974) 501–8.

Ithier, Jean Noël. "Henri Le Saux et le mystère de la Présence: L'expérience advaitine de la conscience du Soi et de la contemplation de la Trinité comme fondement de la rencontre et du dialogue entre l'hindouisme et le christianisme." PhD diss. Université Saint-Paul, 2002.

BIBLIOGRAPHY

Jacquin, Françoise. *Une amitié Sacerdotale Jules Monchanin—Édouard Duperray, 1919-1990*. Paris: Editions Lessius, 2003.

———. "L'immersion d'Henri Le Saux dans l'hindouisme, 1950-1973." In *L'Altérité religieuse: Un défi pour la mission chrétienne*, edited by Françoise Jacquin and Jean-François Zorn, 191-205. Paris: Karthala, 2001.

———. "The Spiritual Journey of Jules Monchanin, or a Passion for the Universal." In *Jules Monchanin (1895-1957) as Seen from East and West: Acts of the Colloquium Held in Lyon-Fleurie, France and in Shantivanam-Tannirpalli—India*, vol. 1, 130-46. Delhi: ISPCK, 2001.

Kalliath, CMI, Anthony. "Swami Abhishiktananda: Theologian of Inter-culturation." *Setu (Bulletin of the Abhishiktananda Society)* 20 (November 1999) 2-11.

———.*The Word in the Cave: The Experiential Journey of Swami Abhishiktananda to the Point of Hindu-Christian Meeting*. New Delhi: Intercultural, 1996.

Kempis, Thomas à. *The Imitation of Christ*. Edited and translated by Ronald Knox and Michael Oakley. San Francisco: Ignatius, 2005.

Lafont, Ghislain. "L'expérience et le discours: Les orientations de H. Le Saux dans *Intériorité et Révélation*." In *Dieu, le temps et l'être*, 295-307. Paris: Cerf, 1986.

Lainé, Noël. *Le droit à la parole*. Rennes: Terre de Brume, 1992.

Lebeau, Yvonne. "Abhishiktananda at the Sivananda Ashram." In *This Monk from India*, 130-34. Rishikesh: Divine Life Society, 1989.

Le Gars, Annaig. *Les Bretons par eux-mêmes: Essai sur la condition bretonne*. Ar Releg-Kerhuon: An Here, 1998.

Lemarié, Joseph. "Henri Le Saux." *Dictionnaire de Spiritualité* 9 (1976) 697-98.

———. "Le Père Henri Le Saux: Swami Abhishiktananda." *La Vie Spirituelle* no. 601 (March 1974) 286-88.

Loudot, Pierre. "A propos d'Henri Le Saux et de l'Advaita." *Studies in Spirituality* 7 (1997) 178-215.

Malkovsky, Bradley. "Advaita Vedanta and Christian Faith." *Journal of Ecumenical Studies* 36, nos. 3-4 (1999) 397-422.

Marmion, Columba. *Le Christ, idéal du moine: Conférences spirituelles sur la vie monastique et religieuse*. Maredsous et Namur, Belgium: Abbaye de Maredsous, 1923.

Mataji, Sr. Vandana. "A Messenger of Light." *Clergy Monthly* 38, no. 11 (1974) 496-500.

———, ed. *Swami Abhishiktananda: The Man and His Message*. Delhi: ISPCK, 1986; rev. ed., 1993; reprint 2000.

McKearney, Andrew R. "Swami Abhishiktananda on Prayer." *New Fire* (1983) 479-84.

McInerny, Ralph. *Praeambula fidei: Thomism and the God of the Philosophers*. Washington, DC: The Catholic University of America Press, 2006.

Mettepenningen, Jurgen. *Nouvelle Theologie—New Theology: Inheritor of Modernism, Precursor to Vatican II*. London: T. & T. Clark, 2010.

Milbank, John. *The Suspended Middle: Henri de Lubac and the Debate Concerning the Supernatural*. Grand Rapids: Eerdmans, 2005.

Miquel, Dom Pierre. "Le Journal du moine Henri Le Saux: 1948-1973." *Lettre de l'Abbaye Saint-Martin de Ligugé* 240 (April-June 1987) 3-6.

Molleur, Joseph. "The Transformation of Dom Le Saux—Swami Abhishiktananda." *Indian Journal of Theology* 39, no. 1 (1997) 35-42.

Monchanin, Jules. *Ecrits Spirituels*. Presentation by Edouard Duperray. Paris: Centurion, 1965.

———.*De l'Esthétique à la Mystique*. Presentation by Edouard Duperray. Tournai-Paris: Casterman, 1955.

BIBLIOGRAPHY

———. *Lettres à Ma Mère, 1913–1957*. Paris: Cerf, 1989.

———. *Lettres au Père Le Saux (1947–1957)*. Paris: Cerf, 1995.

———. *Mystique de l'Inde, mystère chrétien: Ecrits et Inédits*. Presentation by Suzanne Siauve; introduction by Pierre Fallon. Paris: Fayard, 1974.

Monchanin, Jules, et al. *Jules Monchanin: Théologie et spiritualité missionnaire*. Paris: Beauchesne, 1985.

Mott, Michael. *The Seven Mountain of Thomas Merton*. Boston: Houghton Mifflin, 1984.

Mulcahy, OP, Matthew Bernard. *Aquinas's Notion of Pure Nature and the Christian Integralism of Henri de Lubac: Not Everything Is Grace*. American University Studies. New York: Lang, 2011.

Nayak, Anand. "Swami Abhishiktananda (1910–1973): Comme nous, Indiens, l'avons vu. Un témoignage." *Neue Zeitschrift für Missionswissenschaft* 45, no. 1 (1989) 45–56.

Nostra Aetate. Second Vatican Council's Declaration on the Relation of the Church with Non-Christian Religions. Promulgated by Pope Paul VI. October 28, 1965.

Nougue-Debas, Sr. Samuel. "Dom Le Saux ou Swami Abhishiktananda: Monachisme chrétien et renoncement hindou." *Revue Française de Yoga* 27 (January 2003) 127–38.

Oldmeadow, Harry. *A Christian Pilgrim in India: The Spiritual Journey of Swami Abhishiktananda (Henri Le Saux)*. Bloomington, IN: World Wisdom, 2008.

Pacagnini, Juan Carlos. "Swami Abhishiktananda: Un Sannyasi cristiano." *Oriente/Occidente: Revista de Investigaciones Comparadas* 9, no. 1/2 (1990) 43–51.

Panikkar, Raymond. *The Unknown Christ of Hinduism*. London: Longman & Todd, 1965.

Panikkar, Raimon. *Entre Dieu et le Cosmos. Une vision non dualiste de la réalité*. Paris: Albin Michel, 1998.

———. "Letter to Abhishiktananda." *Studies in Formative Spirituality* 3, no. 3 (1982) 429–51.

———. *La Nuova Innocenza*. In *Christianity: Opera Omnia*, Vol. III.2. Maryknoll, NY: Orbis, 2016.

———. *La nuova innocenza*. 50' Puntata 3 di Una serie a cura di Werner Weick e Andrea Andriotto. Lugano: Televisione Svizzera Italiana, 2000.

———. *Tra Dio e il cosmo: Una visione non dualista della realtà*. Dialogue with Gwendoline Jarczyk. Translated by Michele Sampaolo. Rome: Laterza, 2016.

Pelissero, Alberto. "Un'anima inquieta divisa tra due amori: La vicenda spirituale di Henri Le Saux." *Humanitas* 59, no. 5 (2004) 1039–54.

Planson, Glaoud, and Erwan Koshaneg. *Histoire de la nation bretonne*. Paris: Table ronde, c. 1977.

Poggi, Colette. "'Arunodaya', l'aube intérieure et la re-connaissance du 'je suis (aham)', dans le cheminement d'Henri Le Saux—Abhishiktananda (1910–1973)." *Chemins de dialogue* no. 31 (June 2008) 59–92.

———. "'Sur l'étroit sentier des origines,' La traversée intérieure d'Henri Le Saux—Abhishiktananda." *Bulletin francophone du D.I.M.* 43 (January 2011). https://www.aimintl.org/fr/2015-05-29-13-29-48/presentation.

Pont, Daniel. "Henri Le Saux—Swami Abhishiktananda, moine, mystique, bâtisseur de ponts: Colloque de Shantivanam (10–15 janvier 2010)." *Bulletin of Monastic Interreligious Dialogue* 84 (January 2010). https://www.aimintl.org/en/2015-05-29-13-29-49/presentation.

Pope Benedict XVI. *Deus Caritas Est*. Encyclical letter. January 25, 2006. The Encyclical addresses the subject of God's love.

BIBLIOGRAPHY

Pope John Paul II. *Fides et Ratio*. Encyclical letter. September 14, 1998.

———. *Redemptor Homnis*. Encyclical letter. March 4, 1979.

Pope Pius X. *Pascendi dominici gregis*. Encyclical letter. September 8, 1907.

Portier, William L. "Thomist Resurgence." *Communio* 35, no. 3 (2008) 494–504.

Prévotat, Jacques. "Henri de Lubac and Jules Monchanin." In *Jules Monchanin (1895–1957) as Seen from East and West: Acts of the Colloquium Held in Lyon-Fleurie, France and in Shantivanam-Tannirpalli—India*, vol. 1, 58–71. Delhi: ISPCK, 2001.

Rodhe, Sten. *Jules Monchanin, Pioneer in Hindu-Christian Dialogue*. Delhi: ISPCK, 1993.

Rogers, Murray. "Swamiji—the Friend," *Religion and Society* 23, no. 1 (1976) 76–87; reprint, *Swami Abhishiktananda: The Man and his Message*. Edited by Sr. Vandana Mataji. Delhi: ISPCK, 1986; rev. ed., 1993; reprint 2000.

Rogers, Murray, and David Barton. *Abhishiktananda: A Memoir of Dom Henri Le Saux*. Oxford: SLG, 2003.

Royster, James E. "Abhishiktananda: Hindu-Christian Monk." *Studies in Formative Spirituality* 9, no. 3 (1988) 309–28.

———. "A Dialogue in Depth: A Monastic Perspective." *Quarterly Review* 9, no. 2 (1989) 75–92.

Sharma, Arvind. "Sankara's Bhakti and Swami Abhishiktananda's 'Adult Faith.'" *Journal of Dharma* 15, no. 3 (1990) 240–44.

Scheuer, Jacques. "Henri Le Saux: Moine chrétien et renonçant hindou." *Nouvelle Revue Théologique* 116, no. 2 (1994) 238–45.

Schmalz, Mathew N. "The Return from the Further Shore: Theological Implications of Christian Sannyasa." *Koinonia* 5 (Fall 1993) 191–217.

Skudlarek, OSB, William. "Abhishiktananda Centenary Symposium at Shantivanam." *Bulletin of Monastic Interreligious Dialogue* 84 (January 2010). https://www.aimintl.org/en/2015-05-29-13-29-49/presentation

Skudlarek, OSB, William, ed. *God's Harp String: The Life and Legacy of the Benedictine Monk Swami Abhishiktananda*. Brooklyn, NY: Lantern, 2010.

Skudlarek, OSB, William, and Bettina Bäumer, eds. *Witness to the Fullness of Light: The Vision and Relevance of the Benedictine Monk Swami Abhishiktananda*. Brooklyn, NY: Lantern, 2011.

Stephens, Robert A. "Abhishiktananda: The Benedictine Swami." *Tjurunga: An Australasian Benedictine Review* 31 (1986) 42–53; no. 32 (1987) 72–79.

———. "Sri Ramana Maharshi and Abhishiktananda." *Vidyajyoti* 44 (1980) 168–76.

———. "Swami Abhishiktananda." *Clergy Monthly* 38, no. 2 (1974) 80–82.

Stuart, James. "Abhishiktananda on Inner Awakening." *Vidyajyoti* 46 (1982) 470–84.

———. "The Religious in the Church, as Seen by Swami Abhishiktananda." *Vidyajyoti* 57 (1993) 401–13.

———. "Swami Abhishiktananda: The Awakening." *The Mountain Path* 30, nos. 1–2 (1993) 36–42.

Stuart, James, and Odette Baumer-Despeigne. "A Deeply Effective Darshan of Bhagavan." *The Mountain Path* 17 (July 1980) 146–49.

Sumithra, Sunand. "Swami Abhishiktananda." In *Christian Theologies from an Indian Perspective*, 154–58. Bangalore: Theological Book Trust, 1990.

Teasdale, Wayne. "Abhishiktananda's Contemplative Theology." *Monastic Studies* (Autumn 1982) 179–99.

———. "Abhishiktananda's Mystical Intuition of the Trinity." *Cistercian Studies* 18, no. 1 (1983) 59–75.

———. *The Mystic Heart: Discovering a Universal Spirituality in the World's Religions*. Novato: New World Library, 1999.
Theresa, Sister. "Glimpses of Abhishiktananda at an Early Stage." *Occasional Bulletin, (Abhishiktananda Society)* 12 (June 1989) 1–6.
Tholens, Cornelius. "Monachesimo e advaita." *Quaderni del Centro Interreligioso Henri Le Saux* 7 (1990) 111–21.
Thomas, Madathilparampil Mammen, and P. T. Thomas. "Swami Abhishiktananda." In *Towards an Indian Christian Theology: Life and Thought of Some Pioneers*, 203–7. Tiruvalla: New Day Publications of India, 1992.
Tolkien, J. R. R. "Leaf by Niggle." *Dublin Review* 216 (1945) 46–61.
Trapnell, Judson B. "Abhishiktananda's Contemplative Vocation and Contemporary India." *Vidyajyoti* 67 (2003) 161–79.
———. "Catholic Contemplative Engagement with India and Its Theological Implications: Jules Monchanin, Henri Le Saux and Bede Griffiths." In *World Christianity: Politics, Theology*, edited by Anthony O'Mahony and Michael Kirwan, 257–84. London: Dialogues, 2004.
———. "Two Models of Christian Dialogue with Hinduism: Bede Griffiths and Abhishiktananda." *Vidyajyoti* 60 (1996) 101–10; 183–91; 243–54.
Trianni, Paolo. *Henri Le Saux (Svami Abhishiktananda): Un incontro con l'India*. Milano: Jaca, 2011.
Trianni, Paolo, and William Skudlarek, OSB, eds. *Cristo e l'Advaita: La mistica di Henri Le Saux O.S.B. tra cristianesimo ed induismo*. Roma: Edizioni Studium, 2013.
Trinity, Sr. Elizabeth. "The Trinity According to Abhishiktananda." *Indian Journal of Spirituality* 7, no. 3 (1994) 289–311.
Ulrich, Edward T. "Convergences and Divergences: The Lives of Swami Abhishiktananda and Raimundo Panikkar." *Journal of Hindu-Christian Studies* 24 (2011) 36–45.
———. "Monasticism as an Interreligious Meeting Point: A Comparison of Swami Abhishiktananda and Francis Acharya." *Third Millennium* 11, no. 2 (2008) 76–87.
———. "Swami Abhishiktananda and Comparative Theology." *Horizons: The Journal of the College Theology Society* 31, no. 1 (2004) 40–63.
———. "Swami Abhishiktananda's Interreligious Hermeneutics of the Upanishads." *Hindu-Christian Studies Bulletin* 16 (2003) 22–29.
Underhill, Evelyn. "The Essentials of Mysticism." In *Understanding Mysticism*, edited by Richard Woods, 240–60. Garden City, NY: Image, 1980.
Vattakuzhy, Emmanuel. *Indian Christian Sannyasa and Swami Abhishiktananda*. Bangalore: TPI, 1981.
Yedanapalli, Prasad. "Une double appartenance: Le Père Le Saux." *Spiritus* 153 (1998) 372–78.
Yesurathnam, Ragunta. *A Christian Dialogical Theology: The Contribution of Swami Abhishiktananda*. Kolkota: Punthi Pustak, 2006.
Visvanathan, Susan. *An Ethnography of Mysticism: The Narratives of Abhishiktananda, a French Monk in India*. Shimla: Indian Institute of Advanced Study, 1998.
Weber, Eugen. *France, Fin de siècle*. Cambridge: Harvard University Press, 1986.
Wilfred, Felix. "Widening the Horizons: Swami Abhishiktananda (1910–1973)." In *Beyond Settled Foundations: The Journey of Indian Theology*, 53–60. Madras: University of Madras Press, 1993.
Wiseman, James A. "'Enveloped by Mystery': The Spiritual Journey of Henri Le Saux—Abhishiktananda." *Eglise et Théologie* 23 (1992) 241–60.

INDEX

Abhishiktānanda, Swami
    as an acosmic, 9, 44, 101–4, 158
    Amour and Sagesse, 38
    as artist, 104–9, 150–51, 154–56
    assumption and implications of, 1, 4–12
    on Being, 127–35
    in Brittany, 34–37
    on Catholicism, 96
    on contemplative orders, 116–17
    Diary, 71–72, 126, 126n2, 139
    early life of, 14, 34, 37
    experiences, 66–67
    Hindu-Christian Meeting Point, 68, 79, 86
    identity of, 90–95, 139
    importance of study of, 160–62
    in India, 71–73
    leaving France, 40–49
    life in France (*See* France)
    limits of study of, 162–63
    literary theology of, 8–9
    meeting with Monchanin, 13, 153
    Monchanin as first guru (master), 32–33, 57, 60–62
    The Mountain of the Lord, 111, 114, 119
    objections of study of, 163–64
    objective of study of, 152–53
    overview, 154–60
    as priest, 116–21, 154
    profile of, 2–4
    reintroduction, 154
    relocation to India, 31–33
    Sagesse, 79–82
    scholarly problem, 32–33
    social concerns, 1, 9, 104
    spiritual realization quest, 156
    as theologian (*See* theological intuition)
    on vocation, 66
acedia, term usage, 43
acosmic, 9, 44, 101–4, 158
Action (Blondel), 18, 19, 51
active orders, of monks, 39
Ad Gentes (Vatican Council II document), 77
Advaita Vedanta
    Abhishiktānanda's engagement with, 7, 32, 33, 71–73
    Christianity and, 126, 156
    description of, 2, 77, 80
affirmative moments, 146–47
All-India Seminar in Bangalore (1969), 3
Amour and Sagesse (Abhishiktn?nda), 38
Annales de philosophie chrétienne (Blondel), 70
Arunachala mountain, 141–42
asceticism, 39
Athanasius, 40

INDEX

Augustine, of Hippo
  definition of time, 131n17
  on eternal movement, 137
  intelligentia fidei, 97
  internal gift of grace, 71
  literature for novice monks, 39
  on supernatural, 21, 24
awakening, 82–89, 130–32

Balthasar, Hans Urs von, 19, 26, 59, 69
Barnanos, George, 59–60
Basil, 39
Bäumer, Bettina, 93
Baumer-Despeigne, Odette, 44–45, 83, 95, 106n42
Being
  awakening, 130–33
  from becoming to, 159
  Catholic Church and, 132–35
  death and, 129–30
  description of, 128–29
  eternality of, 130–31
  as existing, 127–28
  Grail and, 127–28, 132
  manifestation and, 133–34
Bergson, Henri, 52
Bibcop, Benedict, 38
Blanchette, Oliva, 19
Blondel, Marcel
  Action, 18, 19, 51
  Annales de philosophie chrétienne, 70
  on Augustine's philosophy, 21
  background, 16–23
  character of, 13
  Christianity, adaption to modern civilization, 52
  doctoral dissertation, 18, 19
  double-afference theory, 21–22, 68, 69–71
  extrinsicism, 69
  on *Fides et ratio* (1998), encyclical, 69
  on historicism, 17, 22–23, 69–70
  incommensurability, 20
  Lettre, 18, 19
  on meaning of life, 17–18
  on a middle way, 60
  monophorism, 69
  on outlook on life, 19–20
  on *Pascendi* (1907) encyclical, 20–21, 70
  on the state of the church, 58
  supernatural, philosophy and, 18–19
  on tradition, 62
  on transcendent, 18–19
Boersma, Hans, 26–27, 27n32
Braver, Lee, 138
Brioc (Welsh monk), 34
Brittany
  artists associated with, 35–36
  Celtic heritage, 35
  culture of, 34
  famous people from, 34–35
Brunton, Paul, 141n3

Calloc'h, Jean-Pierre, 16, 16n4
Camaldolese monks, 42
Cassia, 39
Catholic philosophy, 18–19
Catholicism/Catholicisme (de Lubac), 9, 28
Chaduc, Marc, 85–86, 91, 103, 126, 131n20
Chagall, Marc, 35
Charles, Pierre, 41
Charybdis historicism, 23
Chateaubriand, François-René, vicomte de, 34–36
Christian mysteries, 17
Christian philosophy, 18, 56–57
Christian unreadiness, 111–16
church, aspects of, 27
Clervaux Abbey, 41–42
coenobitic life, 42
Coleridge, Samuel Taylor, 151
Congregation of Solesmes. *See* Clervaux Abbey; St. Anne's Abbey in Kergonan
contemplative mission project, 44, 47–48, 54–57
contemplative orders, of monks, 39
Corpus mysticum (de Lubac), 28
Cosmic Christ, 121–24

INDEX

cosmic mountain, term usage, 141
cultural eradication, 15–16

Dante, 148
de Balzac, Honoré, 35
de Chardin, Teilhard, 26
de Lubac, Henri
    background, 23–29
    Catholicism/Catholicisme (de Lubac), 9, 28
    Corpus mysticum, 28
    description of, 13
    on divine order, 6
    on *Guhantara* (*See* Guhantara project)
    on a middle way, 60
    Monchanin and, 52–54, 56n15, 96
    The Mystery of the Supernatural, 25
    on mysticism, 97
    on nature of humans, 77
    Nouveaux Paradoxes, 137
    Paradoxes, 137
    Petite catéchèse sur nature et grace, 23
    on the state of the church, 58
    Surnaturel, 28
    works by, 23n22
de Maupassant, Guy, 35
death, order of "not being," 129–30
Dechamps, Victor, 70
Delatte, Paul, 38
demythologization, 143
Diary (Abhishiktānanda), 71–72, 126, 126n2, 139
Diary (Monchanin), 61, 63–64
Divina Commedia (Dante), 148
divine elevation, 26
dogmatic extrinsicism, 8, 17, 22, 69
double-afference theory, 21–22, 68, 69–71
Doyle, Dennis, 27n32
du Boulay, Shirley, 41, 41n12, 41n14
dualistic ontology, 26
dualistic thought, peril of, 23–24
Duperray, Edouard, 46, 51, 73, 136
Dupois, Jacques, 95
duration, Bergson's conception of, 52

ecstasy, 131n20
Eliade, Mircea, 101
eminence moments, 146–47
eremitic life, 42
Eucharist, 27–28, 102, 157, 163–64
Evagrius, 40
exclaustration, defined, 42
extrinsicism
    Blondel on, 17, 22, 63, 69
    description of, 17, 22
    escaping from, 153
    Kergonan monastery and, 22
    Roman Catholic Church and, 30
    Scylla of, 6, 23

Faber, Frederick William, 39
faith
    Abhishiktānanda on, 85–86
    integrated with life, 29
    philosophy and, 19
Fides et ratio (1998), John Paul II encyclical, 69
finite willed action, as problem of life, 20
Flaubert, Gustave, 35
Fouilloux, Étienne, 23
France
    Abhishiktānanda's departure from, 40–49
    intellectual life of in, 16–23
    life in, 4–5, 14–16, 16n5, 37–40
    Second French Empire, 14
Franco-Prussian War (1870–71), 14
French Catholicism
    intellectual and cultural situation, 5
    political attacks on, 14–16
    pre-Vatican era, 8
French Third Republic, 13–16, 16n5, 18, 63
further directions, 164–66

Gay, Charles Louis, 39
gender-inclusive language, 11
Gispert-Sauch, George, 41, 91, 91n3, 95, 159
Gnanananda, Sri, 2, 5, 32–33
Goel, Sita Ram, 99–100

INDEX

grace
　hidden grace of God, 68
　natural desire and, 78
　spirit and, 24
　supernatural and, 26
Grant, Sara, 68, 86
Gregorian chant, 36
Gregory of Nazianzus, 44
Gregory of Nyssa, 135
Gregory the Great, 39
Gregory XVI, Pope, 36
Griffiths, Bede, 2
Guardini, Romano, 36
Gudin, Théodore, 35
Guennou, J., 96
Guéranger, Prosper, 35
Guhantara project, 61, 67, 73–77, 83, 96, 96n16, 98–99, 146
Guitton, Jean, 62

Hindu-Christian dialogue, 32, 66–67
Hindu-Christian Meeting Point, (Abhishiktn?nda), 68, 79, 86
Hinduism
　Abhishiktānanda's acceptance of, 3
　assimilation in Christianity, 72
　Christianity and, 85, 113–15, 156
　as cosmic religious, 80
　inculturation of, 55
　knowledge and, 79
　Monchanin and, 56–57
　tends towards Christianity, 77
historicism
　Blondell on, 17, 22–23, 69–70
　Charybdis of, 6, 23
　description of, 17, 22
Hugo, Victor, 35
human beings
　essence if, 128
　natural desire for supernatural, 77–79
human nature, de Chardin on, 26
Humani Generis (1650) Pius XII encyclical, 53

"I AM," 85, 87, 132, 151

imagination, individualistic character in, 165
imagining, seeing and, 165
immanence, 19
inculturation, 3–4, 54–55
intelligentia fidei (Augustine), 97
invisible aspect of church, 27
Ireneus, 40

Jesuits of Louvain, 41
John of the Cross, 39, 117
John Paul II, Pope, 69, 78

Kempis, Thomas a, 45
Kergonan monastery. *See* St. Anne's Abbey in Kergonan
knowledge, real and notional, 79

La Fourvière, Jesuit theologate in Lyon, 23
Le Saux, Alfred (father), 2
Le Saux, Henri (later Abhishiktānanda, Swami), 2, 91
Lemarié, Joseph, 117
Lettre (Blondel), 18, 19
Louvain school of missiology, 41
Lumen Gentium (Vatican Council II document), 77, 78

Magisterium, 78
Maharshi, Sri Ramana, 2, 5, 32–33, 44, 108
manifestation, 133–34
Mar'echal, Joseph, 23
Marmion, Columba, 38–39
Merton, Thomas, 42, 44, 94
method of immanence, 19
Milbank, John, 77
monasticism, 39–40
Monchanin, Jules
　on Abhishiktānanda, 13, 46–47, 95
　Abhishiktānanda's first guru (master), 32–33, 57, 60–62
　on Blondel, 52
　on the Catholic church, 51

contemplative mission project, 44, 47–48, 54–59
on de Lubac, 52–54, 56n15, 96
death of, 2, 92n7
Diary, 61, 63–64
meeting with, 13, 50–54, 153
move to India, 2, 57
on revelation, 84
sacramental movement, 146–47
symbol and, 1n1
on tradition, 55–56, 62n23, 84, 135–36
monistic life
descriptions of, 42–43
in France, 37–40
monophorism, 69, 74
monophorisme, 70
moral anxiety, 17
Mother Marie-Gilbert, 147–48
Mount Horeb, 141
Mount Zion, 141
The Mountain of the Lord (Abhishiktānanda), 111, 114, 119
mountains, as unity of worlds, 141
Murray, Rogers, 95
mystery, supernatural order of, 24–26, 27
The Mystery of the Supernatural (de Lubac), 25
mystic, term usage, 69
mystical moments, 146–47
mysticism, 36, 39, 75–76
mythopoiesis, 150–51

nationalism, 15, 16
natural mysticism, term usage, 69
natural order
inquiry of reason, 24
supernatural and, 20, 24–26, 29
term usage, 6–7
negative moments, 146–47
Neolithic Church, 112–15, 122
nonduality, 121, 123n51
noonday demon, 43
Nostra Aetate (Vatican Council II document), 3, 77
notional knowledge, 79

Nouveaux Paradoxes (de Lubac), 137

Origen, 40

Panikkar, Raimon
on Abhishiktānanda, 3, 32, 33, 45, 68, 91, 93–95
on acosmic, 102–3
on Christians, 123
on contemplative orders, 116
on conversion of India, 113–15
cosmism of, 118
on *Guhantara* project, 73–77, 96
names for, 1n1
as priest, 118–20
on Trinity, 98
The Unknown Christ of Hinduism, 113
Paradoxes (de Lubac), 137
Pascendi (1907) Pius X encyclical, 20–21, 70
Petite catéchèse sur nature et grace (de Lubac), 23
philosophy
dualistic thought of, 23–24
faith and, 19
supernatural and, 18
Pius X, Pope, 20
Pius XI, Pope, 2
Pius XII, Pope, 2
Platonic-Christian ontology, 26
Plotinus, 130–31n17
Ponja, Shri Harilal, 74
priesthood, 118–21, 154, 157–58, 163–64
Pseudo-Dionysius the Areopagite, 40, 97n20
pure nature, 26, 71, 78

Redemtor Hominis (1979) John Paul II encyclical, 78
Rémilleaux, Laurent, 51
remythologization, 141–46
ressourcement theology, 40, 159
revelation
objective signs of, 84
from outside, 71, 76
Richard, Louis, 51

INDEX

Rogers, Murray, 32, 93, 99–100
Roman Catholic Church
   All-India Seminar in Bangalore
      (1969), 3
   Being and, 132–35
   Catholic philosophy, 18–19
   as Church of the Awakening, 86–88
   contemplative deficit of, 73–74
   the Councils, 113, 134–35
   distancing from the "I am," 127
   dogmatic extrinsicism, 8, 17, 22
   Eucharist and, 27–28, 102, 157, 163–64
   extrinsicism and, 30
   Fides et ratio (1998), John Paul II encyclical, 69
   French Catholicism, 5, 8, 14–16
   Humani Generis (1650) Pius XII encyclical, 53
   intellectual life of in France, 16–23
   intimacy with God and, 147–49
   liturgical revival, 36–37
   Magisterium, 78
   on modernism, 20
   on mysticism, 97–98n20
   Pascendi (1907) Pius X encyclical, 20–21, 70
   Redemtor Hominis (1979) John Paul II encyclical, 78
   sacramental ontology, 159
   secularization and, 30, 58
   signs of, 27
   social character of, 28–29
   spirituality and, 115–16
   supernatural, term usage, 25
   Vatican II (*See* Vatican Council II)
Rousselot, Pierre, 23

Saccidananda Ashram, 2, 4
sacramental, term usage, 147
sacramental dimensions, 59–60
sacramental imagination
   overview, 140, 154, 156–58
   present crisis, 146–51
   remythologization, 141–46
sacramental movement, 146–47
sacramental ontology
   Being and, 127–35
   within Catholicism, 125
   Diary insights, 126
   reality and, 25–28
   Roman Catholic theology and, 159
   sacramental imagination and, 154, 157
   supernatural, 135–39
   term usage, 27n32, 62
sacramental order, 20
sacramental worldview, 7–8
sacraments of Christ, 27–28
Sagesse (Abhishiktānanda), 79–82
samnyāsa, 2, 54
Scylla extrinsicism, 17, 23
Second French Empire, 14
Second Vatican Council. *See* Vatican Council II
The Secret of Arunachala project, 74
seeing, imagining and, 165
sentimental mysticism, 39
Shantivanam
   Abhishiktānanda and, 76, 91
   founders of, 46, 67
   goal of, 2
   Scriptures and Christian doctrines, 61
silence, as means to communicate, 74, 83
social character of the church, 28–29
Sonnerfaud, Louise (mother), 2
spirit, grace and, 24
St. Anne's Abbey in Kergonan, 2, 4–5, 31–32, 37–39
Stokes, Anne-Marie, 36n6
Storm on the Coast of Belle-Ile (Gudin), 35
Stuart, James, 44, 93, 95
supernatural
   afference of, 21
   Catholic use of term, 25
   dualistic thought of, 23–24
   gift from God, 24
   human being's desire for, 78
   philosophy and, 18
   recovery of, 153
   sacramental ontology, 135–39
   term usage, 6–8

INDEX

supernatural mysticism, term usage, 69
supernatural order, 20, 24–26, 29
Surnaturel (de Lubac), 28
symbols, order of, 133, 134

Teilhard de Chardin, Pierre, 46, 53, 73
Teresa of Avila, 39, 117
theological intuition
    Abhishiktānanda and, 71–73, 95–101, 153–54
    awakening, 82–89
    double-afference theory, 69–71
    Guhantara project, 73–77, 96–97
    overview, 65–66
    preliminary remarks, 66–69
    Sagesse, 77–82
theology, status of, 165–66
Thérése de Jésus, 83
Thérèse of Lisieux, 39
time, flow of, 130–31n17
tradition
    Abhishiktānanda on, 84–85, 88
    Blondel on, 62
    Monchanin on, 55–56, 62n23, 84, 135–36

transcendent, contained in the immanent, 19
Trinity, 98, 132, 134, 146

The Unknown Christ of Hinduism (Panikkar), 113
Upanishads, 86, 92, 117

Valensin, Auguste, 52
van Haeften, Benedictus, 38, 39
Vatican Council II
    Ad Gentes, 77
    Lumen Gentium, 77, 78
    Nostra Aetate, 3, 77
Verne, Jules, 34
visible aspect of church, 27

Winandy, Jacques, 42
World War I, mortality rate, 16n5

Xaveriana journals, 41

Zenonian, conception of motion, 130
Zilboorg, Gregory, 94

www.ingramcontent.com/pod-product-compliance
Lightning Source LLC
Chambersburg PA
CBHW070329230426
43663CB00011B/2261